BLACK GOLD AND HOT SAND

Black Gold and Hot Sand

A History of St Helens

Mike Fletcher

Carnegie Publishing Ltd

Published by
Carnegie Publishing Ltd
Carnegie House, Chatsworth Road
Lancaster la1 4sl
Publishing Website: www.carnegiepub.co.uk
Book Production Website: www.wooof.net

British Library Cataloguing-in-Publication data
A CIP record for this book is available from the British Library

ISBN 1-85936-088-2

Typeset by Carnegie Publishing
Printed and bound in the UK by
The Cromwell Press, Trowbridge, Wilts

Contents

This book is dedicated to Lilian Margaret Fletcher, my mum, a St Helens lass, born and bred, without whose input and support this book would never have been written

FOREWORD

*T*HE HISTORY of St Helens is rich. Like the coal seams that course their way beneath the Borough, it runs deep through the veins of those who sought a better life for themselves and their families. It was through the hard labour of those who worked the mines or built and served the chemical, glass and railway industries, that St Helens became a world-renowned feature of the first industrial land-scape. It was a period of dramatic change – new types of work, new ways of working, and new living environments. People were arriving from different communities and families were having to adapt, some-times just to survive in harsh conditions. The environment itself was changed beyond recognition.

But as the new economy took shape, so the community of St Helens began to emerge. The Borough's residents took pride in their area

Photograph of Councillor Marie Rimmer, Leader, St Helens Council.

and in themselves. Public services developed, leisure facilities expanded and everything that gives a place identity took form.

Eventually the impetus for economic growth turned away from the traditional heartland of the English industrial revolution. Towns like St Helens were once again faced with the pain of changing to meet new circumstances. With the closure of mines especially, the Borough could have lost its will to survive as its people's livelihoods were threatened.

But the great strength of this Borough is its sense of community, built up throughout its history. By drawing on its own innate self-belief, the area has managed to re-emerge with vigour. Physically it has been transformed, socially it is still one of the most coherent communities in the region and economically it is realising its full potential once again at the heart of the powerhouse that is the North West.

To understand where we are now, we must find out where we have been. I am proud that my home town presents itself as a Learning Community because it is by listening to the voices of the past that we come to appreciate the value of what we have today. I hope you enjoy reading the following pages and take some time to reflect on the impact of our fascinating history on our people and our place.

Marie E. Rimmer
Leader of St Helens Council

Acknowledgements

I WOULD LIKE TO THANK a number of people for their assistance with the preparation of this book.

The St Helens Local History and Archives Library has proved invaluable in the research of the town's history. Their collection of relevant material is endless. I would like to thank Ms V. Hainsworth and her staff for their help in pointing me in the right direction.

The photographs used within the book are either taken from my own collection, or have been supplied by the following sources:

I would like to thank V. Hainsworth and the St Helens Local History and Archives Library for permission to reproduce several photographs from their collections.

Several superb old images were kindly supplied by Dennis Whittle, and I am indebted for his overwhelming generosity. These illustrations are credited in the captions as follows: *DW*.

The British Coal Corporation kindly allowed us to reproduce several of their photographs, and these are credited in the captions.

Most of the modern photographs were taken by Anna Goddard, and are credited in the captions as follows: *AG*.

Finally I would like to take this opportunity to thank Anna Goddard and Carnegie Publishing for seeing this project through to the end. It took great foresight to realise that when the original manuscript arrived in 1999 it had potential. It has been a long, slow and often frustrating journey, but three years and two re-writes later, the book has finally been published.

Mike Fletcher,
October 2002

Introduction

*T*HE CREATION AND SUBSEQUENT HISTORY of a town like St Helens is far, far different from that of its north-west neighbours. Towns such as Warrington or Wigan are much older than St Helens, having first become settlements during Roman times and developing through the medieval period. Their histories are both longer and more detailed than that of their younger neighbour. The modern town of St Helens was created from the joining together of four manors and five townships in the middle of the eighteenth century.

The purpose of this book is to chart the creation, progress and development of this town created in the industrial age. The story of St Helens is varied; although its origins are in coal mining, its subsequent development is due to the other industries that the coal attracted.

Origins of the town

The modern town of St Helens was created from the joining together of four manors and five townships – Parr, Eccleston, Sutton, Windle and Hardshaw.

The manor of Parr was controlled by the Parr family from around the thirteenth century. Their grand residence, Parr Hall, was located to the north-west of the manor. The family continued to live there for several generations until 1570, when the demise of the last male heir caused both the hall and estate to pass into the hands of a trustee, a distant relation named William Parr, who sold the hall to his stepfather, Sir Henry Byrom. The Byroms retained the manor, and Parr Hall, until 1713 when they sold it to the Clayton family of Liverpool. Mr Clayton had previously been Mayor of Liverpool, as well as one of its more prominent and wealthy merchants. Sadly John Clayton died soon after the move to Parr Hall, leaving his widow, Elizabeth, and their young daughter, Sarah, to run the estate. Both the hall and estate would pass to Sarah in 1745, following the death of her mother.

The township of Eccleston was owned by the Ecclestone family from the latter half of the eleventh century. The family lived at Eccleston Hall, first built by the Lord of the manor, Hugh Ecclestone, in 1100.

The Ecclestons remained until to the close of the eighteenth century, departing their hall in 1799, after inheriting Scarisbrick Hall, near Southport. Eccleston Hall remained unsold and unoccupied for more than a decade, until it was finally purchased in 1812 by Colonel Samuel Taylor, who had it completely rebuilt in 1836. The Taylors also retained the title of Lords of the manor of Eccleston. Colonel Taylor was later succeeded by his son, also named Samuel.

The manor of Sutton was extensive, including areas such as Peasley Cross, Marshalls Cross, Clockface, Sutton Manor and Sherdley. The Sherdley family had owned their estate since Norman times, building Sherdley Hall there soon after their arrival. Through the centuries several versions of the hall were built, the last of which was erected in 1671, and in later years would be referred to as Old Sherdley Hall. Following the death of the Sherdley family line during the sixteenth century, the estate was taken over by the Bolds, whose estate bordered that of Sherdley. Later it was purchased by the Byrom family, and retained until Sir Henry Byrom sold it to Richard Roughly. His descendants would retain the estate until it was bought by the local industrialist, Michael Hughes, in 1798.

The manor of Windle located to the north of the town, gained its name from the Old English for 'Windy Hill'. The Windle family, who gained the manor during Norman times, built their grand manor house, Windle Hall, high on the hill. Later, the Gerards of Bryn Hall near Wigan, gained the manor through marriage; however, in later years the family would vacate Windle Hall, preferring instead to live at other addresses such as Birchley Hall and New Garswood Hall.

The tiny berewick of Hardshaw, contained within the manor of Windle, had originally been created by the Knights Hospitaller of St John during the eleventh century. Later, their overlords, the Windles, took back the land. The township of Hardshaw, at the centre of the four other townships, had stood on the highway between the two prominent market towns of Warrington and Ormskirk, with other roads leading to Liverpool and Bolton. At its heart stood Chapel Lane, containing a row of cottages, the chapel of St Elyn, and an old inn.

The chapel-of-ease of St Elyn was first built during the second half of the fourteenth century to serve not only the inhabitants of Hardshaw, but the surrounding townships, who were all some distance from the parish church at Prescot. This parish was vast, so these local chapels were erected to save the congregation having to travel such distances to worship at Prescot.

It is thought that from 1330 the Travers family gained the berewick of Hardshaw, and retained control through to 1633. They only lost it, and their grand residence – Hardshaw Hall – following fines levied against them for recusancy. The next owners were the Egerton family

This picture is of St Helens' only surviving wayside cross – though it has long since lost its cross, and only the base remains – which is located in the Catholic graveyard of St Thomas's Chantry. In medieval times similar crosses stood on an ancient highway said to have connected Fiddlers Ferry to Billinge Beacon, at Marshalls Cross and Peasley Cross, which gave the districts their names. *(AG)*

from Cheshire. Years later Mary Egerton left the hall and berewick in her will and testament to Mrs Mary Cotham, a distant relation, who would live at Hardshaw Hall until her death in 1716. Later that same year, the property was purchased from the executors by Thomas Goulden. The Goulden family would retain it through to 1757, when it was sold to Alfred Walmsley-Cotham, a distant relative of Mary Cotham.

This tiny hamlet of Hardshaw including the chapel-of-ease, from which its name was taken, became the nucleus of the town. Early names for the town were based on the original theme, though varied in the spelling: St Elyns, St Elens, St Ellens, eventually leading to the familiar spelling of St Helens (though pronounced locally as 'Sin-Tell-Inns').

It is clear that all would have remained quiet, peaceful and rural in the four manors had it not been for the discovery of coal. Yet its discovery in the sixteenth century was not a significant factor in the development of the townships until the middle of the eighteenth century: the arrival of the Industrial Revolution in Lancashire at that time and the vast change from hand-made goods to industrial manufacture, made that discovery all the more important.

The four independent manors stood on a large section of what was later to be known as the South Lancashire Coalfield. More importantly Liverpool, the major town and port in the region, did not. With the discovery of rock salt in Cheshire, together with the brine already being extracted there, the refining of salt became a major industry. This was transported along the River Weaver and across the Mersey to the Salthouse Dock at Liverpool, where a couple of salt works had been built. The process was energy-intensive, requiring vast amounts of coal to fuel the furnaces. This demand led to the development of transport in the region, with the creation of the early turnpikes between Liverpool and Prescot, followed by the construction of the Sankey Brook Navigation (later referred to as the Sankey Canal).

The coal at St Helens attracted other new industries. The glass industry made a home here, followed by others such as the alkali makers, iron foundries and so on. The berewick of Hardshaw changed dramatically in the nineteenth century, forming the centre of the new industrial town. The population increased and the town grew up around it. St Helens was typical of many industry-based towns; it was created without a specific definition or overall plan. Housing, sanitation, local government, schools, all the common essentials for any town – and something that long-established towns had built upon throughout the centuries – were lacking in this creation. Local benefactors, looking to the greater development of the growing town, had to dig deep into their own personal wealth to ensure that such basic needs were met. It was through their unselfish generosity and community spirit that the town was made a better place. There were many who played a part in the life of the town, such as John Mackay and Sarah Clayton, who brought prosperity here in the eighteenth century. And although there were many who influenced the direction of the town in the nineteenth century, there was none greater than Peter Greenall and following his untimely demise in 1845, his successor, David Gamble. The nineteenth-century town of St Helens owes much to many generous individuals.

By the time the Walmsley-Cotham family rebuilt Hardshaw Hall in 1840, the town was established, and the noise and smell of industry had spoiled the previous peace and quiet. Although over the next forty years the town around them would expand beyond all reasonable expectations, it was the hustle and bustle of this new industrial town that caused the family to vacate Hardshaw Hall in 1884, and relocate to a more rural setting at Springfield Hall in Eccleston.

Although the Victorian town saw its hardships mixed with wealth and prosperity, the town in the twentieth century brought much greater prosperity, together with improvements to working conditions, better housing and a higher standard of health. Yet the new century also brought the effects of two World Wars and the gradual decline of industry, both in coal mining and manufacturing. Long established trades, such as glass-making, were hit by recession – some forced to close, others forced to make massive redundancies. Throughout the period of the 1970s and 1980s the failing economy saw the dole queues rise throughout the country. And towns like St Helens, once vibrant, prosperous industrial towns, were now regarded as failures, described both in the national press and by government as 'unemployment wastelands'. The twelve-month-long miners' strike of 1984/85 brought home the desperation in their industry, though rather than make things better, it made matters worse: the result was the closure of the town's remaining collieries.

However, despite the downturn in the town's fortunes, St Helens weathered the storm and finally rallied. The latter years of the twentieth century have witnessed a resurgence of the town's economic fortunes. Vast redevelopment, of both the town centre and the local infrastructure, has led to a rebirth of St Helens: new industries are being attracted to the town, and retail businesses are taking premises in the newly-refurbished shopping centres. The town is shaking off its old industrial clothes and embracing a new exciting future. The town looks modern, and has a fresher feel about it. I feel that St Helens looks to have a brighter future in the twenty-first century, something that it has lacked for many years.

Chapter One

THE CREATION OF A COAL MINING TOWN

The Phoenix Colliery, which stood off Burtonhead Road, within sight of Ravenhead Colliery, was founded by Benjamin Glover in 1873. Although this could be described as one of the town's smaller collieries, and existed in the shadow of its larger neighbour, it enjoyed some success, in the hands of several owners, and remained in production until 1893. Its above-ground buildings were used for a variety of uses until 1972. Four years later work commenced to transform this entire site for the construction of Pilkingtons Greengate UK5 factory, which occupies the site to present day. (*Reproduced with the permission of the St Helens Local History and Archives Library*)

THROUGHOUT St Helens' chequered history, one thing is certain concerning the creation of the town – it was the discovery of coal that created its prosperity. Coal became the sustenance that fed the Industrial Revolution. Coal had surpassed timber as the main source of fuel, and following the spark that lit the Industrial Revolution, this fuel was in great demand by the new manufacturers, to power their furnaces and machines. The discovery of an abundance of coal here would later attract many industries to the area, thus creating an industrial town. The motto *Ex Terra Lucem*: 'Out of the Earth – Light', was established early on in the town's history, and is still retained today. The coal was the source of the light, the prosperity.

Discovery

Coal was first discovered locally in 1540 at Sutton Heath within the manor of Sutton by members of the Eltonhead family, purely by accident, during the digging a clay pit. Their endeavours struck a coal seam located quite close to the surface. The owners of the land were the Bold family, Lords of the neighbouring manor of Bold: the discovery of the coal led to a dispute between the tenants, the Eltonheads, and their landlords, the Bolds. A compromise was reached, whereby the Eltonheads could extract the coal, less a commission to the Bolds.

Once coal had been discovered in one of the four manors, discoveries in the other three were inevitable: by the following century, coal had been discovered all over the area of what was later to become St Helens – at Windle in 1610, Parr in 1655 and finally in Eccleston in 1660 – and was actively being extracted.

Once coal had established itself as a major source of revenue, the respective Lords of the manor realised that it was to their distinct advantage to have coal mined from their estates. Many of their lordships were directly involved in the early mining ventures, including the Bolds, Gerards, Ecclestons and Byroms, all of whom saw a future in it.

Although many thought that the discovery of coal was beneficial, leading to increased revenue and local employment (other than traditional agriculture), others were not so enthusiastic. It is on record that the inhabitants of Sutton (and in particular Sutton Heath), later objected to the continued mining of coal, and levied their complaints to the Hollands, as Lords of the manor of Sutton. In 1611, for instance, complaints were made regarding the plans of the Eltonheads and Bolds to increase production by sinking new shafts in the area. However, in spite of these objections, much of the local population of the four townships greeted the arrival of the coal industry with the blessing it so rightly deserved.

Early Miners

The early mining activities were very hit-and-miss. Simple shafts were dug in search of coal, without any real understanding the geology of the area. The early prospectors were normally individuals, with little in the way of real capital, and should their searches not discover coal quickly, they were soon in real financial difficulty. Although in certain areas the coal was found close to the surface, in others it was much deeper; and the early makeshift shafts, dug by hand using pick and shovel, did not always reach the coal seams, so they were soon abandoned. Later, with radical improvements in mining occurring all the time, they would be able to sink much deeper shafts, searching for the all-elusive coal.

Early mining was a perilous business: in the rush to reach the coal seam tunnels were often dug without adequate shoring, and roof collapses were common. Flooding in the flatter areas, which made sloughs useless, became a real problem, often leading to the early abandonment of mines. On occasion, a simple bucket and windlass was employed to extract the water in an attempt to reduce flooding and keep the mine open – though more often than not this made little significant difference. Within a few years, however, the arrival of coal-fed steam engines would assist in the pumping of water from the flooded mines.

In the more successful shafts, the coal was mined until the seam was exhausted – or alternatively, until it became too dangerous to continue. In the early years of coal mining there were shafts all over the area, and those left abandoned often had no covering or sign, which could prove hazardous to the unsuspecting traveller!

Mining was actually carried out in Hardshaw, right at the heart of what was later to become the centre of modern-day St Helens. Thomas Greenall had a pit in the area of Bridge Street (at the bottom of the street, close to where the General Post Office stands today) during the nineteenth century; another pit was active on Hardshaw Street;

From this section of the 1894 Peasley Cross map, we can see the Peasley Cross Colliery (*extreme left*). This was opened originally in 1856, as the Peasley House Colliery, though later changed its name to the Peasley Colliery by 1872. Its location, next door to Cannington Shaw (on the present-day site of UGB) provided plenty of trade in close proximity, and good transport links to both the canal and railway. Not the most productive of collieries, it enjoyed limited success. It was purchased in the late 1870s by the Whitecross Company Limited of Warrington, who retained it until 1903, when it was sold to a new company, trading as the Peasley Cross Colliery Company Ltd. It struggled to remain profitable in a highly competitive market, and closed permanently in 1906. (*Reproduced with the permission of the St Helens Local History and Archives Library*)

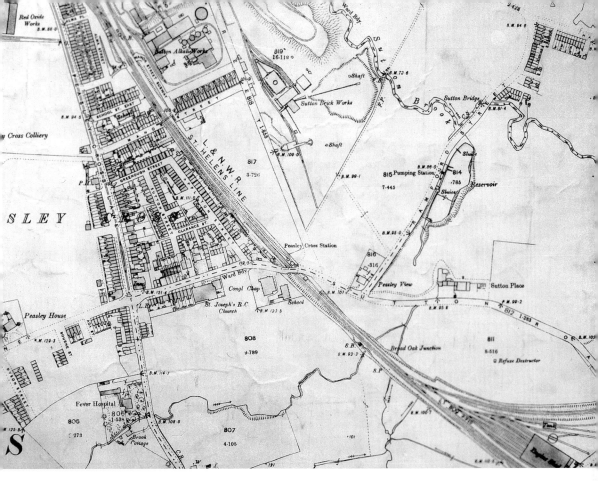

and several more were in operation along what is Duke Street today. These early pits could be established almost anywhere, either by the landowner actively owning and operating the mine, or by a local coal prospector gaining a lease from the landowner in order to mine a patch of ground. There was manipulation on both sides: landowners could charge excessive rates on the coal being extracted, to the point were the coal could be made worthless; or equally, the prospectors could behave in such a manner in their efforts to mine the coal at all costs, that they rendered the land useless. Eventually legislation was passed to protect both parties and eliminate sharp practice, which had led to conflict within the infant mining industry.

Other problems involved subsidence: both on the land, where it could ruin farmer's fields, and around farm buildings, where undermining would cause them to collapse. Examples of mining subsidence have been commonplace around mining towns such as St Helens: buildings lean sharply, and require shoring up for safety, or in the most extreme circumstances collapse without warning. Hollows in the fields, often flooded, are a direct result of subsidence, creating what is often referred to as 'flashes'. Parr Flashes is a good example of this.

A common ploy used to reduce the risk of subsidence was the 'pillar and stall' method, that left sufficient support behind, much of it made from usable coal, to hold up the earth above. This was not cost-effective to the mine owners, however, so a compensation system was introduced to allow 'free coal' for the amount lost underground. (Many of St Helens buildings stand on 'coal pillars', including the hospital and town hall; the coal was bought by the parties concerned to prevent subsidence and protect their structures.)

Eighteenth-century Coal Mining

Following the link with Liverpool (via the turnpike extension) in 1746, St Helens coal mining developed further, as the demand increased at an alarming rate. People with financial backing, either with land of their own or with the finances to purchase suitable land, moved into

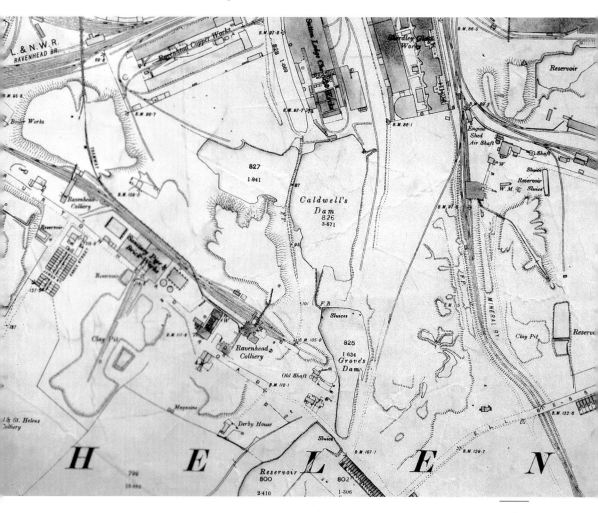

From this 1894 map of
Ravenhead, we can see the
former site of one of the most
productive of St Helens' many
collieries – Ravenhead Colliery.
With an annual output averaging
around 130,000 tons, and with
markets at Garston Dock and
Warrington, this was an asset
that was sought by many.
Throughout the years it was
owned by the Haddocks and the
Bromilows, before a new
company was formed in
September 1871, the Ravenhead
Colliery Company Limited.
Pilkingtons acquired it in 1875,
when they formed St Helens
Collieries Limited. Today this
former industrial site has been
transformed beyond all
recognition, as the Ravenhead
Retail Park. (*Reproduced with the
permission of the St Helens Local
History and Archives Library*)

the coal mining business. Sarah Clayton was one of the town's first coal magnates; after inheriting Parr Hall Estate in 1745 on the death of her mother, Elizabeth, she put great store in the extended search for coal on her sizeable estate. This search was indeed successful and further mining began in earnest. Although the previous owners of Parr (the Byroms) had mined coal, it was in very small amounts. In Sarah Clayton's case, she mined almost the entire estate and for a time she nearly held the monopoly of coal in the region.

In 1766, the powerful Gerard family of Windle Hall had employed the services of the Tarbuck brothers, Robert and John, to extract coal from their estate. Later that year, the brothers were joined in a partnership with Robert Sherratt, who had previously acted as their agent, and together they played a significant role in local mining. Employing this team made the Gerards' new coal operation very successful, making them major players in the coal business; through the years they would become one of the largest families in the coal market, mining not just on their Windle estate, but also at Bryn Hall on the outskirts of Wigan, and later still at Garswood New Hall.

Coal was a wealth provider in more ways than one, for as well as the revenue it created, it brought added wealth through attracting industry, which created further revenue by both renting land and buying coal. In 1771/72, for example, Patten & Co. of Warrington were smelting copper ore at Blackbrook, on land owned by Sir Thomas Gerard of Garswood, on the banks of the Sankey Canal, using Gerard's coal. A wharf was built, which was used by both Gerard's collieries and Patten's foundry.

The discovery of coal led to the creation of coal entrepreneurs: people who did not own land, nor were capable of purchasing it, but would hire out their services to the landed gentry to mine their coal for them, at a price. In some cases they would be mining coal in a variety of mines located on many estates. The Tarbuck brothers were a fine example of this activity, and so too was Charles Dagnall, who was employed to mine coal for families such as the Ecclestons, Gerards and Lancasters (of Rainhill); later he established other such mines in Parr and Sutton.

Thomas Case was another prospector who, through wise investments and family connections, had become a coal magnate in his own right. He had both family and financial connections to Sarah Clayton – in fact he would take over the running of her coal mining interests in 1774. In the following year, Case married Anna Ashton, daughter of John Ashton, co-surveyor of the Sankey Canal. She had inherited some of her father's shares in the canal following his death.

Although Clayton was one of the key figures in the local coal trade, she had her rivals. One of the greatest pioneers and leaders of coal

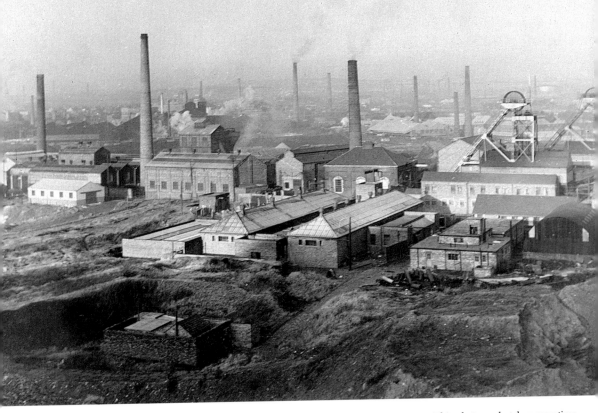

mining in St Helens was John Mackay, a Scotsman, who would also promote the town as an industrial centre. He relocated to Parr from Cheshire, where he purchased a small mining concern, although he only really became established in the industry following his later move to Ravenhead. He leased land at Thatto Heath in 1765 from King George III, and soon after purchased Ravenhead Farm from the Archbishop of York. Here he established Ravenhead Colliery, which would prove to be one of the largest, most productive and long-lasting of the town's coal mines.

When Mackay began his coal mining, initially at Thatto Heath, and later at Ravenhead, he sought the miners he so desperately needed by placing notices locally stating that 'if any ... good colliers ... will apply at Thatto Heath Colliery, they will meet with constant employ and the best encouragement'. Mackay soon built up a great demand for his coal by being one of the cheapest around. In 1771, public notices stated that Mackay had 'lowered the price of coal at his mine to 2 ½*d*. per basket' (each basket weighed 60lbs). And, using the close proximity of the Sankey Canal to full effect, Mackay was soon selling coal, not only to Liverpool and Cheshire, but also exporting it to as far away as America.

Through his connections in the City of London, he managed to pull

This photograph, taken sometime during the 1950s or 1960s, overlooks Ravenhead Colliery, in the direction of the town centre. It offers evidence, if evidence were needed, of the once massive presence of industry in the town: just note the number of smoking chimneys on the skyline. This colliery was one of the first to open in the town, and was in operation for more than two hundred years. (*Reproduced with the permission of the St Helens Local History and Archives Library*) off the coup of the century (in economic terms at least) in successfully attracting the British Cast Plate Glass Manufacturers Company to Ravenhead in 1773. He repeated this success by enticing the Parys Mining Company from Anglesey, North Wales, to set up a copper smelting works also at Ravenhead, just three years later. Both of these companies had been seduced by cheap coal.

Although times were good for the coal proprietors of the area, these were equally trying times for investors; and mistakes, often led by the thirst to corner more of the market, could prove very costly: a combination of bad investments and over-expansion led to the downfall of what were otherwise sound businesses.

However, what was about to occur was something very different. The American War of Independence brought with it an embargo on coal imports into the States. Mackay, who had sold much of his coal to America – exported out of the Port of Liverpool to the American Colonies via the Port of Philadelphia – was immediately affected. The ending of exports meant that the home market was flooded with unwanted coal, and the price fell to an all-time low because of this. Collieries throughout the country suffered while the war continued. Petitions were placed before Parliament by coal proprietors protesting at the state of affairs. Miners and their families were made redundant, and without any income, had to rely on the charity of the local parish to exist while the crisis continued.

This period brought a massive change to the coal industry, and led to the bankruptcy of the more insecure colliery owners. In St Helens there were many casualties. Sarah Clayton and Case went bankrupt, though by far the most surprising casualty was that of the entrepreneur John Mackay. All of these former business giants would be reduced to shadows of their former selves and would die in poverty. Sarah Clayton died in 1779, just a year after her bankruptcy, a broken woman, having lost her family's estate; Case died in 1783; so too did John Mackay.

Following the end of the war with America, the depression ended and the coal market rallied. The market was now going to prove a very different place with the absence of people like Mackey, Clayton and Case. With these powerful, dominating figures out of the way, closer ties were made with the brine dealers of Cheshire: many of the remaining smaller collieries went into partnership with the Cheshire salt dealers. Now, through dual investment, neither side could regulate prices to favour their own position, ensuring that the price remained favourable to all, not just the select few.

Working Conditions

Such was the mining spirit, particularly in the early days, that a miner would often employ his entire family to work alongside with him – both his wife and children. It was common practice for miners' children, as young as four or five, to be employed to work underground.

Although the fledging coal industry was a great employer for the new town of St Helens, the trade was less than fair in its rates of pay. This, together with harsh working conditions, led to the first miners' strike in 1819. This resulted in civil unrest and riots on the streets of the town, matters reaching such a pitch that troops were called in from barracks as far afield as Warrington, Liverpool and Manchester. The hours were indeed terribly long; starting as early as 4 a.m., they could be expected to work underground through to late in the evening and sometimes beyond. Despite this, they lost their fight with the coal proprietors. The strike was broken by the introduction of 'blacklegs' who were brought in from those coalfields not on strike. Work recommenced, this time with even lower rates of pay than before. Further industrial action followed. A much greater strike occurred in 1831, though this too was broken by the colliery proprietors.

As we have seen, it was not just men that worked down the mines,

These photographs offer a glimpse of conditions underground. Life was hard and very dangerous in the coal mines, especially for the early miners. Accidents were common, varying from roof falls to explosions. In 1842, Parliament excluded women from working in these harsh and primitive conditions. (*British Coal Corporation copyright*)

but women and children too. In fact, the collieries were the largest employer of women in the town, as all the other industries – glasshouses and foundries etc. – shunned their employment. Until 1841, when pit ponies were first introduced underground, young boys were employed in backbreaking work of hauling the carts.

However, a feeling was growing throughout the country that it was morally wrong for women and children to have to work underground, in such awful conditions. This led to a number of the more responsible colliery proprietors to take it upon themselves to remedy the situation: for instance, James Lindsay, the 24th Earl of Crawford, proprietor of the Haigh Colliery, near Wigan, took both women and children out of the mines early on, finding them alternative jobs at the colliery above ground; the fourth Duke of Bridgewater (less famous than his predecessor, Francis Egerton, founder of the Bridgewater Canal) took similar action at his Worsley coal mines. Yet for many colliery owners who saw nothing wrong with women and children working in their mines, it would take the passing of legislation to force them to change their working practices. A Bill was passed through the House of Commons in 1842, effectively stopping women and children working below ground. However, despite the benefits to the women's health and well-being, this change in the law did not receive the acclaim it perhaps deserved: the mine owners did not like the change, and neither did the women, who had their pay cut considerably.

There was, of course, plenty of work to be done on the surface: from the early days of serious mining, timber had been used to shore up the seams, and all of the collieries had their own timber yards, where wood, brought in from outside, had to be cut to size and stacked for use below ground later. This change in the law led to the creation of the famous pit brow lasses.

Apart from being a hard life, working in the mines was a dangerous one too. Explosions were common, especially in the early days of mining, though they were to remain a problem throughout the nineteenth century. The common cause for this was referred to by miners as firedamp: the build-up of methane gas. This gas occurs naturally in coal and is highly flammable, and when mixed with air in large enough quantities, becomes explosive. This could be easily ignited by a miner, using an exposed lamp, or lighting a pipe: once ignited, the fire would spread rapidly along the workings and the seam. If miners were not killed by the initial blast or by the fire itself, they would often die from suffocation from the intense smoke and gases created from the burning coal. Huge uncontrollable fires could render a mine inactive for days, even weeks. The problem with firedamp had been known about since the first days of deep coal mining. Pockets of methane could build up naturally in the coal, behind the coalface, and

The introduction of the Davy lamp made working underground that much safer and significantly reduced the risk of accidentally igniting the gases that were naturally present underground. In later years battery-powered lamps were introduced. This picture of Clockface's lamp-room offers an insight into just how many miners' headlamps were needed.
(*British Coal Corporation copyright*)

could be punctured and ignited by a miner's pick by accident, leading to an explosion: these were known as 'blowers'.

Matters had to improve. Initially, the colliery proprietors took the common sense route and began checks on miners – for matches, lighters and pipes – prior to the descent into the mine; this practice would continue throughout the days of coal mining. The invention of the coal miners' Davy Lamp reduced gas explosions, and improved matters further. Eventually battery-powered lamps were introduced.

Even following an explosion, and the subsequent fire, there were other hazards for the miners to overcome: afterdamp is a phrase used by miners when the mines have been filled with harmful gases following a fire or explosion; these were generally carbon dioxide and carbon monoxide (the first will suffocate a person in a confined space, while the second is highly poisonous).

Just a superficial glance through the mining records of St Helens collieries reveals the amount and frequency of explosions. Sankey Brook Colliery suffered a pit explosion on 25 February 1865, and there were two massive explosions at Ravenhead Colliery, on 9 February 1861, and on 28 November 1890. By far the worst of the mining explosions in the area around St Helens was the incident that occurred

at the Wood Pit Colliery, located between Newton-le-Willows and Haydock, on 7 June 1878. At 11.15 a.m., a loud blast was heard over the sleepy village of Haydock. A massive explosion had occurred underground, and it was feared that around 230 miners, who were working underground at the time, had lost their lives. Those that were not killed outright with the intensity of the initial blast were killed by the afterdamp that suffocated them in the dark tunnels beneath the earth. In the final analysis, the death toll was not as high as had first appeared – reaching 189 – though this was by far the worst disaster in the region.

There were many other hazards for the men working below ground apart from explosions and fires. Roof falls were common, where men could be trapped or crushed under tons of debris. The underground railway operated wagons – known as 'bogey wagons' – carrying coal, which either ran with their own momentum down a slight incline, or were hauled by a steam-powered engine, or manually. Many people were run over by these wagons – full or empty – though fewer experienced miners (who knew when to get out of the way) than the inexperienced apprentices. More apprentices were killed or injured during their first week (or even their first day!) down the mines than in their first whole year.

Other incidents occurred while men were entering or leaving the cage that transported them below ground. Early winding gear was prone to creeping, which caused the cage to jerk unexpectedly, and men could get trapped or thrown out. Others actually fell down the open mine shaft – this happened more often than you might think. During the sinking of new shafts many accidents occurred: the sides were prone to giving way, even when shored, and the men working below would become trapped or crushed. Working at the coalface was dangerous too, especially in the early days when men worked in pairs, one using the pick to free the coal, the other (known as a 'drawer') using a shovel to rake out the coal: the drawer, working under the face of the loose coal, could easily be struck by falling coal loosened by the pick.

Again, a quick look at the records of fatal accidents occurring in St Helens collieries shows a recurring problem. Using Ravenhead as a guide to the rest of the town, there were fatal accidents in February 1858, September 1859, November 1862, May 1865. There were four separate incidents in 1866: the first in February, another at the end of March, the third in June, and the final one in October; and there was another death in the June of the following year.

With the increasing number of accidents in the collieries, and in particular the number of explosions, the Government was forced take action. Fuelled by public demand, the Mining Inspectorate was established in 1850; its principal task was to investigate the causes of these accidents and disasters, and find solutions to prevent their recurrence. Although teams of investigators visited collieries throughout the country, they lacked the authority to force owners to change their working practices. However, it was in the interest of the colliery owners (certainly in the case of explosions) to reduce accidents, if only to increase production, so compromise was often reached between the two parties.

Nineteenth-century Collieries

By the turn of the nineteenth century the coal trade was re-established and prosperous. The demand for coal on a national level was constantly growing, and in St Helens, demand by the glass industry amongst others meant that more coal was required. A comparison can be drawn between trade in the two centuries: in 1759, for instance, the glass-makers had bought around 20,000 tons of coal within that year, but by 1820, that figure had increased to around 200,000 tons per annum! The direct result of this upturn in the market was the creation of new collieries.

The area of Ravenhead was one of the most productive mining areas in the town. Although it was dominated by the Ravenhead Colliery, there were several other productive collieries surrounding it. The Phoenix Colliery, which stood off Burtonhead Road to the north of Ravenhead, had been founded in 1873 by Benjamin Glover, though the company took on new partners and changed to Glover, Urmston & Glover in 1886. The colliery itself remained in use until 1893. Later, the above-ground workings were bought by a local man named William Woodcock, and used for a short period as an iron foundry. The former mining buildings continued to be used, for a variety of uses, through to 1972. They were demolished four years later to make way for the construction of Pilkingtons Greengate UK5.

Its immediate neighbour, Burtonhead Colliery, located at the corner of Sherdley Road and Burtonhead Road, had originally been sunk by Jonathan Case in the mid-1770s. Following Case's bankruptcy towards the end of the decade, the mine was bought by Thomas West; however, West himself suffered financial difficulties and had to sell the concern. By 1825, Thomas Caldwell owned the pit for a few years, though a decade later it was purchased by Clare & Company, which later changed to Clare & Haddock. The colliery enjoyed some success during the boom years of the nineteenth century, although it always remained in the shadow of its more powerful neighbour, Ravenhead. After being placed up for auction in 1844 and failing to sell, it remained unsold, and so was eventually closed. However, it was to breathe new life again in the late 1870s, forming part of the Ravenhead Colliery complex.

Sutton Colliery which despite its name was actually located at Peasley Cross, had been opened in 1812 by John Bourne. It stood near Peasley Cross Lane, on land that would later be taken over by Kurtz Alkali,

Two photographs of Ravenhead Colliery. The buildings and spoil heaps to the left of the pictures were originally part of Burtonhead Colliery, originally sunk during the 1770s; it would have several owners before eventually being absorbed by Ravenhead during the 1870s.

Take a look at the state of Burtonhead Road in the bottom picture, probably taken during the 1970s; in stark contrast, this scene today would be very clean and modern, as the home of a McDonalds drive-through and the Ravenhead retail park!
(*British Coal Corporation copyright*)

and later still by the St Helens Gas Works. In 1824, John Bourne formed a partnership with Robert Robertson – trading as John Bourne & Company – and opened the Eltonhead mine later that same year. At the same time, John's brothers, James and Peter, joined the new company. However, by the 1830s, the partnership had split: the Bournes retained Sutton Colliery, while Robinson bought the Broad Oak Colliery at Parr. John Bourne retired in 1859, leaving the company in the capable hands of his immediate family, Cornelius, John, Thomas, James and Peter Bourne. Throughout the remainder of the century, Sutton Colliery maintained full production, averaging 150,000 tons per annum, with markets at Garston Dock, Liverpool and Manchester. During its most prosperous years, its location close to the Ravenhead section of the canal, and later the St Helens Runcorn Gap Railway, made transport and sales of its coal very economical. By the end of the century the coal deposits were reaching exhaustion and its eventual closure came in 1903.

Another colliery nearby, sunk in 1856, was initially known as the Peasley House Colliery, though its name was changed to the Peasley Colliery by 1872. Its location, next door to Cannington Shaw, proved useful. Another neighbour, located across Ell Bess Lane (later Sherdley Road) was Sherdley Colliery, which is thought to have been opened in 1873. Both Peasley Cross and Sherdley Collieries were sold to the Whitecross Company Limited of Warrington in the latter years of the 1870s. Sherdley Colliery was sold by Whitecross (who by now were looking to get out the coal business), to Sutton Heath & Lea Green Colliery Company in 1903. Peasley Cross was sold to a new company, trading as the Peasley Cross Colliery Company Ltd, in the same year, though it proved to be a poor deal, and closed within three years; Sherdley Colliery, on the other hand, proved more productive, and remained open through to 1943.

Just to the north of the Phoenix Colliery stood the Croppers Hill Colliery, which had been opened in 1845 by Bromilow family. James Radley bought the mine in 1850, though it proved an unsuccessful purchase, producing just 40,000 tons of coal per year. Finally, continuous flooding caused the mine to close in the mid-1860s.

In the direction of Thatto Heath was the Greengate Colliery, which was first sunk by William Walmsley in 1869. It was bought by John Cross three years later, who retained it for just four years before selling it to the Greenbank Alkali Company, who operated it as the Greenbank Colliery Company through to its eventual closure in 1915.

The Royal Colliery at Thatto Heath had been founded in 1830 by David Bromilow, and was retained by his family through to 1859, when it was closed. The mine remained idle until 1875 when John Cross purchased it to partner his Greengate Colliery nearby, and began extracting coal once more. It finally closed in the 1880s, and years later, the land was bought by Pilkingtons and used as part of the Alexandra Colliery complex.

By the middle of the nineteenth century, the coal mining industry in St Helens was experiencing its boom years. There were collieries scattered throughout the town. Those located to the east of the town nearest the Sankey Canal, particularly those still used it for the transportation of the coal to Liverpool. The Sankey Brook Colliery, which was owned by the Sankey Brook Colliery Company Ltd, was a successful enterprise and produced around 100,000 tons of coal per annum, with markets at Liverpool and Garston Dock. Its neighbour, Black Brook Colliery, owned by Bromilows, was less successful, producing just 30,000 tons of coal, selling some to the salt mines at Northwich, Cheshire, and some to Liverpool. The company also owned Garswood Colliery, which was the more successful of the two, producing 150,000 tons. Both of these collieries closed in the mid-1860s.

Gerards Bridge Colliery, located close to the New Double Locks (on a site later used by Globe Alkali) had been sunk by Thomas West in the early mining days of the eighteenth century. Following his bankruptcy, it was later owned by Caldwell and McCormack, before being bought by the Speakman family. It was not the most prolific of producers, averaging just 50,000 tons per year, the majority of which was sold to Liverpool. It finally closed in 1874. Its neighbour, Laffak Colliery, owned by John and Thomas Johnson, fared little better, producing 60,000 tons of coal and selling it to both Liverpool and Manchester.

Rushy Park Colliery, at Mertonbank, was operated between the 1820s and 1840s by the Bromilows; its neighbour, Glade Hill Colliery, was also founded in the late 1820s, by James Muspratt, to supply his alkali works. He was later joined in partnership by Robert Daglish Jnr, John Speakman and William Bromilow, though by 1840, Muspratt and Bromilow had left the partnership and the colliery was left in the hands of Daglish and Speakman. They later sold the concern to the Johnson family who owned the nearby Laffak Colliery.

However, in spite of all these collieries' immediate links with the canal, the railway had taken over the bulk of the coal deliveries by the 1860s. Only two collieries still used the canal – Ravenhead and Black Brook – and even these used the railway as well.

By the middle of the century other coal proprietors had appeared on the scene. One of those was Richard Evans. Born in the little village of Munslow in Shropshire, Evans later moved to London, where he had started his working life as a printer and publisher. A few years later, he moved to the north-west, a region of industrial activity, following the construction and opening of the Liverpool & Manchester

railway. He settled in the tiny hamlet of Garswood, between the coal mining towns of Wigan and St Helens. Here he acquired the friendship of two local businessmen – Henry Critchley and William Turner – both of whom had more than a passing interest in the coal mining business. Evans entered the mining business in 1830 with a small pit at Edge Green, near Wigan, which he purchased from Henry Critchley.

From this humble pit he created a coal mining concern that expanded to a significant size – known as the Edge Green Collieries – and over the years, Richard Evans bought several collieries within the St Helens district, including Haydock Colliery, in 1833, which was producing on average 250,000 tons; and Pewfall Colliery, on the St Helens–Haydock boundaries, in 1860, which produced 130,000 tons. Both of these had markets at Liverpool, Manchester, Warrington, and the salt mines of Northwich, Cheshire.

When they were of a suitable age, Richard brought his two sons, Joseph and Josiah, into the business, changing its name to Richard Evans & Sons. Upon his death in 1864, his two sons succeeded him in the running of the business.

Many of the collieries around St Helens had unusual or distinctive names: Southport Colliery, for instance, was nowhere near Southport, but was in fact located off Newton Road in Parr. This was yet another colliery owned by the Evans family; opening in 1894, it would close in 1936. Its neighbour, Havannah Colliery, was one of the earliest to operate, using its location alongside the canal to good effect; it closed in 1927. Broad Oak Colliery, also in Parr, opened in 1790, owned by Bourne and Robinson, reaching its full potential during the nineteenth century: this was the first colliery to transport coal to the docks at Widnes along the newly-completed St Helens and Runcorn Gap Railway, in 1832.

As already mentioned, in the early days of coal mining there were collieries working in what later became the town centre. Hardshaw Colliery was one of the first to open, long before the creation of the town. Through the years this small colliery had several owners, many of whom left their names on the new town's streets: Baldwin and Cotham, for example. In the final years before its closure, Hardshaw's last owners were the Greenall family. Cowley Hill Colliery, located to the north of the town, suffered severe flooding, and the closure of Croppers Hill Colliery led to the closure of Cowley Hill in 1887, unable to keep the waters at bay. Its former site was later bought by the Pilkington Brothers, who built their Cowley Hill Plate Glass Works there.

Many of the collieries were owned by prominent local families, such as the Pilkingtons, Gerards and Gambles, though there were others of similar stature also involved in the industry. David Bromilow, of Haresfinch House (who had relocated there in 1830 from a smaller house on Coalpit Lane, as a representation of his new-found wealth and increased status) bought Blackbrook Collieries, close to the Black-brook section of the canal, in the 1840s. This had originally been owned by James Orrell, of Blackbrook House, in 1790. Today houses have been built over the former site of the colliery. Another local man, James Radley, owned several small collieries within the town, along with the Pocket Nook Smelting Company. Radley was a prominent figure within the town; he was of the first councillors to be elected, and became Mayor of St Helens in 1870.

The prosperous times experienced by the colliery owners in the nineteenth century attracted the attention of other businessmen. Pilk-ingtons, already major players in the glass industry, needed large amounts of coal to power their furnaces. This led them into the mining industry, almost by the back door. Their first steps into the coal mining business were with the purchase of the Green Lane Colliery, within the manor of Hardshaw, in 1845. Their next acquisition was the St Helens Colliery (located off the Grove Street works, close to the crossing of the railway), which had been founded in 1800 by Clare & Haddock and worked through to 1844. It had been abandoned in that year after being placed up for auction and failing to sell; it was bought by

The latter years of the nineteenth century saw the creation of new collieries to the south of the town. Clockface Colliery, pictured here, opened in the 1890s, but was plagued with problems. For rather than striking coal, it struck water instead! This was capped and sold to St Helens Council, as fresh drinking water. New shafts eventually struck coal and the colliery would remain in operation until 1966. Today, the winding gear seen here has long-since gone, and the spoil heaps transformed into a country park.
(*British Coal Corporation copyright*)

Pilkingtons in 1857. Although being closed for such a long period meant that the workings underground were in a particularly poor state, investment meant that coal was being extracted within three years, and the pit soon produced around 130,000 tons per year. Although Pilkingtons' venture into coal mining had been to secure a reliable supply of competitive coal – which meant that it kept the lion's share of the coal for its owned factories – they were soon in a position to sell the excess to Garston Dock and Liverpool.

One of the town's most famous collieries, located close to Ravenhead, was the Alexandra Colliery. This was opened by Pilkington Brothers in 1864, to supply their glass works with coal, it was officially named three years later, following a Royal Visit by the Prince of Wales (later Edward VII) and Princess Alexandra in 1867 (although locally it was always referred to as the 'Cobs').

Ravenhead Colliery, originally founded by John Mackay, remained productive throughout the century. With an annual output averaging around 130,000 tons, and with markets at Garston Dock and Warrington, it was an asset that was sought by many. It was bought by the Haddock family in 1818. Later, the Bromilow family bought a share in the colliery, and the mine was re-sunk to a depth of 900 feet in 1866. Ravenhead changed hands again in September 1871, when a new company, the Ravenhead Colliery Company Limited, was formed. On its board of directors were some familiar names, including D. Bromilow, H. G. Bromilow, James Haddock and David Gamble. Pilkingtons acquired the colliery when they formed St Helens Collieries Limited in 1875 by amalgamating with other coal proprietors including the Bournes, Robinsons, Bromilows and Haddocks, and Radleys.

New Collieries

The latter years of the nineteenth century saw the opening of two new collieries in the south of the town. Bold Colliery was the first of these, opened in 1876 by the Collins Green Colliery Company, though initially it was far from an easy operation. Trouble was encountered almost immediately. No.1 shaft had been sunk to a depth of 607 yards, and No.2 shaft had reached to a depth of just 200 yards, when both flooded to a point where the machinery could no longer withstand it. Both shafts had to be closed, temporarily, while work was carried out to overcome this setback. Once this had been achieved, drilling recommenced, and the No.2 shaft reached a similar depth as No.1. The productive 'Florida seam' was reached (just one of many seams under St Helens) and the extraction of coal began in 1880. So successful was the operation, that in 1890, a third shaft was sunk. Of the three shafts in operation, No.1 shaft was the most active, measuring around twenty-one feet in diameter, while shafts 2 and 3, were much smaller, and measured just sixteen feet in diameter. In 1903 a modern steam engine, supplied by the Worsley Mesnes Company, was employed, which improved the rate of coal being brought to the surface. Throughout the years, the seams of Cambouke, Florida and Wigan were successfully reached, and provided a vast amount of coal, until the mine was eventually closed in the late 1930s.

The second new mining venture was Clockface Colliery (within walking distance of Bold Colliery) which started life in the 1890s. Initially it was also plagued with huge problems, as the newly-sunken shafts, rather than striking coal, found water instead. It looked as though the colliery might have to close even before it had actually begun production: but the water was capped, and sold to the St Helens Corporation as fresh drinking water, and new shafts were sunk that yielded coal. Throughout the remainder of the nineteenth century, and for many years into the next, it produced a profitable output.

By the end of the nineteenth century St Helens was a mining town that could compete with the very best. Its collieries were productive, its prices competitive, and its workers respected throughout the industry. It had a great future ahead.

Chapter Two

THE STORY OF THE SANKEY CANAL

*I*N THE LATTER YEARS of the seventeenth century, the demands on coal mining in the area of South Lancashire were increasing. This was caused by a number of connecting factors. The continued expansion of Liverpool as both a port and as a growing town was one of the reasons. Another was the expansion of the Cheshire brine industry, which required extensive boiling to make salt, which in turn used large amounts of fuel in the process: initially timber had been the main choice of fuel used, but later coal was found to be superior. In 1670, matters were made worse when William Marbury, carrying out test bores on his estate at Northwich in search of coal, discovered rock salt instead.

The growing need for fuel had led to the search for coal in and around Liverpool. This had been painstakingly carried out: the Liverpool Common Council, a group of prominent merchants, had commissioned many experimental test bores, with Alderman Gildart supervising the work himself, but the search had proved fruitless. With this setback, coal had to be found elsewhere. Demand had increased further with the opening of the salt refining works at Liverpool, processing Cheshire's rock salt which was arriving through the newly-completed Salthouse Dock.

It was discovered that Prescot was the nearest coalfield to Liverpool, and so it was from here that both Liverpool and Cheshire gained their coal. It was transported by packhorse: each horse could carry approximately 300lbs of coal on its back, so to transport sufficient amounts, teams of up to thirty horses were employed. Even though Prescot was relatively close to Liverpool, the poor state of the early roads meant that they were only passable in the finest of weather conditions. As soon as the wet months came, these roads turned into a sea of mud and water-filled potholes. With teams of packhorses laden with such heavy loads, it meant that the transportation of coal through to Liverpool and beyond – so vital to its economic success – was erratic at best and non-existent at worst. This was a most unsatisfactory situation, and one that could not be left to continue.

Turnpikes

Matters came to a head in 1725, when the Liverpool Common Council took the step of declaring that a turnpike road should be established between Liverpool and Prescot, and that Trustees should be appointed to ensure that such a turnpike remained in good order all year round. The matter was described as 'Trustees of the Turnpike Roads from Liverpool to Prescot, St Helens, Warrington and Ashton-in-Makerfield', and the Liverpool Common Council decided to construct a turnpike from Liverpool to Prescot in 1726, to make serviceable a road that 'hath been almost unpassable'. The matter was put before Parliament, and received Royal Assent on 26 July 1726. Twenty-one trustees were appointed on a twenty-one year lease, with Messrs Bradshaw and Makin, the principal colliery owners in Prescot, elected as Chief Trustees of the Turnpike.

For the transportation of coal, the situation worked well enough throughout the life of the original lease, and coal was supplied to both Liverpool and the Cheshire 'wiches on a regular basis. All continued to work well until the latter years of the original term of the turnpike, when the supply of coal became erratic, and Bradshaw and Makin began steadily increasing both the rate of coal and the price of the toll along the turnpike. When the lease expired in 1746, following the poor supplies of coal in recent years, the Common Council reviewed the situation.

The solution of the problem was simple enough: extend the turnpike through to St Helens. Here, the new town occupied a greater section of the South Lancashire Coalfield, and as a direct result of this, there were far more collieries, producing much more coal at competitive prices. John Yates, a local surveyor, was employed by the trustees to extend the road through to the coal mines of St Helens, though with the strictest of instructions that he should not exceed the budget of £200 that had been imposed upon him. The extension to the existing turnpike was constructed quickly, reaching the town later that same year, and once again, a regular supply of coal was resumed. On its way to St Helens, the turnpike passed through land owned by the Eccleston family, and later on, land owned by the Gerards. Both families approved the construction of the road, and as a result they were given free passage along it.

The new road was a success, although it did mean that the price of the toll had to rise significantly to cover the cost of the construction, and further improvements were needed to keep the road in operation.

Although the production of coal was far greater from St Helens, further problems would plague Liverpool concerning rising costs – not that the St Helens collieries were overcharging, far from it; their

Carr Mill Dam, a former quarry, was transformed into a reservoir with the re-directing of the Sankey Brook, in order to supply water to the Sankey Canal. The Dam would later become a popular place for picnics, as this photograph indicates. The picture here shows the original sluice, created to supply a regular flow of water into the Sankey Brook and eventually into the canal itself. To the right of the picture stands the Carr Mill Viaduct, erected in the 1870s, carrying the St Helens–Wigan railway across the valley. (DW)

rates were indeed very competitive. It was the cost of transportation along the turnpike itself, which the trustees, doubtless annoyed at the extension through to rival collieries, had increased quite dramatically in an effort to recoup their losses: so high was the toll rate that by the time the coal reached Liverpool it had doubled in price.

Matters rumbled on for a number of years, during which the turnpike was extended further, in 1753, to reach the coalfields of Ashton-in-Makerfield. Later, a new turnpike linked through to Warrington, and Bank Hall in particular, at the request of the influential Patten family.

Nevertheless, the high tolls continued and matters were reaching a point were something had to be done to reduce the cost of transportation. The situation took a more serious turn when tolls were charged on the empty wagons returning to the collieries.

However, the success of the turnpikes not only enabled the transportation of coal to become more reliable, it also opened up the possibility of operating a reliable stagecoach service. There had been stagecoaches in operation long before the arrival of the turnpikes, of course, but their reliability, travelling along the old roads, was in question, with excessive wear and tear on the coaches themselves, not to mention the discomfort of the passengers.

The first of these new stagecoach services ran from Prescot to

Liverpool in 1767, operating a single daily return service between the two towns. Services to and from St Helens did not really begin until 1794. Soon services were criss-crossing the region, and a great many of these passed through St Helens en route to other destinations. Coaches were operating between Liverpool and Manchester, Warrington and Southport, and Liverpool and Bolton.

The Fleece Inn (later the Fleece Hotel, which was demolished in the 1980s) stood on Church Street, and became one of the many busy stopover points on some of the journeys mentioned, where passengers could rest or stretch their legs, and the horses could be watered and changed, before continuing their journey (old stables stood behind the public house long after the stagecoaches had been discontinued). Later, due to the popularity of St Helens at that time, special services began to operate between Liverpool and St Helens.

Despite the success of the stagecoach trade, the pressing concern to the Common Council was the price of coal. It was imperative that a mode of transport be created that could deliver coal to Liverpool at a realistic price. The answer to the dilemma lay not on land, but on water. Years before, the creation of workable navigations of the region's rivers had begun and had proved successful for the free movement of goods and services: the River Weaver, in Cheshire, had been re-worked to raise water levels sufficiently to carry barges through to the Wiches in 1733; the Mersey had been made navigable by Thomas Patten, as far as his copper works at Bank Quay, Warrington in 1698; and Thomas Steers had extended this to create the Mersey & Irwell Navigation through to Manchester in 1732; and the River Douglas had received similar treatment in 1742, making it passable from Wigan through to Tarleton, where it joins the River Ribble.

The Sankey Brook Navigation

With these early successes, the Common Council pondered the question of whether the Sankey Brook – which ran through St Helens and out to reach the Mersey – could be made into a similar navigation. If this were possible, it would solve their transport problems completely: barges could be loaded with coal from the St Helens Collieries and sailed along the waterway to the Mersey, where they could join the river and continue through to Liverpool or across to Cheshire.

Plans for surveying the Sankey Brook were discussed at length at a meeting of the Liverpool Common Council on 5 June 1754, and agreement was reached to conduct such a survey. Two surveyors were instructed to carry out the report on the viability of the project: they were John Ashton, a member of the Common Council, and Henry Berry, the Council's chief engineer. Both men had originated from

In order to raise the canal high enough, Henry Berry created a double lock – the first of its kind in the county. It was a great feat of engineering. Sadly, in 1968, when vast sections of the canal were being filled in by British Waterways, the Old Double Lock was deemed unsafe, and was largely filled in, creating a staircase effect and a waterfall. These two pictures show the Old Double Lock today. (AG)

St Helens, so were ideal choices: Ashton had been the town's bailiff before moving to Liverpool to set up business as a cheese merchant, while Berry, who had served his engineering apprenticeship to a wheelwright from Parr, had later secured a place as a junior engineer under Thomas Steers on the construction of the Salthouse Dock at Liverpool. In fact, following Steers' untimely death part way through the project, Berry was appointed chief engineer to oversee its completion.

The procedure for creating a river navigation was, following the successes of the earlier projects, well established: it involved the dredging of the river bed, widening the banks where necessary, making cuts to straighten out the natural meanders, and thereafter, using locks and weirs appropriately, to control the water level to allow barges to pass along it. This was the straightforward procedure for construction of a river navigation; but the Sankey was a brook, not a river, and that had never been attempted before!

Although both men had been appointed to the task of carrying out the survey, the main responsibility lay with Berry rather than Ashton, as he was the engineer; Ashton held a more supervisory role, being a member of the Common Council. It would be Berry's local knowledge that would prove vital to the success of the navigation, especially in the early stages. Berry had been born in Parr in 1720, and had lived in the township for much of his life before moving to Liverpool. The Sankey Brook passes through Parr, so he knew the brook well; he had played on its banks as a young boy, and doubtless paddled in its waters during the summer months. It would be this intimate knowledge that caused Berry to ponder the viability of the project. He knew, for instance, that the brook was prone to flooding in the wet winter months, yet in stark contrast, during the drier summer months that same brook could be reduced to a trickle. Any attempt to navigate this, in an effort to maintain a consistent level of water over a length suitable for barges to pass, would be almost impossible.

Nevertheless, Berry carried out his survey – for which he later charged the Common Council the princely sum of £66.16 – and reported his findings back to his partner, John Ashton, rather than immediately back to the Common Council. He informed Ashton that the conventional navigation simple was not feasible. And yet, knowing full well the importance of the success of this project to both Liverpool and St Helens, he was not prepared to admit defeat either. Instead he confided in Ashton that a series of cuts, used together to create a 'still water canal' would be the only way of maintaining the required level of water throughout.

The very suggestion of attempting to construct a 'still water canal' as they were referred to then, created a huge problem: not so much in its construction (though that would be difficult enough) but in gaining its approval by Parliament. Any form of transport, be it a turnpike or river navigation, had to be approved by Parliament. This was straightforward when it came to turnpikes or navigations, following so many successes; but passing the idea of creating the country's first canal was out of the question. In 1754, just the year before, a proposal had gone before Parliament to link the towns of Leigh and Salford by canal and had been firmly rejected. Many people, MPs included, simply felt that such a waterway would prove to be unsafe and unreliable.

So both surveyors knew that should they present their true findings and proposals to the Common Council, so as they would surely be rejected by them, not to waste both time and money presenting them before Parliament. The two men chose to resolve their dilemma, to use a modern phrase, by 'being economical with the truth' to their employers: they simply informed the Common Council that the project was feasible, though seemingly difficult, and they were ready to proceed, subject to the Council's and Parliament's approval. All of this goes some way to explaining the apparent secrecy surrounding the construction of the Sankey Brook Navigation (as it was originally called).

With the survey completed, a Bill was drawn up to be presented

In 1761 the Common Council placed a Bill before Parliament to extend the Sankey Canal from the Old Double Locks through to Patten's Copper Works. These two photographs show that section of canal today – taken either side of Blackbrook Road. Like much of the Sankey Canal, these sections are overgrown and largely forgotten. (AG)

before Parliament. The five names which appear on the Bill were all Common Council members, and are listed as follows: James Crosby (Mayor of Liverpool), Charles Goore (the mayor in the following year), Richard Trafford (Senior Bailiff), John Ashton (bailiff in 1749), and John Blackburne Jnr (local merchant).

The Bill was placed before Parliament on 16 December, and was heard on 21 February 1755. Supporting evidence to prove the need for such a navigation – mainly from the parties involved, such as the coal proprietors of the Sankey Valley – was heard by the committee. The Common Council awarded Henry Berry a silver cup, as a token of their esteem, for the work he had carried out in the original survey.

The Sankey Brook Navigation Bill received Royal Assent on 20 March 1755. It read as follows: 'An Act for the Making Navigable the river or brook called Sankey Brook, and three several branches thereof'. The Act went on to say that, where necessary the parties could '... make such new cuts ... canals, trenches or passages for water ...' The wording of the Act was broad enough for Berry to use in defence his intention of constructing a canal, rather than a navigation.

Work began on 5 September at the Warrington end, at Sankey Bridges where a section of brook had already been made into a

What at first glance might appear to be nothing more than a duck pond, was actually a canal basin! Here barges loaded and unloaded materials to and from Patten's foundry and Gerard's collieries. It is hard to believe looking at the place today that it was once such a hive of activity. (*AG*)

navigation some years earlier, with a lock to the river. The Sankey Brook had been named by the Celts during the fifth century, originally spelt Sanchi, and to them it was a holy river. In the centuries prior to the arrival of the Industrial Revolution in the mid-eighteenth century, the waters of the Sankey Brook ran clear, and powered several mills that stood along its banks, particularly at the Warrington end. Work on the construction of the canal was carried out by hundreds of Irish navvies (the term refers to them as navigators) and in complete secrecy; there was no publicity to herald the creation of the new waterway.

Throughout its original length, the canal was raised a total of eighty feet, passing through eight locks and one double lock (from the Sankey Lock, joining the canal to the river, it passed through Bewsey Lock, Hulme Lock, Winwick Lock, Hey Lock, Bradley Lock, Newton Common Lock and Haydock Lock, before reaching the Double Lock). By 1757 much of the canal was completed, reaching the collieries at Parr, and Sarah Clayton's coal mines in particular: she was the first to advertise

in the *Liverpool Chronicle* in November of that year, that 'Mersey flats
were now ready to transport coal' from her Parr Collieries 'through
to Liverpool'. It would be another two years before the canal reached
its terminus at Gerards Bridge.

The total cost of construction reached £200,000. Although the
Liverpool Common Council had funded the original survey, shares
had been offered in the planned navigation. They were advertised
vigorously from Liverpool to Manchester, and were available from the
Liverpool Exchange, between the hours of eleven and one o'clock, on
14 November 1754. Members of the Common Council chose to invest
in the project, though there were equally as many outside investors.
Many of these investors were local colliery owners, as well as other
Liverpool merchants and some from St Helens, all of whom had a
vested interest in the completion and success of the waterway. John
Ashton had invested £9,000 into the canal project (following his death,
in August 1759, his shares passed to his son and three daughters). It
proved to be a sound investment for Ashton and his fellow merchants,
for the canal was a huge success; traffic was brisk from the beginning.

Following the completion of the Sankey Canal, and the efficiency
with which it could deliver coal through to Liverpool, the inadequacies
of the Weaver Navigation began to show themselves: the vessels, loaded
with coal or salt, were slow to pass down this waterway. Complaints
from the Cheshire salt merchants, and equally the Liverpool merchants
dependent on the salt, led to the Liverpool Common Council stating
that it would finance any engineer willing to undertake the modernising
of the River Weaver. This post was filled by the Common Council's
own chief engineer, Henry Berry, fresh from his success on the Sankey
Canal. However, this appointment was to prove to be Berry's final
waterway project: soon after work began creating a new lock and weir
at Pickering's Cut, in an effort to raise the water level, a swell from
the Mersey passed along the Weaver, taking the engineers completely
by surprise, washing away both the lock and the weir and the sides
of the navigation. Although it was clearly not a foreseeable or even a
preventable accident, Berry's credibility was damaged, and he resigned,
returning to his original job at Salthouse Dock. This was be the first
of two heavy blows for Berry for in August of that same year, his
friend and canal building partner John Ashton died. Henry Berry
buried himself in his engineering work for Liverpool's Common Council, work he pursued through to his death in 1812.

In 1761, the Common Council placed a Bill before Parliament to
extend the Sankey Canal in two different directions: an extension from
the Old Double Locks through to Patten's Copper works, and another
from the Sankey Bridges through to Fiddlers Ferry. The first extension
was purely business, at the requests of the Pattens and the Gerards.

The reason for the change to connection to the river from its present position at Sankey Bridges was the tide, which often made entrance to the Mersey difficult and restrictive. Their plan was to extend the canal further down river, to Fiddlers Ferry, where a connection to the river could be more easily maintained. Both plans were approved by Parliament and work commenced on 8 April 1762.

The extension to Patten's Copper Works was straight forward. The extension to Fiddlers Ferry was short – a distance of around three miles – and without the need for locks it was completed quickly, and without any problems. This new connection to the River Mersey, via a sealock, worked well and remained in operation for the next seventy years, only being replaced after the railways arrived to threaten the trade of the canals. Now a new, larger dock was required, further down river, at Spike Island: a new extension needed to be built, gaining Parliament's approval in 1830, and overseen by canal engineer, Francis Giles.

Meanwhile, back at St Helens, a new branch was also planned: leaving the Gerards Bridge section, it would skirt around what was to become the town centre. Work commenced in 1772, and was completed to the Ravenhead terminus within three years. It was quite an undertaking for the canal was raised significantly through the New Double Lock,

The New Double Locks were built in the early 1770s, raising Berry's original canal to the level of the town centre and Ravenhead extensions. These locks, along with other sections of the canal, were rebuilt in the 1880s, and had been rejuvenated again in the early 1990s. *(AG)*

and continued to the town centre where it branched into two sections: one fed the Ravenhead Colliery (and later the Sutton Lodge Alkali Works), known as the 'Sutton Section'; the other headed up to Ravenhead by a more westerly route to its final terminus. By the mid-1770s, the Sankey Canal was a huge success, delivering around 90,000 tons of coal per annum to Liverpool and the Cheshire Salt mines.

Before we proceed any further, let us attempt to answer the question: which was the first English Canal, the Sankey or the Bridgewater? The Sankey waterway is, without doubt, a canal and not a navigation. Although it draws water from some brooks (including the Sankey Brook), it also takes water from specially constructed reservoirs (like Carr Mill Dam), like most canals. So the Sankey Canal was just that, a canal.

Now to muddy the waters, so to speak: when is a canal not a canal? When it's a navigation! Although the Sankey Canal is a canal, it fails to gain the title 'the first English canal' simply because it was built under a Navigation Act, not a Canal Act. The Bridgewater Canal, built in 1759, two years after the Sankey, is a canal, because it was constructed as a canal, under the very first English Canal Act, whereas the Sankey was built under the existing rules as a navigation.

Having said that, it is also fair to say that the construction of the Bridgewater Canal was as a direct result of the success of the Sankey Navigation. Its success proved beyond all reasonable doubt that a 'still water canal' could be constructed safely and made reliable; the early fears that such waterways would flood, leak water, or fail to maintain a decent water level throughout, were all proved false. This approval by Parliament led to a host of other canals being constructed throughout the country: the Canal Age had arrived!

The continued success of the Sankey Canal inspired others to create similar waterways. The Bridgewater, as already mentioned, was built two years after the Sankey, using the water that flowed from the Duke's Worsley Mines, drained by the great slough that John Gilbert had created. Soon 'canal fever' was sweeping the nation, and many more canals were proposed. In the industrial north-west of England, Liverpool was still at the heart of any proposed waterway: the idea of constructing a huge waterway – part canal, part river navigation – from Liverpool to Hull had been mentioned in 1766. This idea was soon forgotten and replaced by the suggestion of a super-trans-Pennine canal, from Liverpool to Leeds, in December 1768. This proposal gathered momentum; it was given the title, the 'Leeds & Liverpool Canal' early on, and its main objective (as far as the Liverpool Common Council was concerned) was to connect with as many collieries as possible; equally, connection to other industrial towns had to be of benefit to the economy of the north-west of England. To the people of Liverpool, the town of Wigan, with its large coalfields, had long been of particular interest, so any proposed route of the new canal would have to pass through or close to Wigan.

Many proposed routes were put forward, together with particular objectives, for consultation; yet from the beginning, the idea of taking the canal out from the north of Liverpool, heading towards Burscough, seemed the most logical direction, as it could connect with many stone and slate quarries around Parbold and Appley Bridge before descending into Wigan. However, other routes were put forward, such as taking the canal from the south of Liverpool, shadowing the river. To the proprietors of the Sankey Canal, any new canal within South Lancashire was seen as a threat to the future prosperity of their own, and so concerned about this were they that they pressed that any such canal must connect with the Sankey. They also proposed the construction of an aqueduct over the River Mersey at Runcorn Gap, to connect the Sankey to the Cheshire Canals, the Bridgewater and Trent & Mersey.

Arguments wrangled for sometime, and at one point it looked as though two canals might leave Liverpool: the Leeds & Liverpool from the north, and another, called the Liverpool South Canal, from the opposite direction, which could link to the Sankey. Following further intense discussions, many of these proposals (including that of the Liverpool South Canal and the Runcorn aqueduct) were dropped simply on the grounds of cost. So the Leeds & Liverpool Canal won, following the earlier suggested route. The canal was a joint Lancashire/Yorkshire project and had committees in both Liverpool and Leeds. James Brindley, now the most sought-after authority on canals since his involvement in the Bridgewater Canal, was brought in to carry out the survey throughout the 127 miles, assisted by John Longbottom, Yorkshire's chief engineer: Brindley was offered the post as chief engineer to construct the new canal, but declined due to pressure of existing work, so his assistant John Longbottom was made chief engineer.

The purpose of the Sankey Canal had been to connect the St Helens collieries to Liverpool, and to reduce the overall cost of transportation: it did all of that and more. The collieries, if not on the route of the canal (and a great many of them were) connected via specially constructed tramways, where wagons could run down to the awaiting barges on the canal. The coal in the town attracted industry, which also made good use of the waterway: the Ravenhead terminus, for instance, was used by the British Cast Plate Glass Manufacturers' Company, along with the Pary's Copper Works. Later many more businesses located alongside the canal to boost the transportation of their goods.

The canals, although a significant step in eighteenth-century transportation, were eventually overtaken by the railways during the middle of the nineteenth century (as we shall see in the following chapter). The St Helens Canal, would eventually merge with its rival the St Helens & Runcorn Gap Railway in the middle of the nineteenth century, and indeed by 1864 that union would be absorbed into the LNWR. Thereafter the canal, now the poor relation to the railway, would enter a period of slow decline that would continue into the next century. The canal saw its last official barge in 1919, at least as far as the St Helens terminus was concerned, although the canal only closed officially in 1931. With the improvements to the road network during that decade, much of the canal was split into sections as the swing bridges were replaced with more permanent structures. Despite the separation of the St Helens end of the Sankey Canal, commercial traffic between the River Mersey and Newton continued until the 1950s: the final cargo from the Sankey Sugar works left in 1959. The canal was finally abandoned four years later and left in a derelict state, the waterway used as a dumping ground for all sorts of rubbish. By

1968, after severe flooding had led to sections of the canal being breached, it was decided that large sections should be filled in. The Sankey Canal had reached the end of the line.

The Sankey Canal Today

Even today, with all the many changes that have taken place in the town, it's still worth taking a walk along the length of the Sankey Canal to get the feel of its importance in the shaping of St Helens and a sense of the industry that once stood alongside it.

The Ravenhead section was filled in during 1898: today Canal Street follows the line of what was once the canal. From Safeway, it is possible to walk along the towpath, past the 'hotties' of Pilkingtons on their original Grove Street works, through to the railway. On the opposite side, the car park and the 'World of Glass' exhibition centre was once the location of the St Helens Foundry. Passing under the railway, on the opposite side of the canal, can be seen one of the last surviving cone-shaped glasshouses, now part of the World of Glass centre. Further along, on the far side of the canal, would have been the other junction of the canal to feed the Sutton Section and the Ravenhead Colliery, but was filled in during the early years of the twentieth century: it would have followed the route of the new Linkway Road for around five hundred yards to its terminus at the colliery yards.

Turning the corner of the canal further along the towing path, the canal is crossed by the last remaining section of the St Helens Runcorn Gap Railway: when the canal was in operation, this was spanned by a swing bridge, which could be operated by hand or from the signal box that stood a little further down the line. On the opposite side of the canal, the open space (now part of the Greenway Recreation Scheme) was once the site of the Lyon Bottle Works yard.

Crossing the canal via the railway bridge, the gas main, which today crosses the canal just a couple of feet above the water level, once crossed on an overhead gantry. Just ahead, on the towpath, the remains of a canal spur can still be seen, which entered into a basin on the former site of the Fountain Soap works and some parts of the Kurtz Alkali works: this was closed at the turn of the century after the Todd Brothers purchased the site (today that site is occupied by the Matalan store). When this canal spur was still active it was crossed by a pedestrian swing bridge. On the opposite side of the canal once stood Almond Michell's Lead Works, and a small stonemason's yard.

Following the towing path up to the main road, there is the remaining half of the road bridge opened by King George VI in 1937 to replace the original swing bridge. Crossing the main road, take the

This section of canal, between Standish Street bridge and the New Double Locks, once served Union Plate Glass, which stood on the left-hand side of the picture, and Union Chemicals, which stood on the right. The St Helens & Lowton railway once crossed the canal here: although the actual bridge has long since been removed, the sides are still visible. In the distance, the tops of the 'Burgies' are just visible: massive banks of waste sand, deposited there by Pilkingtons. (AG) public footpath on the far side and continue to eventually rejoin the next surviving section of canal. Here the section of canal was filled in at the same time the bridge was built, and for many years (through to the early 1990s) the abattoir stood here. Under Corporation Street bridge brings you to the next section of canal, which has been restored in recent years; new stonework laid either side of the canal and the towing path has been covered in tarmac. At the far end of this section of canal, just before the main road, the site of a former railway swing bridge can still be seen; this took the railway into the United Alkali works and Varley's Foundry which stood next door, both on the opposite side of the canal, and through to join the Runcorn Gap line. In fact the remains of the foundry wall still stands there today.

Crossing the road(where the canal now passes through culverts beneath), was once another swing bridge. Over the Sankey, throughout its length, all of the bridges were swing bridges; there were none of the familiar humpback bridges seen across many other canals.

On the opposite side of the road, the canal continues along side the Technology Campus; this was originally the site of the Union Plate Glass Works, owned by the Greenall family. Later, it was bought by Fosters Glass, and later still Rockware Glass. On the opposite side,

the land now taken by the gas depot was once Union Chemicals. Further along this section of canal, the sides of the former railway bridge still stand, even though the line and the bridge itself were removed soon after its closure in the 1960s.

The roadway today leads into the Ravenhead Glass Depot, which was once the site of the Globe Alkali Works, served by a swing bridge across the canal. Just head are the New Double Locks (called this to distinguish them from the original double lock built by Berry at Parr, referred to later as the 'Old Double Lock') built in 1770, to link the new section of canal to Berry's original canal below. Although these locks, like the rest on the canal, were rebuilt in 1884, once the canal had closed this double lock was left derelict for years, before being restored in 1993. A lock keeper's cottage once stood to the right of the towpath, though this has long since been demolished. Straight ahead can be seen the grassy banks of the 'burgies' built from sand and rouge dumped here by Pilkingtons' Cowley Hill works nearby.

Along Berry's original canal, to your left leads to the Gerards bridge terminus, passing under the railway *en route*. The terminus itself no longer exists; it was filled in some years ago. Many people make the mistake of thinking that the Rainford Brook, seen today running into the former canal bed, is in fact the canal, and so passes under the roadway; this assumption is incorrect! The Gerards Bridge terminus stopped short of the road, and followed a line wide of the brook, to the left of the public footpath seen here today (which then formed part of the old towing path). In later years, after the canal had closed, Rainford Brook (which originally ran parallel to the canal) was diverted to run along the canal bed, as it continues to do today. All of this can be verified by viewing the 1894 map of the area, kept in the St Helens Local History Archive. Either side of the terminus stood the Muspratt & Gamble Alkali works, the first of its kind to open in the town – in fact, sections of the old factory wall can still be seen near the road.

Taking the opposite direction, back down the old canal, leads to the former location of Parr Hall, home of Sarah Clayton. This section of canal is very overgrown. On one side of the canal stood the old hall, now modern houses, and on the other was once the embankment for the railway that crossed the canal earlier; today it's open grassland, called Merton Bank Open Space. Further along this section the waters of the canal are directed into the Sankey Brook. Following the brook leads to the Parr section of the canal. Much of this section has long since been filled in, houses stand on what was the route of the canal, and only beyond the school field does the canal begin again.

Here is the original double lock and the first junction of the original canal: one section leads to Blackbrook terminus, the other to Sankey Bridges at Warrington. The Blackbrook section was built to service

The winding gear on the New Double Locks is original and, despite its age, is in remarkably good condition. These locks were in a terrible state for many years, and have only been restored since the 1990s. (*AG*)

the many collieries there, and the silting mill at Stanley Bank, owned by Thomas Patten; remains of the mill can still be seen in the woodlands. It was this section that took the feed from Carr Mill Dam into the Sankey Brook and the canal to maintain the water levels.

The original double lock – later referred to as the 'Old Double Lock' after the construction of the New Double Lock – still survives today, albeit drastically modified. Sadly, unlike the New Double Lock, it was not restored, but dismantled during work carried out to this section in 1978/79: removing the lock gates, the depth of the locks was reduced, creating a staircase effect, through which the water flows like a mini-waterfall. One interesting feature of this set of locks is its width; these locks are much narrower than those seen on other canals, capable of accepting just one barge at a time.

The remaining section of canal has been filled in, though not totally, just sufficient to reduce it to the size of a brook (the original sides can still be seen, along with their stonework in places). This was done in 1968, when the British Waterways Board decided, after continued flooding of this section, not to repair it but to fill it in from this point to Dallam, near Warrington, with the slight exception of a stretch of canal at Newton left for angling. In its place, St Helens Council created the Sankey Valley Way, a footpath which runs along the former canal towing path. Even so, there are sections of canal still remaining: for instance, a little further long two angling ponds are actually parts of the canal, similarly, at Penkford Bridge, near Earlestown, another fishing pond there is a section of canal.

At Earlestown, the canal passed under the famous Sankey Valley Viaduct, constructed in 1829, during the building of the Liverpool–Manchester line. During its construction, which the proprietors of the canal objected to strongly, the Liverpool & Manchester Railway Company had to pay compensation for disruption to the canal: this was negotiated to a lump sum of £500 followed by a disturbance fee of £30 per day while work was carried out there. The arches of the viaduct were built sixty feet high, to allow the Mersey flats to pass underneath without the need to drop their tall masts.

At Newton, a section of canal returns, together with the remains of the Bradley and Hey Locks. Further along the remainder of the canal has been filled in, though on either side of the M6 motorway, the Winwick Lock and Winwick Quay have recently been excavated. The canal disappears once more until the Sankey Valley Park is reached at Warrington, where the canal has been perfectly restored and preserved, and continues intact through to Spike Island where it joins the River Mersey.

Chapter Three

THE AGE OF RAILWAYS

HE GREATEST THREAT TO THE PROSPERITY of the canal network came in the nineteenth century, with the arrival and spread of 'railway mania' throughout the country. For the Sankey Canal the threat was realised with the creation of St Helens' first railway, the St Helens & Runcorn Gap line. Its story is an interesting one; it started as a challenger to the waterway, but ended as its owner, and in some ways, its saviour.

Railways or tramways made of timber had been in common usage both before and after the arrival of the canals. They had been used by the colliery proprietors to move their wagons, both in and outside the mines, and later down to the boats and barges moored on the canal side. But this had been all they had been used for: short journeys, nothing more.

However, one man, Thomas Gray from Nottingham, had promoted their use as a means of transportation of both passengers and freight between towns and cities, though it should be stressed that these were to be used by specially constructed, horse-drawn carts and carriages, not locomotives. He had publicised his radical ideas across the country, seeking the endorsement of the more prominent members of society including the Prime Minister, the Secretary of State for Transport, and the Lord Mayor of London, though without success. Gray's concept of long-distance travel along rails – as opposed to the poor roads – were regarded by most as being a ridiculous and impractical suggestion. He only gained credibility after he approached the merchants of Manchester and Liverpool who, rather than laughing off his ideas, instead saw the merit in the concept he was proposing. To them, anything that would both break the monopoly of the canal and navigation proprietors, and increase the speed in which goods (particularly cotton) could pass between the port at Liverpool and the cotton mills of Manchester, had to be worth investigating.

The concept that Gray had proposed gathered momentum. Surveys were carried out by William James, and the idea of using locomotives rather than horse-drawn carriages was offered after a meeting with George Stephenson during the construction of the Stockton & Darlington Railway. The eventual completion of the Liverpool & Manchester Railway, by George and Robert Stephenson, in 1830, lit the fuse to the 'railway revolution' and led to a number of similar projects being proposed. One of these projects came from the industrialists of St Helens, who wanted a fast and reliable link between the town and the River Mersey, at Runcorn Gap. The possibility of this railway was first raised in 1829, while the Liverpool–Manchester line was nearing completion, and the idea grew, driven by prominent men of the town such as the Pilkingtons, Greenalls and the Welsh industrialist Michael Hughes. However, the interest in the line was not confined to St Helens-based businessmen – one of the early investors was Joseph Crosfield, soapmaker, of Warrington. The industrialists approached a young engineer by the name of Charles Blacker Vignoles, to carry out the task of first surveying the proposed route of the line and, if found to be feasible, to construct it. Vignoles accepted this commission and set about work immediately.

Vignoles was gaining credibility as an engineer, and had actually been involved in the Liverpool–Manchester line prior to this project. The original full survey of the first passenger line had been carried out by George Stephenson (following William James's bankruptcy), and had been faced with huge opposition from landowners whose land the line would have to cross, and the canal proprietors whose interests were threatened. They hampered Stephenson's research at

almost every stage, denying him access to their estates. Opposition also came from the locals living along the proposed route, who feared the arrival of the new form of travel, and gathered in large angry groups to shout abuse at the railway engineers: the worst of this action occurred around St Helens, where stones were thrown at the engineers and some of them were actually badly beaten. All of this harassment led to the production of what was an inferior survey which, by the time it was presented to the Parliamentary committee, was easily discredited by the opposition's lawyers and their experts (who included Francis Giles, recently commissioned by the Sankey Canal proprietors to extend their canal from Fiddlers Ferry to Spike Island). As a direct result of the harassment, George Stephenson had miscalculated the heights involved in the embankments, bridges, both under and over the turnpikes, and so on. The Bill was thrown out. Undeterred, the investors commissioned the Rennie brothers (sons of John Rennie, the famous canal engineer), who had had greater experience in the passing of projects through Parliament, to conduct another survey; in fact, they actually passed the groundwork of this laborious task on to one of the junior engineers within their employ: Charles Blacker Vignoles.

This survey was completed quickly and efficiently, with much reduced opposition from the landowners, and was duly passed by Parliament. However, the Rennie brothers withdrew from the project soon afterwards, when it was stated that despite the poor survey and the rejection by Parliament, the investors still wanted George Stephenson to work on the construction of the line. Although his masters had left, Vignoles remained with the project until 1827, when he too found he could no longer work alongside such a difficult man as Stephenson. Vignoles left on good terms with the investors, however, and this stood him in good favour within the growing railway industry. Almost immediately he acquired the position of chief engineer on the construction of the Wigan Branch Line (which joined to the Liverpool & Manchester) and soon after, secured the contract to construct the St Helens line.

Vignoles carried out the survey of the St Helens line. The proposed route was to begin at Cowley Hill Colliery (close to Gerard's Bridge) and head in a southerly direction, passing through Sutton and Lea Green, where it would join the Liverpool & Manchester Railway, before continuing through to Widnes.

The first proposed Bill went before Parliament in late November of 1829, but was soon rejected, following strong objections from the directors of the Liverpool–Manchester Railway Company: they were opposed to the linking of the two lines, feeling that it would surely led to delays to their services. Plans were revised, adding an intersection

The St Helens & Runcorn Gap Railway, once a vital transport link for the town, has, through the latter years of the twentieth century, become mostly derelict; today only a short section of line is in operation, linking the town to a factory in Sutton. This picture shows part of that still active line, crossing the canal near Matalan. A swing bridge once operated here, allowing barges to pass. (AG)

bridge (the first of its type in the country) over the Liverpool &
Manchester line, and were presented before the House of Commons
on 16 February 1830. This time, without any further objections, it
passed through Parliament easily, receiving Royal Assent from King
George IV on 29 May. This was described as an 'Act for making a
Railway from the Cowley Hill Colliery in the Parish of Prescot, to
Runcorn Gap in the same parish (with several branches there from) …'
29 May 1830. This was not the only Act that was required to construct
the line – further Acts were sought, when necessary, to add sections
and other buildings – but this was the most important, allowing the
project to proceed.

Construction of the St Helens & Runcorn Gap Railway

Although all the meetings of the initial investors of the new railway
had been held at the Fleece Hotel in St Helens, the first full meeting
of the shareholders was held in Liverpool in June 1830. The principal
shareholders at that meeting included, James Muspratt, William and
Richard Pilkington, together with their brother-in-law, Peter Greenall;
Lee Watson of the St Helens Foundry; Michael Hughes, one of the
town's most influential landowners; and Joseph Crosfield, of the Warrington-based soap works. A board of ten directors was elected at the
meeting, with Peter Greenall sworn in as chairman. The newly-formed
company was called the St Helens Runcorn Gap Railway Company.
Charles Vignoles was officially appointed as chief engineer for the
construction of the proposed railway, on an annual salary of £650,
from which he alone was also responsible for the pay his two junior
engineers, Merett and Forth.

Although the length of the line was relatively short, at around eight
miles (especially when compared to the Liverpool & Manchester line),
it was not without its difficulties. Throughout the length, bridges had
to be constructed to carry the line either under or over the roadways,
embankments were required in certain areas to ensure a level line,
and the intersection bridge had to be built to carry this railway over
the Liverpool & Manchester Railway. Over the Sankey Canal, a swing
bridge would be required. But of all the bridges involved in the line,
the intersection bridge over the railway – being the first of its kind
in the country – was to give them the greatest headache, with acute
incline planes having to be constructed either side.

An initial working budget of £120,000 had been awarded at the
shareholders meeting which Vignoles had confirmed that he could
work to. Although a single line of track had been proposed, sufficient

This picture shows the intersection bridge of the St Helens & Runcorn Gap Railway over the Liverpool & Manchester Line. This was the first of its kind in the country, and gave trouble early on, when the inclines were too acute for the early locomotives. The story behind this particular scene is not known: there is much activity alongside the line, and it is commonly thought that the onlookers are awaiting the imminent arrival of a royal train. (*Reproduced with the permission of the St Helens Local History and Archives Library*)

land was purchased to allow the use of a double track at some later stage. Soon after work had begun, the directors informed Vignoles that, on certain sections of the line at least, a double track was to be laid. The primary objective of the line was to deliver coal to the docks more quickly and cheaply than its rival the canal – with this in mind, branch lines were proposed to connect the collieries to the railway, so wagons could be loaded and transported through to Runcorn Gap.

Construction of the line was split into three sections, and tenders for the work were put out to various construction companies, with the best bids securing the contracts; J. J. Thornton & Sons were successful in securing two of the three main sections of the line, while Benjamin Seed & Company gained the third. Vignoles, as chief engineer, remained in overall control of the subcontractors, and supervised the construction throughout. Although in the initial stages there had been no objections from the landowners across whose land the railway would pass (unlike the Liverpool & Manchester line), once construction was under way some landowners insisted on a higher price being paid due to the disruption they were experiencing. Despite the railway company's deep reservations, this extra money had to be paid to ensure the line remained on schedule, though it would affect the budget greatly.

The construction of the docks at Widnes led to further problems. The canal proprietors had put a bill before Parliament at the same time as the railway company, to seek to extend the canal from Fiddlers Ferry to Spike Island: this was approved. Following this success, the canal proprietors also petitioned Parliament, pointing out to them that, in all fairness, the docks of both rival companies should be built side by side, and completion of both docks – canal and railway – should be simultaneous. Parliament accepted the canal proprietors' claims regarding fairness, and passed the appropriate Bill, insisting that both docks should be completed together, to avoid any thoughts of favouritism to either party. Once again, construction was placed out to tender, and was secured by Nowells & Sons of Dewsbury, who also supplied the stone used in the docks' construction. Both docks were completed, and opened for trade, in July 1833.

Meanwhile, by 1831, with the project looking more expensive than originally predicted, Vignoles informed the Board of Directors that to remain close to the original budget he would have to reassess the entire project, making the necessary cuts were appropriate. This he succeeded in doing, although at some cost to the standard of the line: he reduced the overall size of the docks, dropped the double tracks (including the proposed double track over the intersection bridge crossing the Liverpool & Manchester line), and opted for just one connecting line to that railway (on the Manchester-bound track) rather than the two that had originally been planned. Yet regardless of these cuts, by the summer of 1832 the railway was far from being finished, and once again was way over budget. Further cuts were made, this time to the number of branch lines connecting the railway to the collieries – which was to prove to be a costly mistake in the future. Even with these cuts, the Board of Directors had to approve a further loan of £40,000 to ensure completion; in fact, the cost of constructing the St Helens Runcorn Gap Railway was to finish close to £200,000.

The acute incline planes, built either side of the intersection bridge crossing the Liverpool & Manchester railway, proved to be a real headache for the engineers. The angle was so sharp that the locomotives of the day – especially with fully-loaded wagons – simply could not haul themselves up the steep slope. Initially, men and horses were employed to assist the locomotives, although later it was decided that a stationary engine was a much better solution. It worked well, and with a steel cable attached to the front of the locomotive, it could be hauled up quickly and easily. This engine was supplied and installed by St Helens Foundry.

The first train to travel along the newly-completed line, loaded with coal from the Broad Oak Colliery in Parr, did so on 28 November 1832, watched by hundreds of fascinated onlookers. This was a test run, and the locomotive delivered its cargo safely to Runcorn Gap, making good time along the new line. The line did not officially open until 21 February of the following year. The completed docks opened for trade on 24 July, capable of handling vessels in excess of 200 tons. Even when the railway was fully open, as a direct result of the cost-cutting measures, only three collieries had connecting branch lines (which included Broad Oak), although Ravenhead Colliery, one of the largest and most productive of the town's collieries, was connected up to the railway in the following year.

Transport Developments

With the arrival of the railways as the new means of passenger transport, many of the long-standing stagecoach operators gauged it as a major threat to the prosperity of their own businesses, and 'the beginning of the end'. Some, such as Bartholomew Bretherton at Rainhill, chose to retire rather than attempt to compete against this new, faster rival. Other stagecoach operators, entrepreneurs of their day, actively encouraged the railways by investing in them (in the case of Peter Greenall, this meant becoming chairman of the company). Others saw the arrival of the railways as a means to further trade; for instance, a service was established soon after the opening of the St Helens Runcorn Gap Railway operating a connecting coach service for railway passengers between the stations at Peasley Cross and St Helens Junction, the first of which ran in September 1832. Later, another service operated between Peasley Cross station and St Helens town centre; and although a relatively short distance, it was a popular service.

By the middle of the nineteenth century more coach operators had arrived on the scene. One of the larger operators was the Liverpool Road and Railway Omnibus Company, which was owned by the Busby family, and operated services between St Helens and Liverpool from 1860, with stables at Prescot. At first the service only ran daily; yet within a couple of years, intense demand had increased this to three or four trips per day.

Merger Talks

Meanwhile, competition between the two rival forms of transport – canal and rail – was now intense. In an effort to remain competitive, and avoid losing customers to the railway, the directors of the Sankey Canal drastically reduced their transport rates. Although the railway was certainly quicker than the canal, it did not manage to steal much trade. By 1836, for instance, three years since the opening of the railway, only seven collieries had branch lines attached. This led to a large difference in the amount of coal each company moved: the canal in that year transported around 170,000 tons, while the railway moved just 130,000.

In 1834, the original contract to operate locomotives on the railway had been awarded to the Viaduct Foundry at Newton-le-Willows, but by 1841 that contract had been cancelled and awarded instead to the St Helens Foundry. Although Messrs Watson and Daglish were prepared to operate far more locomotives on the line than their predecessors, they refused to cover the running repairs to the railway track that the previous operator had; they had found the line in a poor state of repair, even such a short space of time after completion. Later, however, the St Helens Foundry did negotiate a separate contract to cover repair and renewal of track for the railway.

By 1843, the shift in business to the canal rather than the railway was even greater than before: during that year the canal handled just over half a million tons of coal, compared to less than half that by the railway. And yet neither side was winning the battle, as their price-cutting was really starting to affect profits. A proposal to amalgamate the two companies had originally been put to the Board of Directors of the railway by Joseph Crosfield back in 1838, but had been firmly rejected by the canal proprietors. By 1843, with matters worsening, another proposal of amalgamation was presented; this time both sides were prepared to sit round a table and discuss the matter; nevertheless, the talks broke down. The following year Crosfield died and the railway Board lost one of its greatest campaigners. It would take another two years before a formal plan for the railway company to buy out the canal proprietors completely was finalised: the plan was put before Parliament and received Royal Assent in July 1845. Henceforth, the new company – which now held the monopoly on transport in St Helens – would trade as the St Helens Canal and Railway Company.

The sudden deaths of two prominent men from the fledgling railway company in consecutive years of 1844 and 1845 proved to be a massive loss – Joseph Crosfield, for his negotiation skills, and Peter Greenall for his leadership – and one that the company would struggle to overcome. Later that same year, the new Board of Directors, now chaired by Gilbert Greenall since his brother's death, reviewed their financial situation: they brought in the railway engineer, John Meadows Rendel, to survey their entire operation, and look at ways of reducing overall running costs and securing greater income for the future. His report was sweeping and thorough. It proposed that the Board close the docks at Runcorn Gap, and replace them instead with much larger docks situated further down the river at Garston. He also suggested that their railway network be significantly expanded with the construction of two new lines, one from Gerard's Bridge through to Rainford, and another to Eccleston. This second line, to reach Eccleston, was later dropped following objections from the Grand Junction Railway Company, who had already submitted plans to construct a railway from Huyton to St Helens. Nevertheless, a branch line was constructed to Eccleston though on a different route, for freight (this would later service Pilkingtons' Triplex Works). But the first proposal, of a line from St Helens to Rainford, with stations at Gerards Bridge, Moss Bank and Crank (before joining the Liverpool–Wigan line, and creating Rainford Junction) went ahead as planned, and was a huge success. Later, a further extension, from Rainford Junction to Ormskirk, was built in a joint venture with South Lancashire Railways, with a further connection to Southport.

However, the most significant proposal made in the Rendell report would also prove to be the largest undertaking: the construction of a branch line, from Widnes to Warrington, connecting to the St Helens Runcorn Gap line, via Fiddlers Ferry. This was adopted after being strongly backed by George Crosfield, who had taken the place left by his father on the board (the reason for Crosfield's enthusiasm was obvious: the new railway passed alongside Crosfield's works at Bank Quay, offering tremendous improvements to their transportation). This new line was put before Parliament and received Royal Assent in July 1847. So important to the railway company's plans was this new line that construction was commenced immediately; it was later extended, to reach the newly-built docks at Garston.

In the same year as the new Widnes & Warrington line was begun, one of the greatest difficulties experienced on the original St Helens & Runcorn Gap Railway was being addressed. Robert Daglish, director of the St Helens Foundry, proposed the reduction of the acute angle of the incline planes at Sutton, which in spite of the introduction and use of a stationary engine had plagued the line from its creation and still caused delays to traffic. His plans were readily accepted by the railway company and work began in November of the same year, reaching completion in February 1849.

A Passenger Railway

The St Helens Runcorn Gap Railway had been built principally with the transportation of coal in mind, yet following the success in passenger traffic on the Liverpool & Manchester line (which accounted for much of its annual revenue), passenger stations had been added to the line. The first such station for the people of St Helens was built at Peasley Cross (parts of this still remain today, seen from Sutton Road Bridge). However, the location of this station was hardly close to the town centre, and as the years went by, the directors of the line could see that they were losing valuable income by not catering for the general public. With this in mind, the terminus of the line was extended towards St Helens town centre and a new station was built, on land along side Raven Street opposite the Raven Hotel. Work began on this line and the station in February 1849: the booking office was built in nearby Salisbury Street, and a total of thirteen lines were added. The first passenger train left there in December of that year. To coincide with this, further work had been carried out to the main line; many more branch lines were added, connecting to all the major collieries, foundries, glass houses and copper works.

Although St Helens now had its own passenger station, it had missed out on connection to the first passenger railway – the Liverpool & Manchester – years before: the original plan, as surveyed by George Stephenson, took a more direct route that would have passed through the centre of St Helens. This route was altered in the second survey, carried out by Charles Vignoles, following objections from the Earls of Derby and Sefton, as it would have passed too close to their respective estates at Knowsley and Croxteth. Moving the line further south away from these estates meant that it also moved away from the centre of St Helens. The line just touched the district of Sutton, which later led to the creation of St Helens Junction Station, joining the St Helens Runcorn Gap Line to the original Liverpool & Manchester Railway.

This lack of a link to Liverpool led Peter Greenall, the most promi-nent businessman in the town, to launch a private coach service in 1827 called the Regulator, which operated a regular service between St Helens and Liverpool. Later Greenall rented out this service to a local man named Lawton, who maintained it for a number of years thereafter.

At last the people of St Helens knew that shortly they would gain a connection to the Liverpool & Manchester line. However, within the next couple of years things were going to change: both the Grand Junction Railway Company and the St Helens Canal and Railway Company would be taken over by one of the fast emerging railway giants: the London and North Western Railway Company (LNWR). In 1851, a meeting was held at Prescot by the directors of the new company to discuss the construction of the Huyton-St Helens line, followed by further meetings in St Helens. However, the commencement of work on this new line was delayed until 1868 by landowners' objections.

The new line joined the existing Liverpool & Manchester just west of Huyton, and continued to St Helens, via Prescot and Thatto Heath. Work was slow, hampered by having to cut through the natural sand-stone at Thatto Heath. Another difficulty was crossing the Pilkington Grove Street Works: this was achieved by the construction of a steel viaduct. Despite the difficulties encountered *en route*, the line was

St Helens has two railway stations: one in the town centre, on Shaw Street, connecting to both Liverpool and Wigan, and the other, St Helens Junction, at Sutton Oak and connecting to the Liverpool & Manchester Railway. The original nineteenth-century Shaw Street Station was demolished and replaced with a modern building in 1961. During the 1980s the station was revamped again, changing its name to this time to St Helens Central. (AG)

finally completed in 1871. A new station was built at St Helens, St Helens Shaw Street, which opened on 17 July of that same year (the old Raven Street station closed soon after). Prescot Station opened later the same year, as did Thatto Heath, followed in July 1891 with a new station at Eccleston Park. Within a few years, by public demand, an extension was added to the line to take it to Wigan.

With both freight and passenger numbers increasing, St Helens witnessed the building of its third town centre station in 1895; Central Station, built on the corner of Corporation Street and Central Street. Originally only open to freight traffic, within five years it had begun catering for passengers too. This was a very popular station in its heyday, handling much of the town's traffic, transporting goods and passengers through to Manchester, via Lowton. It closed to the general public in 1952, but remained open for freight until its complete closure in January 1965. Today, the Law Courts, Police Station, Grosvenor House and a car park occupy its former location.

Decline of the St Helens & Runcorn Gap Railway

Meanwhile, the original St Helens Runcorn Gap Railway line would remain in use. It carried freight and munitions throughout both World Wars, and saw good times during the 1950s, 60s and 70s. However, by the late 1970s and early 1980s, the line was witnessing a huge reduction in traffic and rapidly becoming redundant. Within a few years the operation of the line was scaled down further, leading to some sections being shut completely. Today, only a very short section of single track remains in operation: running from the main line at St Helens, passing over Peasley Cross Lane and under both Sutton Road and Baxters Lane bridges, it services a single factory in Sutton.

The vast majority of the railway line bed remains, and a variety of embankments, bridges and cuttings, passing through Sutton, Clock-face, Sutton Manor, Bold Heath and onward to the outskirts of Widnes. As it stands today, it is in dereliction, a post-industrial eyesore. A more fitting use for the heritage of the town's first railway would be to turn it into a linear path or park, along the same lines as the Rainford Linear Park. I live in hope.

The huge railway sidings and locomotive sheds off Baxters Lane remained in operation until the 1960s, when they were finally closed. Soon after work began on taking up the tracks and converting the huge sheds into a supermarket, which it remained until recently. Now the building and land stands derelict, awaiting demolition. Further sidings, originally built to service Ravenhead Colliery and Pilkingtons' Grove Street works, have also been drastically reduced in recent years (certainly since the construction of the Linkway Road, which passes through their former location). Today, only a small section of the sidings remains, feeding off the main Liverpool–Wigan line, to trans-port raw materials through to Pilkingtons.

The 'swinging sixties' saw great changes to the nation's railway network following the sweeping report of Dr Beeching, and the picture in St Helens was no exception. The once popular St Helens–Rainford line was a victim of these cuts, having lost its passenger service in 1951; it closed completely in 1964, and its track was taken up just three years later. Today, a small section passes over Gerards Bridge, to service Pilkingtons' Cowley Hill works. The route of the old line can still be determined however: the two remaining sides of the former bridge that once crossed Washway Lane signifies that Scafell Road opposite was actually the path of the old railway line, heading through to the former Moss Bank station (today a public house); and Rainford's Linear Park is actually the bed of the old railway line.

Also in the 1960s, rumours that the Huyton–St Helens railway line was to close proved unfounded. Instead, the original Shaw Street station was demolished, and replaced with a more modern-looking building, using glass supplied by Pilkingtons. Its overall cost rose to around £80,000 and it reopened on 17 November 1961. More recently, during the 1980s, the station was revamped again, now with a long-stay car park, and a change of name to St Helens Central. Improvements

The passing of the 1870 Horse Tramways Act led to the foundation of the St Helens & District Tramways Company, nine years later, and soon horse-drawn trams were employed on the majority of the town's streets. Although the passing of the St Helens & District Tramways Act, 1882, allowed steam-powered trams to be employed on some of the town's more difficult routes, the Council took the view that they would not be used on town-centre streets, so as not to offend shoppers with smoke and fumes. Streets such as Westfield Street, Church Street, Cotham Street and, as this photograph indicates, Bridge Street, maintained their traditional horse-drawn trams. (*DW*)

came to the Liverpool–St Helens–Wigan line throughout the latter decades of the twentieth century, with more regular services – including express services direct to destinations such as Preston, Blackpool, Lancaster and Morecambe – operated by First North Western trains since privatisation during the late 1980s.

Public Transport

The latter years of the nineteenth century witnessed an increased demand for reliable public transport, not just from town to town, but within the towns themselves. The passing by Parliament of the 1870 Horse Tramways Act led to the founding of the St Helens & District Tramways Company in 1879, which announced plans to construct tramways along specified routes to districts such as Prescot, Peasley Cross and Haydock. This was a rather ambitious plan, and would involve lengthy construction, including the installation of swing bridges over various sections of canal crossed *en route*. This grand plan was later reduced in scale as the company experienced financial difficulties, and the first of the routes to open was from the town centre to Toll Bar in 1880, though within a year it had been extended to the neighbouring town of Prescot. This early success was followed by the completion of tramlines to Dentons Green, and in the following year, Marshalls Cross. The building of the Tram Depot and stables for the horses was completed in Hall Street in the same year. On the original main routes the horse-drawn trams operated a twice-hourly service and overall ran a good, efficient service, which was popular and made good efforts to maintain its timetables. However, there were notable exceptions to this; the double-decker trams, to cope with the increasing number of passengers, proved to be too heavy a load for the horses to cope with, especially on the steeper routes. This ultimately led to increasing delays to the service which, as one might expect, led to complaints from the public.

A Bill had recently passed through the House of Commons – the Mechanical Power Tramways Act – allowing the use of steam-powered trams to replace horses and avoid delays on some of the hilly routes. This seemed to be the answer to the problems, and both company and Town Council agreed that a small number of these steam-powered trams should be purchased for use on their more demanding routes.

With the assent of the St Helens & District Tramways Act, 1882, the first of these new steam trams came into operation. Nevertheless, the Council took the position that such trams should not be used on

The take-over of the St Helens tram network by the Atherton Brothers brought massive changes – the most significant of which was the introduction of electrified trams. The first electric tram left the town centre, filled to capacity, for its short run through to Toll Bar on 20 July 1899, arriving at its destination on time.

These new trams offered a smoother and often quicker ride, and were soon employed on the town's more demanding routes. They proved to be very popular with the travelling public, as can be judged from this photograph.

However, they were prone to disconnection from the overhead lines, as the picture opposite clearly demonstrates! (*DW*)

the town's main streets – Westfield Street, Church Street, Cotham Street and Bridge Street – so as not to offend the shoppers and shopkeepers with their smoke and fumes: here, instead, the traditional horse-drawn trams would continue in operation, with connecting services to steam trams once outside the town centre, located at the top of Westfield Street and Liverpool Road.

By 1889, the financial difficulties experienced by the St Helens & District Tramways Company had reached breaking point, and later that year they were taken over by a consortium of tramways companies from Yorkshire wishing to expand their business links into South Lancashire. The Town Council lifted the ban it had imposed on steam trams operating on the town's main streets, and so steam-powered trams were used on all the town's routes, regardless of the gradients, and horse-drawn trams were withdrawn.

Although this new operator actually ran the services much better than its predecessor, it still experienced problems: the lack of investment in the tramlines through the years meant that the new, larger trams, together with their steam engines, placed excessive weight, wear and tear on the lines. These lines had never been designed for this sort of use, having originally been laid for the much lighter horse-drawn trams.

Following the St Helens Corporation Act, 1893, the entire tramway system, including the lines around the outlying districts, was taken into public ownership and administered by the Borough Council. They ran it well; services were made to run more frequently and the routes were expanded throughout the borough. It remained in public hands for five years, until the Council decided that it could be made more efficient by leasing it to one contractor, which would be responsible for running the service and its maintenance, although the operation would be overseen by the Council, which retained the authority to penalise the contractor should standards in service decline.

Several companies tendered bids for the contract, but it finally went to the St Helens & District Tramways Company which, once gain, was in new hands: this time owned by the Atherton Brothers, who also owned BICC in Prescot. Due to their extensive knowledge of cables and electricity, they had an impressive plan for operating electric powered trams, not only in St Helens, Prescot and Liverpool, but right across the whole of South Lancashire. They were granted a lease by St Helens Council to operate the service within the Borough of St Helens, for a term of twenty-one years.

The Atherton Brothers carried out their plan with precision, laying power lines throughout the area, ready to feed the new fleet of electric trams. With the network of power lines laid, the first electric tram left the town centre, filled to capacity, for its short run to Toll Bar on 20 July 1899, arriving at its destination on time. Within a matter of days, these new, quicker electric trams were replacing many of the main routes previously operated by steam trams, such as the St Helens to Prescot service. By the end of the first year, most of the major routes within the town had been converted to electric trams, and by the end of the following year the task was completed.

The town's electrified tram system, was running well; the service was running to schedule, the public approved of the punctuality, and the owners, the Atherton brothers, were doubtless pleased with their investment. However, by 1914, with the St Helens & District Tramways Company's lease (founded in 1898), nearing its expiry, the company began talks with St Helens Council to have the original lease extended, or, better still, a new lease drawn up. Both of these options were firmly rejected by the Council and, from September 1919, the Council took control of the tramway network once more.

Although the electric trams were popular with the inhabitants of St Helens, there were still areas of the town not linked to the network which, as a result, had no public transport service. These included the isolated mining villages of Clockface and Sutton Manor. This situation had caused concern for a number of years and was finally addressed in 1914: Councillor Thomas Abbott was appointed to create the first motorised bus service in the town. Working with the

Dromgoole family, who owned a transport company called County Carriers, he started a bus service between the Market Place, in the town centre, and Sutton Manor. These services were dramatically increased following the Act of Incorporation of 1921, which gave the Corporation the right to operate its own motorised bus service. Within a matter of weeks, services were linking areas such as Rainford, Billinge and Rainhill; later further services were added through to Parr, Burtonwood and Warrington. Special early services were operated for the miners, to coincide with the times of their shifts.

The electric trams were eventually replaced by trolley buses. These were originally brought in purely as a temporary measure, for use on the routes where the tramlines were in a poor state and needed repair. However, the popularity of these vehicles were to take the Council by surprise, and their use was to be made permanent. This was a blessing for the Council, as the trolley buses did not need tramlines to run on, so their constant repair and replacement was no longer required and they were eventually taken up. Plans to extend the tramlines were dropped, and the finances that had been allocated for their renewal and maintenance were freed to purchasing a new fleet of trolley buses. By 1927, the service was fully installed throughout the Borough.

The trolley buses remained popular with the people through the decades – even if they did often disengage from their overhead power lines (especially around sharp corners), leaving the bus and its passengers stranded until it could be reconnected once more! By 1951, they began to be withdrawn from the town's major routes, and replaced by the new motor buses; this was a gradual change, and it would take a decade before the last trolley buses were finally decommissioned in 1961.

Chapter Four

THE CREATION OF A GLASS-MAKING TOWN

*A*LTHOUGH COAL WAS THE INITIAL SOURCE of success and prosperity of St Helens, it would be the manufacture of glass that it became best known for. Companies such as Pilkingtons that began in the town would become world-famous, taking the name of St Helens with them.

The making of glass was not a new enterprise. Like many industrial skills such as copper smelting, it had been practised by our ancestors through the centuries: it was only following the Industrial Revolution that these skills were brought together on a larger industrial scale. It is widely known that the Romans made glass; in the North West region, places such as their camp at Wilderspool, near Warrington, were very active in the glass-making process. Later, in medieval times, glass was made on a small scale in the North West, particularly around parts of Cheshire such as Delamere Forest. By the fifteenth and sixteenth centuries, glass was being made on a small localised scale around Ormskirk, using timber-fired furnaces; other evidence suggests that similar furnaces were used closer to home, at Carr Mill, around the same period.

Glass manufacture only really took off in South Lancashire during the seventeenth century, following the Civil Wars, and the rise of Liverpool as an independent port. Around the period, records show that the Huguenot family had a small glassworks at Warrington in 1650; in fact, Warrington had a prosperous glass industry until the end of the eighteenth century. The first such works to open in Liverpool did so in 1715, by Josiah Poole. Later the Huguenot family (who by this time had changed their surname to Leaf) opened another glass-works, in Sutton: this was the first recorded glassworks within the area of modern-day St Helens. Fifteen years later, Seaman & Company opened a glass bottle manufacturing works in St Helens, while a similar process was being carried out at Thatto Heath.

In the early days of glass manufacture, the quality of the glass being produced was, by later standards, pretty inferior. This was largely due to the poor choice of sand being used in the process, which was taken from any available source: pits, streams, or river beds. Only much later was sand sought with a low iron oxide content, which produced a purer quality of glass. Equally the alkali used in the process then was taken from plant and tree extracts, which was of a much poorer consistency to that later produced commercially.

Glass is made from a mixture of sand, limestone and soda. Heated in a furnace to a temperature of around 1500°C, these materials will produce a liquid that can then be formed into a variety of shapes. When the liquid is cooled under carefully controlled conditions, to a temperature of around 500°C it becomes a solid. The sand is the main component in the process, forming the glass itself; the soda is there purely as a flux, and the limestone's task is to stabilise the mixture, making the glass less brittle and more durable. To produce these temperatures the original furnaces had been timber-fired, though later they switched to coal, when it was realised that coal reached these temperatures quicker and more consistently.

By the eighteenth century, the vast majority of the world's glass was made in France, in the small town of St Gorbain in particular. By this time, the demand for glass in England, and plate glass in particular, had reached a very high level; so it was decided, to cope with demand, that plate glass should be manufactured here.

Various like-minded investors came together with the concept of forming a new company that would, initially at least, employ French workers to pass on their expertise in producing plate glass. They appointed a former French glass worker, Philip Besnard, to survey their proposals for attempting to produce glass in this country on an industrial scale, and to see if indeed it was feasible: his findings were greatly encouraging to the investors, proving that it was perfectly possible to make glass here.

With this, the investors applied to Parliament to secure the rights of incorporation for the new company (to be called the British Cast Plate Glass Manufacturers Company) to provide them the protection of limited liability should the project fail. A Commons Select Committee was formed, to look more closely at the proposal, and review Besnard's findings. They consulted other eminent sources before finally ruling in favour of the project: the Act of Incorporation was passed by the House of Commons in April 1773. Able to proceed, the investors raised the necessary capital required to fund the project, in total £60,000, of which two-thirds was raised from joint stock.

First Steps into Glass-making

Finding the location to build the factory was the next matter on the agenda: offers of possible sites had been arriving since the project had received approval from Parliament. Initially, it looked as though

Newcastle, with its huge coalfields, was the favoured location. But this was later dropped in favour of a new North West town that was booming: St Helens. Here was not only an abundance of coal, but quality sand (known as Shirdley Hill Sand) found throughout the town, which had the perfect iron oxide content for glass-making. Furthermore, the town's close proximity to the Cheshire salt wiches, together with the excellent transport facilities available with the Sankey Canal, made this town the ideal location. Also at St Helens the investors had a landlord, in John Mackay, who was also one of the largest coal magnates in the area, and who was willing not only to provide the site for the factory but supply it with coal from his nearby collieries at reduced rates.

The new factory, which was built at Ravenhead in 1773, was not only the first plate glass works in the country, but also the largest factory in the country (measuring 113 yards in length and over 50 yards wide). Much of the size of the factory was taken up by the huge casting hall where the plate glass was made.

The first works manager was a Frenchman, Jean Baptiste Francis Graux de la Bryure, who had worked at St Gorbain, the location of the premier glass-makers of France. He brought with him other French glass workers, both to operate the factory, and to educate the English workforce (many of whom were local) in the expertise and techniques of glass-making. Nevertheless, despite the knowledge of the French workforce, they encountered problems working in England; one of the

By the nineteenth century, St Helens was literally overflowing with glassmakers – though some were more successful than others. This is a drawing of the Union Plate Glass Works at Pocket Nook, founded by Gilbert Greenall in 1837. This factory played a significant part in the town's glass making heritage.

It proved to be a profitable venture, assisted as it was by the close proximity of the railway, and it remained in business through to 1899. (*Reproduced with the permission of the St Helens Local History and Archives Library*)

greatest was working with coal-fired furnaces, having always worked with timber-fired furnaces in France; they experienced difficulty achieving the correct temperatures in these more efficient furnaces. Many other problems were to arise during the early years of production, though these were addressed and did not affect output for long. By far the greatest setback to the factory's initial success was the excessive duty levied on glass once it was made: this was payable, regardless of whether the glass was ever sold or not.

The productivity of the company only really started to increase after the death of Graux in 1787: the year before, a Boulton & Watt engine had been installed, making some of the processes automated, which increased the factory's output. But by far the greatest improvements came following the appointment of Robert Sherbourne as general manager in 1792: Sherbourne proved to be a manager well beyond his time, with the foresight that the company needed to forge ahead. In order to speed deliveries of coal, he had a short and private section of canal cut between the factory and the collieries at Thatto Heath in the latter years of the 1790s; however, it should be stressed that this was never, at any time, connected to the St Helens Canal.

Sherbourne's talents were not just confined to improving transport, however, for he pioneered the introduction of new working practices to the factory. Some were elaborate, others just common sense, such as covering the pots to prevent foreign bodies entering the molten glass during the process, which made the finished articles better than before.

The casting tables used in the factory copied those used in the French glass factories, in both their design and assembly, which meant copper laid on stone blocks: although this was the norm, it was far from satisfactory, as molten glass poured on to these tables often cracked. This matter was only really resolved in 1843, with the introduction of iron plate, and the new tables were also built on castors so they could be easily moved around the factory.

One of the long-term difficulties of this pioneering glass company was its ownership. Following the expiry of the twenty-one year term of incorporation, the directors of the British Cast Plate Glass Manufacturers Company approached Parliament to gain another term. This was rejected, and left the Board of Directors little choice but to sell the company, before their creditors called in their mounting debts and, ultimately, the receivers. The factory was purchased by Thomas Oakes in 1794, for the sum of £105,000, on the strict proviso that it could be bought back in the future, should the original directors ever be granted a further term of incorporation. Four years later, following that much sought-after award of incorporation, the former directors bought back their company.

The works remained in their control through to 1841, when they were leased to Cockburn, Blake & Grant. The next owner was Edward Sullivan, who gained control in 1860. However, his connection with the company did not last long, for it was bought in 1868 by the London & Manchester Plate Glass Company, of Sutton Oak, on a ninety-nine-year lease. In the following year, the business changed its name to the British Plate Glass Company Limited.

Despite the change of name, the Ravenhead operation was run simultaneously with the Sutton works and remained profitable. However, increasing competition on the world glass market forced the owners to sell Ravenhead to a new concern in 1894. Thereafter the business traded as the British Plate Glass Company Ltd. By 1901, the business was suffering financial difficulties and was put up for sale, eventually being bought later that year by Pilkingtons. Following the purchase, the facility was run down, and later much of the huge site was used for storage space. It remained so until the building suffered a huge fire in 1974, which damaged the structure so severely that it had to be demolished.

The creation of the British Cast Plate Glass Manufacturers Company was just the start of the glass industry's interest in the new town of St Helens. Soon afterwards, other companies either relocated here, or founded their operations in the town.

One such company that founded was here was the Eccleston Crown Glass Works. This started in 1792, when Angus and George Mackay (relatives of John Mackay, who had died in 1783), formed a partnership with Thomas West, to make window glass. Initially they traded as Mackay West & Company, before later becoming Eccleston Crown Glass. Their business venture was successful; from their premises in Eccleston they would maintain the local monopoly in window glass through to the 1820s.

Later the partnership would break up, after the company came under investigation by the authorities, suspected of avoiding excise duty on their glass. These investigations revealed that their initial suspicions were indeed valid, and Thomas West was found guilty of fraud; later, as a direct result of this, he was made bankrupt. The Pilkington Brothers would later purchase the premises owned by Eccleston Crown Glass.

By the nineteenth century, St Helens had become the one of prime centres of glass production, not only in England but throughout Europe: the town's many factories were responsible for more than half the glass made in England. Now, for the first time, the output of glass from this country could rival that of France. The glassmakers of St Helens were famous throughout Europe. By far the most famous of the town's glass companies was Pilkingtons, which formed in 1826 (their story covered in the following chapter); but there were once many more glass manufacturers in the town, and this is their story.

The Best of the Rest

The Cannington Shaw Glass Bottle Company opened in St Helens in 1866, with a small glasshouse at Marsh Crossing. Four years later, with trade increasing, they acquired the premises of the Sherdley Glass Bottle works at Peasley Cross, close to the Ravenhead Colliery section of the canal. The Sherdley Glass Works furnace – pictured here – still survives today, situated at the rear of the former United Glass Works, and the Linkway Road. Although a listed building, it is in a very poor state. Surrounded by wire fences (though it can be viewed from the road embankment), it is clearly unsafe. (AG)

Although the twentieth century was one of domination by Pilkingtons over the local glass market, things had not been so easy in the previous century, when the town had more than its fair share of rival glass-makers. Soon after the arrival of glass-making, the skilled glass-makers became the best-paid of all the workers in the town; later, with the advent of other competitive glass-makers, skilled workers were in relative short supply, making them worth their weight in gold and able to demand high rates of pay; head-hunting of workers, from one company to another, was a common practice within the town.

The Union Plate Glass Company was built on land owned by the influential Greenall family, at Pocket Nook, alongside the canal. It had been formed by Gilbert Greenall, of the brewery family, in 1836: he would be joined by his brother, Peter, in 1842. William West, a relation of the disgraced Thomas West, was appointed as works manager. Its location on the edge of the canal, together with its close proximity to Gamble & Crosfield's alkali works, made it a most viable business. During the boom years of the 1850s, the company expanded its site and became, at least for a short period, a major employer in the town, and became a limited company in 1864. However, it was fortunate that it chose to expand when it did, for a decade later the Civil War in the USA made life extremely uncomfortable. Through its many years of operation, although it did not become the largest of the town's many glass-makers, Union Plate Glass was one of the largest, and became very well known and successful. However, the changing pattern of world markets can, and does, catch smaller companies unaware. Sadly this was the fate of Union Plate, for it went into voluntary liquidation in 1899. Despite its closure, the sale of the site and its relative assets would take sometime to fully complete. The site lay empty for a few years before Foster & Sons Glass Company, looking for larger premises than their current works on Atlas Street, took over part of it in 1908, and expanded further, taking all the former Union Plate site by 1912.

Brothers John and David Foster, who had both served their apprenticeships at the Atlas Foundry, had established their own business in 1878 by purchasing the Navigation Boiler Works. Trading as D. & J. Foster, they relocated to Pocket Nook in 1890. Following David's departure in 1893, the company traded as John Foster & Co. Ltd, still in the boiler trade. As a company they only switched to bottlemaking in 1900, initially trading as Fosters Glass Bottle Manufacturers Ltd: it later changed its name after Foster's eldest son – also named John – joined the company. Foster's were successful on their new site, competing against rival companies within the town, and indeed around the world; they became a Public Limited Company in 1919. They continued to trade from the Pocket Nook site until 1968, when they became part of the Rockware Glass Corporation. Rockware prospered here too, although only for a short period of time, for by the late 1970s they had become a victim of the recession. They would be the last glass-maker to occupy this site.

In 1837, a new glass company entered the town at Sutton Oak, the Manchester & Liverpool Plate Glass Company, opening its purpose-built factory – designed and built by local architect John Whittaker – on the corner of Robins Lane and Lancots Lane. The key investor here was the soapmaker, Joseph Crosfield, of Crosfield & Son, Warrington. The glass industry was a tough, competitive industry to operate in, where only the strongest survived. Sadly, this new venture was one of those that did not; despite considerable funding by Crosfield, within four years it had passed into liquidation.

This was not the end of the story, however, for in 1846 the site was purchased by the London & Manchester Plate Glass Company. This new business venture, managed by the Blinkhorn family, had far greater funding than its failed predecessor and as a result was able to compete against its rivals. The company prospered and expanded its manufacturing base in the 1868, by purchasing the British Cast Plate Glass Manufacturers Company at Ravenhead. Both sites

remained profitable through to the end of the century, when a turn-down in business forced them to sell both. The Ravenhead site was bought by a new company in 1894, trading as the British Plate Glass Company Limited, and Sutton Oak site was sold to Pilkingtons Brothers in 1903, who used it for warehousing. It would never again be used to manufacture glass.

Another of the town's glass companies to become a major player in the world markets was United Glass Builders (UGB), which specialised in bottlemaking. This company was formed by the uniting of smaller glass bottlemakers into a larger concern that could compete against the bigger manufacturers.

One of the companies to later join UGB was Nuttall & Co. Their origins can be traced back to 1845, when a small glasshouse, originally founded by the West family at Thatto Heath, was purchased by brothers-in-law Francis Dixon and John Merson, trading as Dixon & Merson. Soon after this purchase the partners built a new glasshouse at the Ravenhead terminus of the Sankey Canal, which later became their main manufacturing site. Nine years later, Merson left the partnership, selling his fifty-per cent stake in the company to his partner. This was not to be Merson's last venture into glass-making, however, for soon after he opened a new glasshouse in Salisbury Street, trading as John Merson & Co. Sadly this venture only lasted five years before Merson was forced to sell out to the Lightfoot brothers, who made bottles there for another ten years.

Meanwhile, Dixon was running the original company alone. Although times were hard for the smaller glass companies such as his, he persevered. In 1859, with the sudden death of his uncle Thomas Nuttall (one of the major landowners in the area, who lived in a large mansion known as Nuttall Hall), he inherited a sizeable fortune, which provided a welcome boost to the company's capital. From that year, the company changed its name to Dixon-Nuttall. Things went well for the business in the next few years, but a severe downturn in the glass market in 1870 caught the company unprepared, forcing it into bankruptcy. Nevertheless, fortune favours the brave, and just a year later, after finding new investors, the company was trading once more, this time as Nuttall & Co. It would join the union of the United Glass Builders in 1912.

Another small glass-maker to join the union was Cannington Shaw. R. Cannington and R. Lawson had been in partnership making glass in Bristol in the early years of the nineteenth century, though the partnership would end after John Cannington, son of the founder, relocated his business in Liverpool in 1850. By 1866, John Cannington had been joined by his brother, Edwin, and family friend, John Shaw, to form the Cannington Shaw Glass Bottle Company. They moved to St Helens in the same year, opening their first glasshouse at Marsh Crossing. In 1870 they acquired the premises of the Sherdley Glass Bottle works at Peasley Cross, close to the Ravenhead Colliery section of the canal. Their original furnace, part of the Sherdley Glass Works, still survives today, situated at the rear of the former United Glass Works, and the Linkway Road: surrounded by wire fences (though it can be viewed clearly from the road embankment), it is in a poor state and clearly unsafe. Cannington Shaw later bought out Tobias Royle in 1873, who had been making both window and plate glass from his works at Sherdley since 1851.

In 1890, the company (which was going from strength to strength) purchased Lyon's Peasley Cross Glass Bottle Works, which stood alongside the canal and across the railway from their own factory. J. Henry Lyon, the son of a local mineral water merchant, had ventured into glass bottlemaking in 1857, purchasing a glasshouse at Thatto Heath from Merson & Dixon before buying the Peasley Cross Works, which had been founded seven years earlier by William Riley. Following Lyon's death in 1879, the company had been managed by his two sons, William and John. At the same time as buying the Lyon works,

United Glass Builders – UGB – was formed on 31 March 1913 by the amalgamation of several glassmakers, including Nuttalls, and Cannington Shaw. Work concentrated at their Peasley Cross site, seen here, which underwent periods of expansion to cope with the huge growth in trade. Through the years, UGB became the town's premier glass bottle maker. Sadly in 1999 the factory was forced to close, unable to compete on world markets. It was a massive loss to the town. Three years on, the factory has been purchased, but its future will not lie in glassmaking. (AG)

Cannington Shaw also purchased Sutton Lodge from the Eccleston family, and demolished it to build their new furnace on the site.

In 1892, the company changed its name to Cannington Shaw & Co. Limited. Cannington Shaw's former Sutton Lodge Chemical Works had been bought by United Alkali in 1890, and closed just six years later. The site remained derelict for around four years before being purchased by Cannington Shaw, in order to build a new glass works.

Like Nuttall & Company, Cannington Shaw joined in the creation of United Glass on 31 March 1913; it also included the Alexander Glass Company of Leeds and Robert Cadlish & Sons. The new company, trading as United Glass Bottle Factory Limited, now held sites at Ravenhead, Sherdley and Peasley Cross, and was by now the largest glass bottlemaker in the town. Through the years, the factories at Ravenhead and Sherdley were closed, to concentrate production at their Peasley Cross site, which expanded to cope with the huge boom in trade. United Glass became the premier glass bottlemaker in the town, and did well on the world markets (later diversifying into table-ware too). The factory was fully automated in 1932, which met with an initial harsh response from the trade unions.

UGB was registered as a holding company on 1 March 1959, prior to it becoming a subsidiary of Distilleries Co. Ltd, of the USA, with its own autonomy, trading as United Glass (England) Ltd.

St Helens glass-making heritage
is promoted and remembered in
a special museum called 'The
World of Glass'. These two
pictures show exterior and
interior views of a reconstructed
glasshouse. A visitor to St Helens
during the nineteenth century
would have seen these
cone-shaped chimneys right
across the town! (*AG*)

By the mid-1960s the Sherdley factory was becoming increasingly
out of date, and plans were drawn up to construct a new, modern
factory, much larger than its predecessor, using the land previously
occupied by McKecknies and Red Oxide. McKecknie's foundry had
been closed by United Alkali in 1927, as part of the exodus to Widnes.
Three years later it had been bought by St Helens Corporation, the
factory demolished, and the site left empty. Red Oxide had closed in
1961. UGB bought both areas of land.

With the extra land acquired, construction work began, including
the building of two modern furnaces to the south of the site in 1966,
and the new factory was ready to start production in early 1967. The
old Sherdley Glass works was used through to the late 1970s. In 1970,
a change in the management structure led to a change of name, from
United Glass (England) Ltd, to United Glass Containers Ltd. The new
factory boosted production and led to a period of increased profitability
for the company.

Sadly, by 1999, the story of United Glass came to an end, for the large Peasley Cross site had to close. Government grants to similar companies trading in Northern Ireland put United Glass in a position where it could no longer compete against them on the world markets, and was therefore forced to close: it was a sad end to a company with such an illustrious history. Recently the site has been bought by a new company (although not in the glass trade), and scheduled for redevelopment.

The Future of a Glass-making Town

The picture of St Helens as a glass-making town is one of decline and closure. Where there were once many companies manufacturing glass – from plate glass to bottles and drinking glasses – scattered around the town, today that picture is less rosy. The closure of one firm after another – from Rockware to UGB – has left a hole in the town; and in 2001 came announcement of the intended closure of Ravenhead Glass, after around 200 years of success. This announcement meant not just the loss of around 300 jobs, but that a once-mighty glass-making town had been reduced to one manufacturer, Pilkingtons.

A Heritage in Glass Manufacture

Although St Helens glass-makers have withered on the vine, their memory, and indeed the glass-making heritage within the town, has been maintained by the opening of the World of Glass heritage centre which opened to the public in 2000. This fascinating 'working museum', located at the centre of the town, offers a historical insight into the art of glass-making. The combination of a modern building and the use of Pilkingtons' original glasshouse enables the centre to present a picture to its many visitors of glass manufacture throughout the ages.

Chapter Five

THE STORY OF
PILKINGTONS

O F ALL THE GLASS MANUFACTURERS in St Helens, the most
successful and, as a result, the most famous, is surely Pilkingtons. Although they were not natives of St Helens, through the years
their name would become synonymous with the town. The Pilkington
family can trace their origins as far back as the Battle of Hastings,
when they had crossed the channel with William the Conqueror.

William Pilkington's family were farmers and lived at Horwich on
the outskirts of Bolton, where they had tended the land for years.
Nevertheless, young William chose not to follow in his family's foot-
steps in traditional agriculture, but instead sought a career in medicine.
In 1779, at the age of fourteen, he was successful in gaining an
apprenticeship with the doctor of the neighbouring village of Blackrod,
Dr William Fildes. Having completed his training – where it was clear
that young William had a talent for medicine – he secured a place as
a junior doctor at St George's Hospital, London. In the meantime,
two unrelated events occurred that in later years would have a direct
bearing on not only the life of Dr William Pilkington, but also his
future family: first, Dr Fildes relocated his general practice to the new
town of St Helens, sharing it with a Dr Walker; and second, William's
great-grandfather, Richard Pilkington, inherited Allerton Hall and estate, near Liverpool.

On completion of his term at St George's, William Pilkington
travelled north again, first to visit his parents at Horwich, then across
to Allerton to see his great-grandfather. *En route* he visited his old
employer, Dr Fildes, in his new practice at Chapel Lane, St Helens;
during their conversation, William was offered the chance to join the
practice as a junior partner. This he accepted, and following the death
of Dr Fildes, he became a full partner in the practice and took it over
completely after Dr Walker retired.

The practice operated from small premises on Chapel Lane, close
to the chapel of St Elyn: Chapel Lane later became Church Street.
In 1794, William Pilkington married his childhood sweetheart, Ann
Hatton, the daughter of a tanner from Parbold. William's sister, Elizabeth, later moved to St Helens after her brother had set up his practice.

While living in the town she met, and later married, John Rylands, who owned a draper's shop close to her brother's surgery. Later they had a son, who was named John after his father. John Rylands Junior would, in later years, become one of the most successful and famous of the Manchester 'Cotton Kings': following his death, his widow donated funding for the creation of the now-famous Rylands Library, in Manchester.

Dr William Pilkington supplemented his income by selling wines and spirits, along with medicines, in a small apothecary shop, attached to his surgery (this was common practice for doctors at the time). In fact trade from the shop proved to be so profitable that Dr Pilkington chose to retire from general practice in 1813, to concentrate solely on his business.

William and Ann had several children, but the two most important of these were Richard and William, born in 1795 and 1800 respectively. Both of these sons lived in St Helens, attended Morley's School on College Street, and both secured apprenticeships: William worked as a distiller for Preston's of Liverpool, who were friends of his father; while Richard, the elder of the two brothers, worked for Liverpool merchants Ewart Meyer & Co. as a bookkeeper. William was the first to join his father in the family's wines and spirits business, followed by Richard within a couple of years. Thereafter, the business proudly traded as William Pilkington & Sons. They were still in their Church Street premises (on the corner of Church Street and Bridge Street, today occupied by Burtons Menswear), and trade continued to be good; although the halving of the duty paid on spirits in 1826 certainly came as a welcome boost.

Also in 1826, Dr Pilkington chose to retire. Leaving the business in the safe hands of his sons, he moved to the grand mansion of Windle Hall. This was owned by Sir John Gerard, Lord of the manor of Windle, and the Pilkingtons rented it at £300 per annum, although within a few years the family was in a position to purchase the hall, which they retain to this day. Dr William Pilkington died in 1831 (his wife Ann had died some sixteen years before) and he left behind an estate valued in the region of £25,000. Of their many children (they had eight in total, three sons and five daughters), Richard and William proved to be the most successful, though the third son, Thomas, became manager of the wines and spirits business later. Of the five daughters, only one married: the eldest, Eleanor, who made a success-ful union with Peter Greenall, owner of the town's largest brewery and one of the most prominent local businessmen, in 1821.

Following their father's retirement in 1826, the two Pilkington brothers, who now ran a very profitable business, wanted to invest in other prosperous companies within the town. One such venture was

The St Helens Crown Glass Company – the forerunner to Pilkingtons – had been founded at Ravenhead in 1826, by the Bell brothers, Peter Greenall, the Pilkington brothers, James Bromilow and John Barnes. The following year the company bought land at Grove Street, alongside the canal, for £800. Pictured here is the blue plaque, seen on the wall of their Watson Street and Grove Street offices, confirming that this is where the 'Pilkington story' began. (AG)

the Bell Glass Company, which had been founded in 1822 by brothers John and Thomas Bell. They had previously taken over some small premises at the Ravenhead terminus of the Sankey Canal (originally built and used as an iron foundry) to manufacture flint glass. Within a few years the company was experiencing financial difficulties and looking for an injection of capital from new investors. Both William and Richard Pilkington put money into the business, as did their brother-in-law, Peter Greenall, along with James Bromilow (one of the foremost colliery owners) and his solicitor, John Barnes. The new company changed its name to the St Helens Crown Glass Company.

This new business did rather well in the local glass market, and before the end of the year had outgrown its original premises. A decision was made by the investors to relocate; purchasing land off Grove Street, alongside the canal, they build a new, larger glasshouse

the following year (the land at Grove Street was a sound investment, costing £800).

However, by April of the following year things began to change: the Bell brothers withdrew from the partnership; and in February 1829, both James Bromilow and John Barnes left the company, following an argument with Peter Greenall, who suspected them of defrauding the company (although his suspicions could not be proved there and then, they were later found to be correct). The five remaining partners bought the shares that had been held by the Bell brothers equally between them; though when Bromilow and Barnes left the business they refused to sell any of their shares to Greenall, so the Pilkingtons bought them instead. These changes left the business trading with just three directors, and although it was still the St Helens Crown Glass Company, it was referred to locally as 'Greenall & Pilkingtons', with the greatest emphasis on the name Greenall. The Greenalls were by this time the town's premier family, possessing status as well as wealth. Through the early, difficult years of the company, it had been the Greenalls' reputation, and the connection they held with Parr's Bank of Warrington (which had been founded in 1819 by Peter's father Edward Greenall, together with Thomas Lyon and Joseph Parr), that kept the business afloat.

By 1836, Pilkingtons' original business in wines and spirits – which had been managed by their younger brother Thomas since 1826 – had struck poor times, and was now trading at a loss. The sudden and rather unexpected decision by Thomas to resign from the business in 1836 caused the two older brothers to take the immediate step of closing the business, selling off the remainder of the stock, and renting out the premises.

Peter Greenall, the town's foremost businessman, had been successfully elected as Member of Parliament for Wigan in 1841 (following a failed attempt in 1837), and it was his commitment to this office, together with his other business activities, that led him to resign as a director of the St Helens Crown Glass Company. Although the business's balance sheets were in much better shape than they had been in previous years, the Pilkingtons were in no position to buy Greenall's shares at once, so a deal was arranged between the two parties whereby the shares would be purchased over the next few years, by instalments of £250. This transaction was only fully completed in 1849, making William and Richard Pilkington sole proprietors of the company. However, the sudden death of Peter Greenall in 1845 (he suffered a stroke while visiting William Pilkington at his home at Millbrook House), had meant that the estate had been administered since that time by Peter's brother, Gilbert Greenall.

Following completion of the transaction, the company changed its

Pilkingtons' original glasshouse, opened in 1826, has been transformed in recent years into a wonderful museum – 'The World of Glass' – where visitors can see at first hand the skills employed in the art of glass-making. (*AG*)

name to Pilkington Brothers. The two men took on different roles within the business to ensure its continued success: Richard controlled the day-to-day running of the factories, while William travelled all over the country, seeking out new trade and reinforcing existing customers.

The glass company prospered, pioneering new techniques and bettering those of their competitors: in 1832, a new technique had been discovered for improving the manufacture of window glass, by using a cylinder to roll out the sheet glass. Polished glass came along just eight years later. These improvements stood the company in good stead, for a depression that started in the late 1830s continued into the following decade, and saw many of Pilkingtons' competitors go to the wall. The boom in the glass trade returned by 1845, following the lifting of the excise duty on manufactured glass. The repealing of the much-despised window tax in 1851, when properties were taxed on the number of windows they possessed) boosted the fortunes of the business still further.

William, although the younger of the two brothers, had been the first to marry, to Charlotte Boyes of Parr Hall in 1824. Richard did not marry until 1838, to Ann Evans. William's children, then, were older than Richard's and William's eldest son, William Roby, was the first to join the company as a fully fledged partner, in 1853, at the age of twenty-six.

In the same year, Pilkington Brothers had started to expand, purchasing the premises of the Eccleston Crown Glass Company along with other smaller glasshouses in the town. The 1860s were a particularly hard time in the glass trade as the American Civil War prevented the continuation of the very lucrative trade with the States. Although Pilkingtons weathered the storm, many of their competitors did not, and were either forced to close or suffered long-term hardship.

Richard Pilkington had not felt worried by the promotion of his nephew William Roby to the position of director in 1853, for he felt that the growing success of the family business should be shared by the entire Pilkington family; and that surely the same honour would be granted to his children, once they were old enough. He was wrong, however, for when Richard's eldest son, William Windle (so named to distinguish him from his cousin) reached the age of twenty-six, rather than being made a director like his cousin before him, was offered the more inferior post of works manager by his uncle. This infuriated Richard, and led to a serious argument between the two sides of the Pilkington family that, if unresolved, could have split the company in two. Thankfully for the continued prosperity of the business, agreement was reached whereby all future descendants of the two founding Pilkington Brothers would gain equal status within the company.

By now, the two founding brothers, William and Richard, were reaching old age. Richard Pilkington, who had taken over Windle Hall following the death of his father, retired there himself, leaving his eldest son, William Windle, to run the business in his absence; he was joined later by his brother, Richard Pilkington Junior. Richard Pilkington enjoyed his retirement, and died at Windle Hall in 1869 aged seventy-four.

William Pilkington, on the other hand, who had begun his married life living over his father's wines and spirits shop in Church Street, later moved to Millbrook House. On retirement he moved to Eccleston Hall – which he had bought earlier from the Taylor family – leaving his two sons, William Roby and Thomas, running the company with their respective cousins. William Pilkington died in 1872 while visiting friends in North Wales, aged seventy-two.

As the eldest of the second generation Pilkingtons, William Roby became Managing Director and senior partner following the retirement of both his father and uncle. He was a good manager and ran the company well, gaining a high status within the town: he became Deputy Lieutenant of Lancashire in 1887, and in 1892 could have been made a baronet, but declined the offer. Joined on the Board of Directors by his brother Thomas, and cousins William Windle and Richard, together the second generation Pilkingtons continued to run a successful glass business.

Ravenhead 1894. Pilkingtons' Grove Street would undergo massive expansion five years after this map was produced. The filling in of the Ravenhead section of the canal – so dominant in the centre of this map – allowed the closure of Grove Street, and its replacement with a new thoroughfare which followed the line of the former canal, named Canal Street. This simple change brought massive benefits to Pilkingtons, allowing them to build new offices and warehouses, as well as gaining access to Greenbank. (*Reproduced with the permission of the St Helens Local History and Archives Library*)

Throughout the century improvements to the glass-making process continued to be made. The silvering of glass to produce mirrors had been attempted several times through the years, though it was a most hazardous process and not always successful. This procedure improved in 1873 when Pratt & Company pioneered a new process at their Peasley Cross works, which was later adopted by Pilkington Brothers.

In the same year, Pilkingtons began looking for a prime site to open a plate glass works. By coincidence, 1873 was the centenary year of the opening of the British Cast Plate Glass Manufacturers' Company, the very first plate glass works in England. Initially, the Board of Directors favoured a site at Blackbrook, close to that section of the canal. However, despite its advantages, this was later dropped in favour of a much larger site at Gerard's Bridge, which was also close to the canal but with superior railway links. This location, a large part of Cowley Hill, was to prove ideal for the extra land could be used to dump the waste sand left over from the glass-making process. Much later the area was expanded to Washway Lane by purchasing Stubbrook Farm and two abandoned collieries. Three years later, in 1876, Pilkingtons purchased Ravenhead Colliery to join with the other smaller

Pilkingtons demolished its Jubilee offices in the 1930s, replacing them with more modern offices, built on the same site. Designed by Herbert J. Rowse, they were officially opened in 1940. By the early 1980s, they had been abandoned and left derelict, and would remain so through to the late 1990s, when they were purchased by the Grosvenor Housing Association, who transformed them into apartments. (AG)

collieries bought in 1845, which all traded as St Helens Collieries: this ensured that Pilkingtons' furnaces always had a sufficient level of coal at low prices.

By the end of the nineteenth century the company had taken its expertise abroad, setting up manufacturing operations in South Africa, Australia and many European countries. However, this expansion into world markets had not been at the neglect of the original St Helens base, for as the nineteenth century drew to a close, changes were occurring closer to home with the further expansion of the Grove Street site.

Expansion had actually begun in 1879, when Pilkingtons had bought the original Ravenhead Glass Bottle works from Cannington Shaw. They demolished the factory and used the area to store sand and construct railway sidings instead. Further moves to expand the Grove Street works followed. The Bridgewater Alkali Company, which occupied land between Grove Street and the canal, had gone bankrupt in 1878, and within six years the site was put up for auction and acquired by Pilkingtons. Here they built their Jubilee Works in 1885 which were extended five years later by acquiring the former Navigation Boiler Works from the Foster brothers. Completion of the Grove Street site came in 1897, when the Todd Brothers' Bridgewater Forge, which stood on Pilkington land, was forced to relocate after their lease expired. The factory was later demolished, and warehousing built.

The superb railway links that had been created meant that the company was no longer dependent on the canal for its transportation, and more importantly, the Ravenhead section of the Sankey Canal alongside the Grove Street works was no longer required. Pilkingtons sought an Act of Parliament to have this section officially closed, and so gain permission to fill it in. This was agreed by the House of Commons in 1898. Once the back filling of the Ravenhead section was successfully completed, the construction of Canal Street took place: Pilkingtons also extended their Grove Street site, building their Jubilee Offices with its distinctive clock to celebrate the Jubilee of Queen Victoria the year before.

The closing of the canal gave Pilkingtons two distinct advantages: first, with the creation of Canal Street running parallel to Grove Street, they convinced the Council that Grove Street, as a through road, was surplus to requirements and should be made private – which it was, allowing new buildings and warehouses to be erected; and second, Canal Street offered improved access to the area of land opposite, known as Greenbank.

Parts of Greenbank came into Pilkingtons' hands in 1891, with the closure of the Doulton Pottery Company, and further land at Greenbank was acquired when Greenbank Alkali Works, which had been taken over by United Alkali in 1890, closed in 1922.

The company was forced to create new, larger railway sidings and a storage area for sand between Grove Street and Ravenhead Colliery in 1920 by purchasing Bibby's Copper Works. The need for these facilities was the lack of sand available locally. From the creation of the earliest glasshouses in the town during the eighteenth century, all of the town's many glass companies had used local sand and by the latter years of the nineteenth century, local supplies were running low and other sources had to be found. Pilkingtons opened a new quarry on the outskirts of Rainford in the early 1880s to cover the local shortfall though by the turn of the century they, like other companies within the town, were importing sand from Europe.

However, despite the influence the company had over the town, and their seemingly endless buying power, Pilkingtons did not always get their own way. By the 1930s, the company was still eager to increase the size of the Greenbank site, and made an offer to the Glover Rope Works (which stood to the rear of Greenbank Alkali) whereby they could relocate to the former site of the London & Manchester Plate Glass Site at Sutton Oak (which Pilkingtons owned) in exchange for their current site. Glovers flatly refused to move!

Nevertheless, the Greenbank acquisitions made a significant difference to the Grove Street Works. The timber yards, which had previously taken up much space on the Grove Street site, were trans-ferred to Greenbank; which allowed greater expansion on the Grove Street site. The two sites were connected via tramways, where engines hauled goods back and forth until the 1980s, when Greenbank was sold off for housing.

Pilkingtons demolished their Jubilee Offices in the 1930s, replacing them with more modern offices on the same site designed by Herbert J. Rowse, which were officially opened in 1940. By the early 1980s they had been abandoned and left derelict, and would remain so through to the late 1990s, when they were purchased by the Grosvenor Housing Association and transformed into apartments. Pilkingtons built a new, modern head office at Eccleston in 1965. A tall tower made from distinctive blue glass, it was designed and built by architects Fry, Drew & Partners: it dominates the St Helens skyline and can be seen from miles around. It was constructed on the site of former cornfields, with a picturesque lake in front, popular with the local anglers.

The company, which had been trading as Pilkington Brothers since 1845, became a limited company in 1894. The turn of the century had seen great changes in the company's management structure. William Roby died in April 1903. This left his brother Thomas and his cousins William Windle and Richard Pilkington running the ex-panding company. Richard died in 1908, William Windle in 1914, and

Thomas in 1925. Now the family business moved into a third generation.

William Roby's two sons, William Lee and George Herbert, had worked under their father, though both men chose to retire early in 1907. George Herbert's eldest son, Geoffrey, joined the company two years after the retirement of his father. Thomas, William Roby's brother, had two sons, Thomas and Alan; the latter joined the company in 1904 as company secretary through to 1919; the former was killed during the Boer War.

The other side of the Pilkington family fared much better. Richard's four sons, Arthur, William Norman, Guy and Ernest, all joined the company. William Windle also had four sons, though only two – Henry and Austin – decided to follow their father and join the company.

Austin became company chairman, though had to retire prematurely after contracting tuberculosis. His position as company chairman was filled by Richard Pilkington's eldest son, Arthur, who served through to his death in 1921. In the same year the company lost another director when Alan Pilkington chose to retire. Austin, who had recovered from his illness and was now in excellent health, took over once again as chairman, assisted by his younger brother Cecil.

The company suffered a period of decline during the 1920s culminating in their worst financial year in 1931, which saw annual profits

Pilkingtons' head offices stand on Alexandra Street, off Prescot Road, Eccleston, and were built in 1965. Its tall tower, made from distinctive blue glass – designed and built by architects Fry, Drew & Partners – dominates the St Helens skyline, and can be seen from miles around. *(MF)*

plummet from almost £600,000 the previous year, to just over £135,000. The poor financial state of the business led to a disagreement between Austin and Cecil, and caused both men to leave the Board. For the time being their brother-in-law Edward Cozens-Hardy took over the position as chairman, though he was replaced by Geoffrey Pilkington in the following year. The company entered a period of transition, which by the end of the decade saw Pilkingtons acquire the enviable position as the only British manufacturer of plate glass.

Geoffrey served as company chairman through to 1949 – steering the business through the difficult war years – and saw the profits grow year-on-year. His eventual replacement was Sir Harry Pilkington, who turned out to be just as good a businessman as his predecessor: he was made Lord Pilkington in 1968, and heralded as one of the most outstanding business leaders of his age. The company continued to prosper, leading the world in the innovation of glass. Their Research & Development department, which opened in 1938 on Watson Street, had been driven hard in an effort to define and improve manufacturing techniques; the technique of producing float glass was created in the 1950s by Alastair Pilkington, keeping the company ahead of the competition.

Safety Glass

At the start of the twentieth century, with the increase in the motor trade, early experiments into creating laminated glass were carried out by a man from Swindon, named John Wood. Although his ideas were promising, he was unsuccessful in acquiring the necessary financial backing required to set up his business. Meanwhile, across the Channel in France, Edouard Benedictus had been carrying out similar tests into laminates. He was more successful than Wood, and was able to raise the investment to establish a laboratory, where he designed the first safety glass suitable for automobile windscreens. He successfully patented his designs in August 1909, and used the trade mark of XXX; later this changed to the written words, Triple X, before finally adopting the single word, Triplex.

With early success in France and other parts of continental Europe, the Benedictus company wanted to offer rights of production to a glass company within the United Kingdom market. Approaches were made to Pilkingtons early in 1911. Although Pilkingtons were interested in the innovation of the Triple X brand, they were sceptical as to its success within the British market, and the terms offered for the rights to manufacture in this country were heavily stacked in the French company's favour: so Pilkington declined the offer.

By 1925, the Triple X brand had grown in stature tremendously.

This photograph shows the tall chimneys of Pilkingtons UK5 and 6 factories. These were built on the former site of the Greengate potteries and colliery. UK5 opened first, coming on line in 1979; UK6 was delayed, though finally opened in 1992. Both of these factories, ultra-modern and hi-tech in their operation, were designed to lead the company into the twenty-first century, and was judged locally as a major investment in both the town and its workforce. (AG)

They had opened a factory in the Midlands, the heart of the British Motor Industry, and were experiencing fabulous trade. This caused the Pilkingtons Board to rethink their initial rejection and in that same year, they placed their first order for toughened glass from Triple X. Such were the sales of this glass that the Board later took the bold step of purchasing large quantities of shares in Triple X.

The Austin Motor Company had agreed to purchase all its windscreens from Triple X, and this huge increase in demand led to an agreement with Pilkingtons to buy all of their sheet glass from them. In 1929, Morris Motors of Oxford placed a vast order with Triple X for safety glass: by now, the company held almost the monopoly for safety glass with the British Motor trade. Within the same year, the respective Boards of both Pilkingtons and Triple X entered into talks for greater unity of their two companies; the result was the formation of Triplex (Northern) Limited, and the announcement that summer of the intention to build a specialist factory to make safety glass on land owned by Pilkingtons at Eccleston. On completion of the new factory, its works manager was Lewis Forbes, who had joined Pilkingtons in 1921 at the Cowley Hill Works.

Through the following years, Pilkingtons steadily increased their capacity of shares within Triplex and finally, in 1965, they acquired

complete control of the Triplex company. Through the boom years of
the British Motor Trade – especially in the 1950s – the company
witnessed a huge boost in sales and profits, the Eccleston-based factory
working to full capacity to maintain the output required. However, in
more recent years Triplex has not fared quite so well, with many of
its workers being made redundant.

Fibreglass Limited opened at Ravenhead around the start of the
Second World War. Although, understandably, trade was greatly reduced throughout the war years, it re-established itself in the late
1940s. This became yet another boom market for Pilkingtons: glass
fibres had a variety of uses, and the success of the product led to the
opening of many plants throughout the world. The first of these
opened in Argentina in 1948; South Africa followed in 1954, Singapore
in 1971 and Jamaica the following year, to name just a few.

Further Expansion and Modernisation at St Helens

To remain the key player in the glass industry, the company had to
modernise its now ageing St Helens operation. Plans were drawn up
in the early years of the 1970s to create two new factories, to be known
as UK5 and UK6. A site was found at Greengate and earmarked for
redevelopment. Work began on clearing the remains of the collieries
and brick works that occupied the Greengate site in 1974. Construction
of the first factory, UK 5, commenced just three years later, reaching
completion in 1979; it produced its first glass in 1981. Its sister plant,
UK6, was delayed, finally opening in 1992. Both of these factories,
ultra-modern and hi-tech in their operation, were designed to led the
company into the twenty-first century, and were judged locally as a
major investment in both the town and its workforce.

Pilkingtons became a public limited company in 1970. Three years
later Lord Pilkington retired, and was succeeded by Sir Alastair Pilkington, who held the position through to 1980, when the current
chairman, Sir Anthony Pilkington took over. By the 1980s, with all
the investment that had gone before, the company was the largest
producer of both flat and safety glass in the world. Profits were up,
not just on the world stage but in the UK. Another technical break-
through came in 1985 with the creation of the Pilkington K Glass: a
single-pane double glazing unit that is a superb insulator, letting heat
in without allowing it out again.

The company, which had been trading as Pilkington Brothers PLC
since 1970, changed its name to Pilkington PLC in 1986. However,
this new-found success made Pilkingtons the target for an acquisition
when, on 20 November, BTR made an aggressive takeover bid. The
company was secure in that it had the backing of its Board, its

shareholders and the support of the people of St Helens and the town council. The process was settled inside two months and the takeover failed, though it had cost Pilkingtons almost £10 million to win.

In the latter years of the twentieth century Pilkingtons has seen its original St Helens operation change quite substantially. Although its presence in the town – with its five sites – has not been diminished, the size of its workforce has. By the 1990s, and through to present day, the company employs fewer than 6,000 workers in St Helens, compared to its overall world-wide employment of almost 60,000. Nevertheless, Pilkingtons are still the world leader in glass manufacture today, and in spite of the reduction in their workforce, they remain the town's single largest employer. Overall, it would seem fair to say that Dr William Pilkington could be rightly proud of the company that his two sons Richard and William created, for where others failed, they alone succeeded.

Chapter Six

THE STORY OF AN
INDUSTRIAL TOWN

S T H E L E N S, as an industrial centre, was created rapidly. Soon after the commercial mining of coal began companies, both old and new, were attracted to the 'new town' to be close to that vital source of fuel. The early industrial area formed to the west of the town centre at Ravenhead, principally at the instigation of one man, John Mackay.

Although a Scot by birth, Mackay spent much of his life in Cheshire and had married well: his bride, Millicent Neate, was of a wealthy London family, and brought with her a dowry of around £3,000. The first land that Mackay bought at St Helens was in Parr, where he set up his first colliery, though later he bought land at Thatto Heath and eventually Ravenhead Farm, where he opened the largest of his collieries. Ravenhead would be the site of his industrial development; here he attracted vast amounts of labour, and built cottages to house them.

Foundries

It was not just a labour force that Mackay attracted to Ravenhead, but industry too. Following his coup of bringing the British Cast Plate Glass Manufacturers Company here in 1773 against stiff opposition from other parts of the country, he then brought Pary's Mining Company of Anglesey, North Wales, just three years later. In September 1776, Mackay leased a section of land alongside the Ravenhead section of the Sankey Canal to the Pary's Mining Company, for them to establish a copper smelting works. Its location was ideal, close to the canal so as to transport the copper ore through from the mountains of North Wales, and send out the finished products in the same manner; and with coal sold to them by Mackay from his collieries at concessionary rates, together with complete use of his stone and lime quarries.

The Pary's Mining Company was owned and operated by three partners: Edward Hughes, Thomas Williams and John Davies. They sent Edward's son, Michael Hughes, then aged twenty-nine, to run the new venture as works manager. He brought with him a number

Michael Hughes came to St Helens from Anglesey in the September of 1776 to manage the Pary's Mining Company's copper foundry which had opened at Ravenhead. He rented a house near the foundry at first, but later, as his wealth increased, he purchased Sherdley Hall estate and had a new hall built there. Although his copper business closed in 1815, he and his family remained in the town. His son, the second Michael Hughes, sold the estate to the town, and this later became Sherdley Park. His grand home, Sherdley Hall – seen here around the turn of the century – was demolished in the 1940s. (DW) of workers from the Anglesey copper works, to pass on their knowledge to the other workers employed here, who had been recruited locally. To house the men he had brought with him, Hughes had built a row of cottages (located between the canal and Watson Street) that was referred to as Welsh Row. The copper business prospered; by 1796 they were purchasing 600 tons of coal per week. Sadly, the recession of 1815 was just too much for the copper works to handle, and it had to close.

Michael Hughes, apart from managing the business, would later become one of the most important figures within the town, and actively promote it. He originally lived at The Tickles, a house built on land owned by the Eccleston family, which he rented although the cost was covered by the business. Hughes later chose to rename the house Sutton Lodge. He was a man with an eye for a good investment and soon began buying up land around the town: he purchased estates in Sutton and Lea Green, and bought the Burtonhead Estate from Thomas West (following the trouble he created for himself over the avoidance of glass duty while running the Eccleston Crown Glass Company). Hughes bought the Sherdley Estate for £3,150, and soon after increased its overall size by buying Costeth House Estate which bordered it from William Greenall who, like West, was in financial difficulties. This was followed by further purchases in Eccleston, and his largest-ever purchase, the Sankey and Penketh Estates near Warrington, from Thomas Claughton.

Hughes took an active interest in both the well-being of the town and its inhabitants. Seeing that transport was vital to the town's continued success, he took a keen interest in the turnpikes and other roads. Having been made a trustee of several turnpikes in the area, he used the waste copper slag to re-surface many of the roads throughout the region.

He married twice, first to the daughter of the vicar of Prescot, then following her death in 1798 to Ellan Pemberton, daughter of a major landowner in Sutton. He had six children from his second marriage including his heir, Michael Hughes Junior, born in 1810.

Although he had lived at Sutton Lodge since arriving from North Wales in 1776, and it would appear he enjoyed living there, Hughes was eventually forced to leave after Nicholas Ashton opened a small colliery nearby (on land owned by the Ecclestons) and employed the use of a Newcomen engine, which produced such noxious fumes that Hughes could stand it no longer. Initially, he thought of returning home to Wales, though later reconsidered and commissioned architect John Harrison to design and build a new, larger Sherdley Hall on the estate he had bought in 1798: this grand mansion was completed by 1800.

Michael Hughes was made Lord Lieutenant of Lancashire in 1806, and later that same year became a Justice of the Peace. He was indeed a great statesman, and worked tirelessly for the benefit of the town and its people. His son, Michael Hughes Junior, did not hold the same feelings for the town, and did not continue the work begun by his father: he did, however, leave his estate to the people of the town on his death.

Although the Pary's Mining Company's copper business was successful and, largely due to its location and connection with Mackay, became famous within the area, it was not the only one of its kind locally. Thomas Patten, from Warrington, had set up a similar copper smelting works at Blackbrook in 1772, on land owned by Sir Thomas Gerard, from whom he purchased his coal. It was, in fact, the Patten family that brought copper smelting back to the fore within Lancashire with the opening of their Bank Quay works at Warrington in 1717; they were equally famous for their residence, Bank Hall, which later became Warrington Town Hall. Such was their influence and success that they created the first navigation of the River Mersey to transport their materials. The decision to open this second works here in St Helens had been influenced by the abundance of coal around the town, which would reduce their transportation costs substantially.

Following the closure of the Pary's Copper Works, the site remained derelict through to 1829 when it was purchased by a new concern, the St Helens Smelting Copper Company Limited. This new venture lacked the finances to have any great longevity, and was taken over in 1834 by the Ravenhead Copper Co. However, despite greater investment in the plant, the company was bought out within four years by John Bibby & Company of Liverpool who retained the site, making it prosperous once more. They remained at this site through to 1860, when they chose to relocate to new premises not far away on the edge of Pilkingtons' Grove Street site. Once again the former Pary's factory lay empty, until it was purchased in 1867 by the St Helens Smelting Company, owned by Keates & Rawlinson. William Keates, the senior partner, had another copper concern within the town; through a partnership trading as Newton Keates, they operated the British & Foreign Copper Company, with foundries at Peasley Cross and Parr.

In the mid 1860s the Brookland's Copper Company opened a small foundry on the side of the canal, near the St Helens Foundry,. Within a decade the company had been bought by W. Roberts & Co. Ltd. By the late 1870s they had begun trading as the St Helens Lead Smelting Co. Ltd, although within the next decade, they had been taken over by Quick, Barton & Burns, who occupied a site on the other side of the railway on Salisbury Street. They remained in production through to 1925, later changing their name to the Mitchell Lead Works.

Another copper foundry opened at Peasley Cross in 1871, trading as the Duncan McKecknie Copper Works. McKecknie, a Scot by birth, whose family had moved to Cheshire, had previously been a partner in the Old Quay Works at Runcorn. Having gained sufficient experience in the copper smelting trade, he wished to open his own establishment in this busy industrial town. The company, extracting copper from low grade ores, benefited from its chosen location – it stood on land between both Sutton and Peasley Cross collieries, which ensured a regular supply of coal for its furnaces. Despite competition and difficult times, this venture succeeded where others had failed. Through the years McKecknie's were so successful that on the twentieth anniversary of the company's founding – in 1891 – Daniel McKecknie was placed in an enviable position to negotiate a favourable deal in his company's takeover. The buyer was United Alkali, and the sweetener in the deal resulted in Daniel McKecknie securing a seat on United Alkali's Board. However, the surrender of his family business did not exclude McKecknie from keeping his hand in the foundry trade. His sons, Daniel and Alex, formed a small foundry in Widnes in the same year, backed and supported by their father. When the great exodus of the alkali companies began in the early 1920s, both United Alkali and McKecknie's followed the rest to Widnes.

As well as copper, other foundries soon arrived in the area, the largest being the St Helens Foundry. This was located alongside the canal in the town centre, opposite Pilkingtons' Grove Street works (today, their former site is taken up by a multi-storey car park and The World of Glass Museum). The foundry was originally started by Birkett & Postelthwaite in 1798, although within a few years it had been taken over by the Fletcher family (no relation!) before being bought by the Watson family in 1813.

John Watson had owned a similar foundry in Liverpool, which he had operated until his death in 1800. This unexpected bereavement left the business being run by his widow and two young sons, Lee and John. Although Mrs Watson took over the day-to-day running of the family foundry, she wanted to move away from Liverpool. By 1813, the family had put their original premises in Liverpool out to let, and had relocated to St Helens, purchasing the St Helens Foundry. Within seven years, the foundry had been placed in the hands of her two sons, though Lee Watson, the older of the two lads, was in charge: this was reflected in the trading name of the foundry as Lee Watson & Co.

When the Watsons had bought the foundry it was experiencing a period of low trade; most of it consisted of simple foundry work, and carrying out basic repairs. After the Watsons had established themselves, trade did increase, and further orders came from as far afield as South Africa. However the business required greater investment, and so a partner was advertised for: and answered by an eminently qualified engineer from Wigan, named Robert Daglish.

Daglish had been the manager of the successful Haigh Foundry in Wigan, owned by Alexander Lindsay, Lord Balcarres, located within the Haigh Hall Estate in 1804. There he had increased the output of the foundry considerably, securing new orders, including the building of the Laxey Wheel for the Isle of Man, which on completion was so large that the foundry had to enlist the services of the local farmers, together with their horses, to haul this huge wheel up the steep mill brow. While at Haigh Foundry, Daglish designed and built his famous 'Walking Horse' locomotive engine, which was later used to great effect in the local collieries. Within a few years Daglish had left the Haigh Foundry and took up a position as manager of the nearby Orrell Colliery: there he became an authority on both railways and collieries, and later acted as a consultant to the British & American Railway Promoters Association. He was indeed the ideal partner for the Watsons, and together they successfully increased the business of the St Helens Foundry.

Daglish's son, also named Robert, was born in 1809 and started work at the St Helens Foundry in 1830, following an engineering apprenticeship in Bolton. Four years later he married Harriet Speakman, daughter of one of the most wealthy coal dealers within St Helens. This marriage led to further orders for the foundry and also

Ravenhead, 1894. This section of the Ordnance Survey map demonstrates just what a diverse range of industry was once in operation close to the town centre. Within such a small area stood many of the town's notable manufacturers: Ravenhead Copper Works, Sutton Lodge Chemical Works, Sherdley Glass Works, McKechnie's Metal Extracting Works, Brookland Copper Works, St Helens Lead Works and St Helens Foundry, to name just a few. (Reproduced with the permission of the St Helens Local History and Archives Library)

brought him closer to his boss, Lee Watson, who had married Harriet's sister Alice a decade earlier.

Robert Daglish Junior worked hard for the company. He had studied the work of both his father and brother-in-law, and in 1850 took over the running of the foundry. He was an excellent manager, and during the time he was in charge of the business, it reached new heights, securing contracts with many railway companies (including the St Helens Runcorn Gap Railway), supplying bridges, locomotives and repair and maintenance contracts to the new network of lines. By the time of his death, in 1883, Robert Daglish Junior, had seen his foundry more than treble in size. St Helens Foundry became a limited company in 1900 – trading as Robert Daglish & Co. Ltd – though the twentieth century would not be as successful as the nineteenth. After attempting to weather a number of poor financial years, and carrying debts, the company went into voluntary liquidation in February 1934. The work-force was laid off and the plant and equipment was sold. Demolition of the factory and site commenced in 1939. Nothing remains of it today.

Apart from the St Helens Foundry, there were many others within the town: the Caledonian Foundry on Crosfield Street, the Phoenix on Old Warrington Road, and the Victoria, on Liverpool Street, which opened in the same year as the St Helens Foundry. The Liver Foundry, located in Arthur Street, specialised in brass work; while the Varley Foundry, at Pocket Nook, alongside the canal, worked both iron and brass.

The Varley Foundry had its origins in the Waterloo Foundry (the site of the Technical College today). With tiny premises on Waterloo Street, the foundry had opened in 1837, begun by brothers James and Jesse Varley. The partnership ended, due to a family squabble, in 1857: James retained the original business, though relocated to new, larger premises at Pocket Nook, and brought in his two sons, James and Henry. Jesse Varley founded a rival concern, the Brookfield Foundry, on Foundry Street, which remained in business through to 1875.

The Varley Foundry expanded its operation at Pocket Nook by purchasing the Atlas Foundry in 1908. The Atlas Foundry had been created by John Cook, and was managed by his nephew, Thomas Robinson; though originally it had started life on Bridge Street in 1841, trading as the Bridge Street Foundry. However, such was its early success that it had outgrown its premises on Bridge Street within a couple of years, and had to relocate to larger premises on Atlas Street. The foundry prospered, and Robinson's two sons, Joseph and Thomas, joined the business, later succeeding their father. The company closed in 1907, and the site, which then neighboured the Varley Foundry, was bought by them soon after.

Another acquisition by the Varleys was their neighbour, the Pocket Nook Smelting Works, which stood in front of the Atlas Foundry, and had been started by Alex Arrott in 1851. However, by the end of the decade, coal proprietor James Radley had bought Arrott out. He retained the foundry through to 1888, when it was bought by William Marshall, who struggled to make it profitable, and in the end lost the battle: the site was placed for auction in 1892, and acquired by John Varley. The expanded Varley Foundry – which changed its name to John Varley (Ironfounders) Ltd in the early 1970s – continued to trade here through to the end of the end of the decade, finally closing in late 1979 a victim of the recession.

The years of the Napoleonic Wars at the turn of the nineteenth century had brought trade to many foundries throughout the country, in the manufacture of both musket and cannon shot. But the arrival of the railways gave the biggest boost, as it both increased the trade of the foundries and the ease in which they could transport their heavy cargoes. Just like the collieries and the glass industries, St Helens' foundries had relied upon the Sankey Canal to transport both raw materials and finished goods, but the arrival of the railway and the construction of branch lines meant they could connect directly to the main railway network. The Varley Foundry line, for instance, line came off the main St Helens–Wigan Railway, and crossed the canal via a swing bridge (although the swing bridge has long since gone, traces of the sides are still visible today). The expansion of the railway network throughout the nineteenth century – referred to as 'railway mania' – was a huge boost to their trade: the demand for iron rails, bridges, locomotives etc., led to massive orders being placed with local foundries, and to the creation of many more such operations.

Two Scots, Haddon William and Charles Todd, came to St Helens from their native Aberdeen to establish the Bridgewater Forge on Watson Street in 1859. They were later assisted by Richard Pilkington who, as their newly-acquired brother-in-law, came in as a silent partner: a partnership that lasted until 1864, when Pilkington retired. In 1872, the foundry relocated to premises alongside the canal, changing its name to the St Helens Ironworks; its fortunes were boosted by receiving a massive order from the St Helens Railways to supply both iron rails and bolts.

The foundry enjoyed success here and were reluctant to move when their lease, granted by Pilkingtons, ran out in 1897. This time they purchased the former Phoenix Foundry, located off Raven Street and alongside the canal. This foundry had been started in 1865 by Thomas Williamson but had soon failed. It was bought by William Varley in the following year, and traded as Varley & Simpson through to 1878, when they moved out to larger premises at Pocket Nook. The Todd brothers invested a great deal of capital and modernised the premises, and by the turn of the century wanted to expand the site: they bought

Tinkers soap works in 1904, and the Kurtz Alkali factory in 1908, filling in their canal basin soon after.

Engineering companies were not only located in the centre of the town. In Sutton Oak there were a great many such companies opening, inspired by the railway at St Helens Junction. William Neill founded his small ironworks here in 1895. This would later become Capper Neill's, a notable employer in the area. Also at Sutton Oak, Edward Burrows opened his ironworks close to the newly-completed St Helens Junction, where he was successful in manufacturing steam engines for the booming railway industry: his engines would be used by almost every factory in St Helens, all of whom had their own links to the railway network. Burrows later sold the business to James Cross, who was also involved in the manufacture of locomotives.

The Brewing Industry

Through the early years of the industrial town, the presence of so much activity led to a great demand for liquid refreshment: in the early days, this was brewed within the homes of the workers, either for their own consumption or shared amongst family and friends. By the end of the eighteenth century, this practice had fallen into decline, people preferring to visit one of the many public houses that had opened throughout the town, supplied by small local breweries.

Although there were many such breweries in the town, by far the most well-known was Greenalls. Thomas Greenhalgh was born in 1733 in the neighbouring town of Warrington, the first son of Richard and Phoebe Greenhalgh. The family soon relocated from their native Warrington to the manor of Parr, where Richard had purchased a small, though workable, farm.

When Thomas became a young man, rather than following his father into the farming business, he took a position at the local Parr Stocks Brewery. Thomas worked well here, and in 1754, he married Mary Turton, whose father, John Turton, owned and ran the brewery. Together they would have three sons: Edward, William and Peter.

Following the sudden and unexpected death of John Turton later that same year, his widow Mary inherited the family business, and placed her son-in-law Thomas Greenhalgh in charge. Thomas proved to be a gifted manager, and the business went from strength to strength under his control. By 1762, just eight years since he took control, the brewery's trade had increased so much that Thomas knew he could go it alone, and left to open his own brewery. Later, Mary Turton sold part of the Parr Stocks Brewery to a close family friend (and distant relation) Joseph Greenough; following her death a few years later, the brewery was purchased outright by Greenough.

Meanwhile, Thomas had decided to alter the spelling of his surname from Greenhalgh to Greenall. Both he and his wife had looked for premises for their business venture – called Greenalls Brewery – and had settled on a prime site, off Hall Street at Hardshaw, right in the centre of the developing town. From this grand location Greenalls prospered, and in a short space of time supplied almost all of the vast number of public houses that were open in the town. Yet Thomas's ambitions were not fulfilled this one site; he had plans to expand his activities much further. In 1786 he purchase the Saracen's Head Brewery at Wilderspool near Warrington, for the estimated sum of £15,000, and two years later opened a third venture in Liverpool. Thomas placed his eldest son Edward in charge of the Liverpool brewery, which traded as Edward Greenall & Company; and to oversee the Warrington venture, he purchased a large house at Wilderspool, though still retained his Hall Street residence in St Helens. The Warrington venture proved a financial leap too far, and so Thomas took on two business partners, William Orrett and Thomas Lyon, though the St Helens brewery remained in sole Greenall control.

Thomas Greenall's business interests did not stop at breweries, however, for he saw himself as an entrepreneur. In 1777 he went into partnership with a Billinge nailmaker by the name of John Rigby, which lasted seven years. He also joined in a business venture with Thomas Eccleston, lord of the manor, to construct a cotton mill there in 1792. This proved to be a costly affair, however, and ultimately ended in failure. In 1800 he purchased Hardshaw Colliery, which stood alongside Greenalls brewery; this proved a wise, and indeed profitable move, which compensated for the losses incurred in his disastrous cotton mill saga.

Thomas died in January 1805 and was succeeded by his eldest son Edward, followed later by his younger brothers, William and Peter. Edward, like his father, was an excellent manager. He had been placed in charge of the Liverpool venture from the beginning, and after taking over the entire company he took the family business to even greater heights. The company took a greater share of the trade by opening and purchasing existing public houses, initially in St Helens, and later in other towns such as Warrington, Liverpool and Manchester.

Edward had married in 1791 and had five sons and two daughters. His first son, Peter Greenall, was born in 1796, while the family was living in Thomas Greenall's house at Wilderspool, near Warrington. Peter moved to St Helens in 1818, taking over the running of his father's Hardshaw Brewery. Marrying Eleanor Pilkington, the eldest daughter of Dr William Pilkington, on 6 March 1821, made a powerful union of what would later prove to be two very influential families.

Although Peter had a lucrative position as manager of the Hardshaw

Brewery, his business interests were not to stop there; like his grandfather, he had a flair for business, and was a natural entrepreneur. He invested capital into the Bell Glass Company with his brothers-in-law William and Richard Pilkington in 1926, and eleven years later, joined his brother Gilbert in the Union Plate Glass Company; he established the first water supply to the town in 1826, and six years later, formed the town's first gas company; he became chairman of the local railway company in 1830 before taking charge of the family business in 1835 following the death of his father, Edward Greenall at the age of 77; and became MP for Wigan in 1841. He promoted the town of St Helens widely, becoming its greatest ever statesman, and took a very active role in its continued development. His sudden and untimely death in 1845, from a stroke, robbed the town of a great man. Following Peter's death, the family brewing business was taken over by his brothers, Gilbert and Thomas; at St Helens, the Hardshaw Brewery was managed by Samuel Robinson.

Although Gilbert was the driving force behind the company, much of the day-to-day running of the company was carried out by his brother Thomas, and at Hardshaw by Samuel Robinson. Gilbert maintained a supervisory role. Sharing his time between the breweries, the chairmanship of the St Helens Runcorn Gap Railway (which he had inherited from Peter) and Union Plate Glass seems not to have daunted him, for in 1847 he followed the path set by his late brother into political office, becoming the MP for Warrington.

The following year brought disturbance to the company, with the death of Thomas, aged just fifty-six. This led to Thomas's eldest son, Edward, joining his uncle as a partner in the breweries. This partnership worked well, and continued through to 1853, when Edward was forced to take early retirement due to ill-health. Gilbert brought in his other nephew, John Whitley, whose father had married Gilbert's sister, Isabella, some years before.

More unhappiness was on the horizon for Gilbert, for in 1861 his wife Mary died. They had no children. Gilbert married again three years later, this time to a Warrington woman, Suzanne Rapp. Together they would have three children: a son, named Gilbert after his father, and two daughters, Suzanne and Bertha.

The influence of John Whitley on the success of the company was rewarded in 1867 when he was made a full partner along with his brothers, William and Peter. Despite this new partnership, the company continued to trade as Greenalls Breweries. The company changed name in 1880, following the death of John Whitley, to Greenall Whitley & Company Ltd; at the same time a new Board of Directors was created, and a place was given to Joseph Robinson, who had replaced his father, Samuel, in 1847 as manager of the Hardshaw Brewery.

Gilbert lost his parliamentary seat for Warrington in 1868, though he regained it six years later. His work, both publicly (he was made a Justice of the Peace in 1873) and within industry, was rewarded in 1876 when he was made a baronet. He retired from the company in 1892 (succeeded by his son Gilbert, as chairman, and Peter Whitley as senior director), and died two years later, aged eighty-eight.

The Hardshaw Brewery formed a major role in the company throughout the remainder of the nineteenth century and long into the twentieth. However, by the late 1970s when the Board of Directors rationalised the business, Warrington was deemed to be the main site, and Hardshaw was sacrificed. It closed in 1979, with production and many of the jobs transferring to the company's Wilderspool Brewery at Warrington.

Other Breweries

There were other breweries in the town; in fact, in the early years many of the larger public houses actually brewed their own beer in the yards at the rear of their premises. Other major breweries included Parr Stocks Brewery, which continued in business run by the Greenough family; the Phoenix Brewery at Sutton Oak, owned by Charles Wilcox & Sons; and John Cross had a brewing operation in Sutton. Ralph Tickle and William Hill owned an establishment in Dentons Green during the early years of the nineteenth century, although they sold it to Charles Speakman in 1821, who also sold beer from his Market Street premises (Speakman Road at Dentons Green is named after him, and the brewery he bought and ran nearby); the Greenall family would buy this venture in 1866.

Other Industries

Unlike every other Lancashire town, St Helens had almost no cotton or textile industry. There were, from time to time, one or two mills operating in the town, although they never amounted to much. The best known of these was Eccleston Mill, built near Spray Bridge (which no longer exists; the stream has long been piped, but it would have passed near the Lingholme Inn of today), and was noted, not so much for its trade, but its owners: Thomas Eccleston and Thomas Greenall, from two of the most influential families in St Helens. It cost around £1,500 to build the four-storey mill and expand the nearby brook to construct a mill-race (this was known locally as the 'Cotton Cut', and sections of it still remain in Eccleston). The mill was not successful, and soon fell victim to the depression facing the cotton industry towards the end of the eighteenth century. The building lay empty for a while before Robert Kirkham, a Liverpool cotton manufacturer, leased it briefly from the Greenall family in 1800. After him came Richard Wigan, who struggled to make the mill profitable, and ended in bankruptcy in 1817. Following this the mill was used as warehousing space, before finally being demolished.

One company that is often remembered by the more senior residents of St Helens is the Red Oxide works at Peasley Cross. What particularly stays in the memory are the red stains on the road and pavements around Peasley Cross from the red dust that was scattered by the winds – and the red rivers that flowed down Peasley Cross Lane every time it rained, which stained shoes and rotted socks! This company, the Liverpool & Hull Red Oxide Company Ltd, had opened on Warrington Old Road, next door to the Sutton Lodge Chemical Company in 1891. It would remain in operation there through to 1961, before it relocated to Hull.

Another well-known company in the town was British Sidac Company Ltd. A Belgian company manufacturing plastic sheet used in the wrapping of food products had opened in Sutton in 1934, on the former site of the London & Manchester Plate Glass Company. Through the intervening years they became a major employer in the village and area of Sutton Oak. When they closed in the late 1980s, the effect on the local economy was profound, placing large numbers on the dole queue.

Of the town's many indicators of its industrial past most prominent were the tips, from colliery spoil heaps to chemical waste dumps, many of which have long since disappeared. However, some former tips that have never been removed, and through the years have become a local landmark, are the 'burgies' located between the St Helens–Wigan railway line and the Sankey Canal, standing either side of Mertonbank Road (once Coalpit Lane). These were made from sand and rouge, used in the production of glass, largely from Pilkingtons' Cowley Hill Plate Glass Works nearby. They stand tall, today covered in grass and trees (the latter were planted purposely to ensure against landslides) and form a perfect habitat for local wildlife.

Quarries

Apart from coal being taken from the ground around St Helens, clay too was extracted from huge 'clay holes' or pits, scattered throughout the town: there were clay pits in areas such as Ravenhead, Clockface and particularly at Peasley Cross, where St Helens Hospital was once surrounded by them!

The clay industry witnessed great times during the eighteenth and nineteenth centuries, with the huge demand created by the construc-

Apart from mining, the ground under St Helens had other minerals, including sand and clay, which produced the industry of potteries, producing anything from bricks and tiles to teapots! The capacity of St Helens potteries was legendary. Many thousands of bricks were produced and were used to build many of Liverpool's docks, including the world famous Albert Dock. (*Reproduced with the permission of the St Helens Local History and Archives Library*)

tion of mills, factories, warehouses and houses, particularly in the 1840s. This was not only locally driven; indeed, St Helens clay bricks were used in the construction of many Lancashire towns, and many of Liverpool's riverside warehouses and docks were built with bricks made here, including the famous Albert Dock.

Potteries too were opened, such as Greenbank Pottery, owned by Mort & Simpson, who also owned the Herculaneum Pottery in Liverpool. Later, in 1850, the Ravenhead Brick and Tile Company was founded by Horn and Kelly and their bricks were used in the construction of bridges, tunnels, houses and factories throughout the region. The expansion of the sewer system in St Helens caused the company to change its name in 1875 to the Ravenhead Sanitary Pipe & Brick Co. Ltd. The apparent boom in sewer pipes was short-lived, for by 1880 the company had abandoned this line and reverted to making bricks, changing its name to the Ravenhead Brick Works in the process. The company retained this site through the years, and was bought by its long-time rival, Roughdales Brickworks Ltd, in 1960.

Roughdales Fire Clay Company, founded at Chester Lane, Clockface, in 1879, became one of the town's most famous brick firms; they also started making clay pipes used in the laying of the town's expanding sewer system, after they had acquired a further site at Greenbank. A neighbouring pottery at Greenbank was owned by Henry Doulton & Co.

The St Helens Tile & Brick Works, located to the rear of Phoenix Colliery, opened in 1881, inspired by the building boom of the late nineteenth century. However, by 1890 it had been taken over, and traded as the Liverpool & St Helens Brick Co. Ltd. By 1900 the company had changed hands yet again, this time bought by Wood & Co., who traded as the 'Old Teapot Works'. In 1935 they were bought by J. Bate & Son, who also opened a mining operation in the same area. They retained the name of the Old Teapot Works, and operated the site through to its closure in 1974.

Another brick works opened in 1933 at the top end of Jackson Street, beside the Chemics, in 1933 founded by Laithwaite & Booth who traded as T. R. Booth. Its close proximity to the former Kurtz Alkali factories caused it to be referred to by locals as the Kurtz Brick Works, so much so that the company actually changed its name to this later on! The site was operated through to the late 1960s. Later the quarry was used a council refuse tip.

Companies such as these employed huge workforces, as they were very labour-intensive, and workers were needed to move both raw materials and the finished articles; the work was both hard and demanding, in the heat and dust of the coal-fired furnaces.

The Ravenhead Brick & Tile Company was bought by Roughdales in 1960, though the works continued its production through to 1970, when the shortage of clay locally caused it to relocate to Upholland, near Skelmersdale. The former site, with its tall and distinctive brick chimney, stood derelict and was demolished in the mid-1970s. Later construction of Pilkingtons' ultra-modern, state-of-the-art Greengate UK5 plant began. Unlike the other scars left behind by the town's various traditional industries the disused clay holes, particularly those located at Ravenhead, were put to good use and became massive refuse tips during the late 1970s and 80s, and were landscaped during the 1990s to form part of the Ravenhead Greenway Project.

Of course, the industrial town was not only the preserve of large labour-intensive industries: smaller firms and cottage industries, such as nail-making, blacksmiths, hinge-making, shoe and clogmakers – even watchmakers – also played their part and made the town prosperous.

Chapter Seven

A CHEMICAL TOWN

*M*ANY OF THE CURRENT RESIDENTS of St Helens might well be surprised to discover that the old town was not just a home to engineering, but that it also attracted many companies concerned with the growing chemical industry. In fact there was a time, from the 1820s through to the 1920s, when St Helens was very much considered to be a chemical town. The chemicals produced at that time were alkalis, principally salt cake and soda, both used extensively by the town's glass industry.

However, despite this link with the chemical trade, the town of St Helens did very little in the soap trade compared to its neighbour Warrington, which is noted for its soap manufacture, with giants such as Crosfields and Lever. Nevertheless, St Helens did have one successful soapery: F. W. Tinker, who began in 1852 from small premises alongside the canal, trading as Fountain Soap. It remained in operation, aided by the close proximity of the many alkali works in the town, through to the end of the nineteenth century; the factory was later purchased by the Todd Brothers.

The first alkali factory to appear in the town was opened in 1828 by two men from Northern Ireland, trading as Muspratt & Gamble. Josiah Christopher Gamble was born in 1776, near the village of Enniskillen, Ireland. He was brought up in a strict Presbyterian family and was ordained as a priest in 1799, taking up a position in Belfast six years later. He later attended Glasgow University, where he studied chemistry. This education caused him to decide to leave the church, and instead to set himself up in a small chemical business. This venture was a success, and he later relocated to Dublin to be closer to a ready supply of coal and salts, both vital components in the process. It was during his time in Dublin that he met his future business partner, James Muspratt, who had founded a similar operation of his own.

Soon a move to England would be forced upon them after the tax levied on salt rose so dramatically that profitable alkali manufacture became impossible. Muspratt left Dublin first, in 1823, and set up his chemical business in Liverpool. Gamble hung on in Ireland for as long as he could, finally deciding to cross the Irish Sea in 1828.

Gamble met up with Muspratt on landing at Liverpool, and together they discussed the future. Muspratt was dissatisfied with his factory's location, and Gamble was yet to find premises for his. The sensible answer was to join forces in a partnership. Both men were of a mind that they wanted to relocate to the South Lancashire Coalfield, yet remain close to the Cheshire salt: the obvious location, to satisfy both of these requirements, was the growing industrial town of St Helens. Also Lancashire had become a busy county; the Industrial Revolution had made a welcome home here, and with the Lancashire towns expanding, the demand for soda was high, providing both men with an ideal market.

They opened their washing soda factory in St Helens at Gerard's Bridge in 1828, close to the New Double Locks, on land leased from the Greenalls. The canal not only offered that vital link to the Cheshire salt and a link to greater markets throughout Lancashire, but also a ready supply of water for use in the manufacturing process: they extracted water direct from the canal, and nearby Rainford Brook, with the full consent of the canal proprietors.

In 1830 Gamble, now fifty-four, married Hannah Gower, the daughter of a Dublin solicitor. Together they had four children, one son, David, and three daughters, all of whom died as children. In the same year, Gamble and Muspratt had a disagreement on the future of the company: Gamble, who was seventeen years older than his partner, considered himself to be both older and wiser than Muspratt, whom he considered to be youthful and impetuous. Eventually the disagreement led to the profitable partnership breaking up. Muspratt moved to the newly-created railway town at Newton-le-Willows, called Earlestown, to start his own soda business the following year, while Gamble chose to remain in St Helens.

However, Gamble traded alone – for a period of four years – before taking on new partners, James and Joseph Crosfield, the Warrington soapmakers, who wanted a cheaper supply of soda needed in the manufacture of soap. Together they traded as Crosfield & Gamble Alkali. They were joined in 1837 by Simon Crosfield, younger brother of Joseph and James.

In the same year, the new company purchased the Gerard's Bridge Alkali Works – which stood on both sides of what was then Gerard's Lane (later College Street) and alongside the terminus of the canal (today the site of Gerard's Bridge Council Depot). This small concern had been created by Edward Rawlinson, a local solicitor, in the late 1820s as an iron foundry, and had been managed by his brother-in-law, a Mr Williams. It moved into alkali production in the early 1830s, though the uncertainty of the market meant that it was bankrupt by 1833. The site was auctioned three years later, and acquired by Crosfield & Gamble, at what must have been a bargain price.

Sutton Alkali had been formed by Andreas Kurtz. From premises alongside the canal, it would expand to become the largest of all the town's alkali companies. This photograph, taken around 1890, shows just part of the huge Kurtz industrial complex along the canal between Lyon's Yard and Peasley Cross Lane. (*Reproduced with the permission of the St Helens Local History and Archives Library*)

Although the alkali company was successful, the Crosfields' main interest was their Warrington-based soapery, and they insisted that this business must always come first. Joseph Crosfield withdrew from the partnership first, in 1843, followed by his brother James the following year. Gamble, once again, traded alone; he was later joined by his son, David, changing the company name to J. C. Gamble & Son.

Josiah Gamble had originally lived in a rented house on Duke Street soon after coming to St Helens. As the company grew, so too did his wealth and stature within the town, and he moved to a quiet farmhouse that stood on land that would later be taken by Central Station. In 1839, he moved to a large detached property in Marshalls Cross, known as Sutton House – later the Cottage Hospital – which he rented from Michael Hughes. J. C. Gamble died there on 27 January 1848.

David Gamble succeeded his father in the running of the family business. He had gained a schooling in the town, and later a degree in chemistry after attending the Universities of Glasgow and London. He not only continued to make the business profitable, but was also one of the greatest supporters of the town and its inhabitants: through the years his influence and generosity made the town of St Helens a

Peasley Cross, 1894. Andrew Kurtz founded the Sutton Alkali Company Ltd in 1842, when he bought the debts of the Darcy & Dierden alkali works, an insignificant chemical company which had begun three years earlier. Over the years, Kurtz would become one of the largest of the town's many chemical companies, operating on three major sites: originally formed on the canal side (near Fountain Soap), between Lyon's Yard and Peasley Cross Lane, it would expand to cover the site later taken by the gas works, and a large area of land alongside Langtree Street (later renamed Jackson Street after local blacksmith Joseph Jackson). Kurtz died on 31 March 1846 and was succeeded his son, Andrew George, who would prove to be just as good a businessman as his father, leading the company to even greater success. This section of the Peasley Cross 1894 Ordnance Survey map shows just how dominant Kurtz (or Sutton) Alkali became, covering huge areas of land on both sides of Peasley Cross Lane. Much of the centre of this map is now occupied by the St Helens Retail Park. (*Reproduced with the permission of the St Helens Local History and Archives Library*)

much better place. His services to the town were recognised in 1868, when he was elected as the first Mayor of the newly-incorporated borough: he was also made a baronet in 1897.

Looking to expand his chemical empire, David Gamble founded the Hardshaw Brook Chemical Company in 1869. There had been a chemical company trading here before, created by John Keane & Richard Sadler in 1864, though it failed to be profitable and it closed just four years later. Gamble purchased the site the following year.

David Gamble sold his original alkali works at Pocket Nook in 1879 to Globe Alkali – a company that had started in Runcorn trading as Wigg Brothers Steel, and had earlier bought Crosfields Alkali – but retained the Hardshaw Brook Chemical Company. Globe Alkali was successful, and expanded considerably within a matter of years, purchasing more land from Gilbert Greenall. They became part of United Alkali in 1890, and eventually closed in 1922. The land was bought by the Corporation eight years later. Hardshaw Brook Chemicals also joined United Alkali in 1890, and traded on that site through to 1928. St Helens Corporation purchased the site and the buildings two years later, creating the Hardshaw Brook Depot which stands there to the present day.

Gamble and Muspratt's initial success later attracted more alkali companies to establish in St Helens. Newton & Keats set up their first factory in Sutton 1831, while the Belvir Mining Company opened their alkali works in the town centre in the same year.

Another of the town's chemical companies was founded by Andreas Kurtz (later referred to as Andrew). He was born on 16 September 1781 in Reutlingen, Baden Wurtemburg, Germany. He moved to France as a young man to study chemistry. Later, he took his knowledge and expertise to America, working in their all-important gunpowder trade. Some years later, he travelled to England, working for a chemical company on the banks of the Thames before his work brought him north, initially to Manchester, then Liverpool. His connection with the town of St Helens began in 1842, though in rather strange circumstances: a family friend, John Darcy, had been lent sufficient finance by Kurtz to begin his small chemical company on the banks of the St Helens Canal in 1839. Darcy had married a Miss Dierden and had joined in partnership with his brother-in-law, Richard Dierden. The new company soon encountered financial difficulties, which led Darcy to ask Kurtz for more money; this he refused. Darcy then attempted to muddy the waters concerning his growing liability with his creditors, claiming that Andreas Kurtz was actually a silent partner, and therefore should be equally responsible for the company's debts. Darcy and Dierden ended in bankruptcy, though not before Kurtz had been dragged into court, and had spent a significant amount of money on litigation, defending himself from implication in the insolvency of the company. To settle the matter, Kurtz bought the assets of the Darcy & Dierden alkali works, and established a company of his own. His company – the Sutton Alkali Co. Ltd – would later become the largest of the alkali works within the town, operating on three major sites: originally built on the canal side (near Fountain Soap) between Lyon's Yard and Peasley Cross Lane, it would expand to cover the site later taken by the gasworks, and a large area of land alongside Langtree Street (later renamed Jackson Street, after local blacksmith Joseph Jackson). Andreas Kurtz died on 31 March 1846, and his son, Andrew George, succeeded him. Andrew George Kurtz would prove to be as good a businessman as his father, and would led the company to greater heights, successfully purchasing land that had once surrounded Sutton Colliery from the Bourne family in 1856, in order to extend his operation.

St Helens' reputation as an industrial town attracted more chemical companies. John Marsh & Company set up what was later described as the Parr Alkali Works within the manor of Parr in the early 1830s, which proved successful, and enjoyed more than forty years trading before it was forced into liquidation in 1878.

An unsuccessful chemical company was Greenbank Alkali, which was started by brothers, William and Samuel Clough, who took over an abandoned soap factory on the Greenbank in 1835. However, the chemical business was not for the faint-hearted, and many, including the Clough brothers, found it difficult to make it profitable; they closed in 1841. Three years later the factory was taken over by Spenser & Churchill, who traded as the British Patent Alkali Company. They were a much bigger concern and had some successful years, though they too were out of business by 1856.

The site was bought St Helens Alkali the following year. This company had been founded in 1852 by William Bateman, who had served his time at the British Patent Chemical Company. He set up his factory on land adjacent to the canal off Corporation Street (today the site is occupied by St Helens Glass). The business was working well, and the expansion by purchasing his former employers' site at Greenbank proves just how well the company was faring. However, if only to offer further proof that the chemical trade was a risky business, St Helens Alkali went bankrupt in 1865. Both sites were sold to Henry Menzies & Sons, trading as Greenbank Alkali, who remained in control through to 1890 when they were amalgamated into United Alkali. The company reminded here through to 1921.

The alkali companies of the nineteenth century came in a variety of sizes, some large, some small. One of the smaller operations stood on the bank of the canal just off Watson Street (later used as warehousing by Pilkingtons) facing the St Helens Foundry. It had begun in 1851, with the partnership of Richard Watkins and John Parker. This venture proved precarious, however, for within four years the company had gone out of business, and the site was purchased by the Parr Alkali Works, later trading as the Bridgewater Alkali Works.

The Union Chemical Works (which stood on the opposite side of the canal to the Union Plate Glass Works, a site now occupied by the gas depot) had been founded in the 1850s by Llewellyn Evans, the former manager of the St Helens Foundry. Evans, like so many other Victorian small businessmen, struggled and had to resort to taking a business partner – James McBryde – on board. It would appear by all accounts that McBryde was a shrewd businessman, and clearly knew what he was doing joining in partnership was Evans, as by 1873 McBryde had bought out Evans completely.

Such was the trade in the chemical industry within the town that other companies, not directly connected with the alkali trade, were tempted to join in. Cannington Shaw, for instance, a well-established company in the town's glass industry, formed the Sutton Lodge Chemical Company in 1875, adjacent to their Peasley Cross glass bottling plant. Although the venture was fairly successful, towards the end of the century competition in the trade had created new, large consortiums, against which smaller firms such as Sutton Lodge found it hard to compete. This competition finally forced them to sell the business to one of their larger rivals, United Alkali Company Ltd, in 1890.

An Unhealthy Environment

Although the alkali trade was welcome in St Helens as a major employer which brought much prosperity, the locals living near these factories were less pleased. The factories produced noxious smells, and such potent fumes that they could turn brasses green! These gases were in fact hydrochloric acid, emerging untreated from the factories in the steam. Complaints followed, but of mere residents the chemical industry took little or no notice, and carried on regardless.

The situation was the same for Muspratt at Newton-le-Willows. He faced litigation on countless occasions for pollution. The St Helens companies avoided court proceedings by paying out masses of compensation. It was a tactic that worked, at least in the short term.

The first serious attack on the chemical industry in St Helens came from Sir John Gerard, Lord of the manor of Windle. He had recently moved to the newly-built mansion, New Garswood Hall, after his estate at Bryn Hall had become uninhabitable through excessive coal mining. With the completion of the hall, Sir John had commissioned the services of Repton, the famous landscape gardener, to create the most beautiful gardens; it would be these splendid gardens that brought him into direct conflict with the alkali firms of nearby St Helens.

As the acid drifted on the winds across from St Helens to his estate, the fumes were still potent enough to kill both the flowers and plants in his garden. Sir John took legal action against the offending factories, and although the matter was settled privately before it reached the courts it put the factories under notice that they must begin to clean up their act.

Nevertheless, within a short space of time, things were as bad as before. Further complaints followed, though this time they were taken up by the most powerful man in the area, Edward Stanley, Earl of Derby. From his estate at Knowsley, he too had noticed the effect the acid fumes were having on the town and surrounding countryside, much of which he owned.

Edward Stanley, Earl of Derby, was a formidable politician. Having first become Prime Minister in 1852, succeeding Lord John Russell, he regained the premiership in 1858 and again in 1866, succeeding Lord Russell for the second time. However, as Leader of the Opposition at the time of the complaint, as well as a member of the House of Lords, Lord Derby took the matter before Parliament in 1863. He was able to persuade the Government to form a select committee to look into the mounting complaints: in fact, Stanley himself headed the committee. They took the matter seriously. Members of the committee interviewed all concerned, before eventually reporting their findings and conclusions before Parliament. The result was the passing of the Alkali Works Regulation Act 1863, which forced the factories concerned to drastically reduce their toxic emissions, or face severe fines.

Although the chemical trade within St Helens had enjoyed a great many years of high profits, by the later years of the nineteenth century trade had become far more competitive, and remaining buoyant, especially on world markets, was becoming increasingly more difficult. Talks were held for a number of years, between the larger of the town's alkali manufacturers, in an effort to amalgamate under a common banner. By 1890, the individual alkali companies – including Sutton Alkali, Hardshaw Brook Chemicals, Union Chemicals, Greenbank Alkali and Globe Alkali – had joined, and became known as the United Alkali Company, all using the famous Leblanc process.

Despite the amalgamation, the chemical industry was still a very hazardous environment, both for the workers and the surrounding residents. This fact was emphasised when the former Kurtz factory, off Langtree Street, now a member of United Alkali, suffered a huge explosion on 12 May 1899.

This major incident was caused by the simple accident of a barrel

Kurtz Langtree Street factory, by this time part of United Alkali, was the scene of a massive explosion on 12 May 1899. This picture depicts the aftermath, and the massive destruction which it caused to the factory. A single spark, caused by a barrel falling from the back of lorry, caused a series of events which culminated in a massive explosion and the death of five men. The blast was so intense that it was felt over twenty miles away, and was reportedly heard as far afield as Oldham. (*Reproduced with the permission of the St Helens Local History and Archives Library*)

falling from the back of a lorry which was being loaded in the main yard. As the barrel fell, the metal rim struck the cobbled floor hard, causing a spark which ignited the chlorate-soaked wood. The fire spread very rapidly indeed, much quicker than anyone could have possibly imagined. It reached the settling tanks on the opposite side of the yard, causing them to explode.

Five men were killed immediately in the blast, all of them local, their ages ranging from twenty-one to sixty-four. A further nine people were seriously injured, while over a hundred were hurt, mostly by flying glass and debris. A large gas tank on the nearby Corporation yard was punctured, though thankfully failed to explode, otherwise the incident could have been far more severe. As it was, the blast was felt over twenty miles away, the flames shot over seven hundred feet into the air, and the noise of the explosion was heard as far afield as Oldham.

The End of an Era

The alkali industry would eventually leave St Helens by the 1920s, though not as a result of the complaints from the town's residents! The decision to abandon a town that had brought the industry such prosperity lay in an increase in charges, on both the canal and railway, that in light of the competitiveness of the trade, had a dramatic effect on business: it took twelve tons of raw materials to produce just one ton of soda, so, simply, they could not afford the increase in the cost of transportation. It was a logical conclusion that their factories would need to move closer to the salts: the solution was Widnes, close enough to the Cheshire Wiches, and at the opposite end of the Sankey Canal, close to the coal supply. What St Helens lost, Widnes gained; and today, Widnes is famous as the capital of the chemical industry.

An Industrial Legacy

During the nineteenth century, St Helens reached its peak as an industrial town: more than half the glass used in the country was made here; more than a quarter of all the alkali produced in Britain came from here; and again, more than half the copper smelted in the country was processed in St Helens. All this intense production left waste which had to be dumped somewhere, and would leave scars on the town long after those industries had left. In fact, many of these eyesores remained around the town through to the 1970s, and some later still. These included the spoil tips left by the collieries, which at one point almost encircled the town.

The chemical industry left its waste behind, too. These tips piled as high as the town's colliery spoil heaps. The reason for this is that, particularly in the early days of the alkali trade, the manufacture was wasteful: two tons of waste were produced for every ton of soda, and

The once dominant St Helens chemical industry left its mark on the town. When the companies departed St Helens in favour of Widnes during the 1930s, they left their waste behind. Huge mounds of waste, referred to locally as the 'chemics', which stood like mountains either side of Jackson Street, as this photograph taken in the 1950s clearly shows. Sceptics said that they could never be moved – they were wrong, as by the end of the following decade, these 'mucky mountains' had disappeared. Today their former locations are occupied by industrial estates.

(*DW*)

that mounted up through the years, especially when there were so many firms. All of the chemical firms within the town produced waste: there were deposits left alongside the canal near the New Double Locks, from Globe Alkali; Sutton Lodge Chemicals deposited their waste around their factory (though much was later used to fill Caldwell's Dam, at the rear of their factory); and other waste, such as that left by Greenbank Chemicals, was piled high and remained on Greenbank throughout the period it was owned by Pilkingtons, and was only moved just prior to the construction of the houses there in the 1990s.

However, of all of the chemical piles scattered throughout the town, by far the most memorable were the old 'chemics'. These occupied the land adjacent to Jackson Street, and stood tall, like mountains towering over the town, for years. Residents of the town – of a certain age – recall the 'Chemics' with fond memories: as children they had played on these hills, with their almost 'moonlike' surface. All against their parents' wishes no doubt, though attempting to hide the fact that you'd been up there was pointless: the corrosive nature of the waste meant that it discoloured your shoes and socks (and rotted them if they weren't cleaned afterwards) … a dead giveaway to where you had been playing!

Through the years, several attempts were made to remove the waste; contractors would begin in earnest, then abandon the work once the enormity of the task was realised. Everyone said that as the waste was so toxic and corrosive that it could never be moved: they were wrong. Pickavance, a local haulage contractor, took on the challenge in the late 1960s and succeeded where many others had failed.

Sutton Alkali, the company that had produced much of the waste (later part of United Alkali) donated the land to the Town Council, for 'appropriate use', though at that point the Council not did have the finances to redevelop the site. When the waste was finally removed, much of it contained lime, which was sold to the fertiliser industry, while other parts were so tough, that they were used as hardcore on many of the region's new roads. Once cleared, many of these former dumps have been redeveloped into recreation areas, and more importantly, industrial parks to attract today's new hi-tech industries.

Beechams

Another chemical company that would become linked to the town of St Helens, though not in the same way as the alkali producers, was that of Beechams, a company renowned for its 'Beechams Pills and cough mixtures'. Its former site at the bottom of Westfield Street was equally famous, with its distinctive, telltale smell, associated with its various products.

Thomas Beecham was born in Oxford in 1820, although his family had relocated to the north of England during the 1840s: originally to Liverpool, where Thomas met and married his wife, Jane Evans, and in 1847 to Wigan. It was in Wigan, during his late teenage years, that he gained an interest in medicine, and soon after began creating his very own herbal pills at home, which he later sold to family and friends. These pills proved to be successful at curing ailments, and within a seemingly short space of time, word had travelled of their healing properties, so much so that people were knocking on his door from far and wide to purchase them. This initial demand was the first step on the road to the forming of his business empire and the opening of his first shop, in Wigan.

Jane, his young wife, gave birth to their son Joseph in the summer of 1848, and their daughter Sarah two years later. Jane also assisted him in the shop, dispensing the new remedies and various medicines. Further success followed; as well as the shop, they had stalls in the markets of neighbouring towns, including St Helens. All went well until Jane mistakenly misread a label on a bottle of pills, that ultimately led to the death of a customer's child: although Beecham was fully exonerated, the shame locally meant that the family had to leave Wigan in 1859.

He chose St Helens as the place to start again, it being the nearest, most prosperous town, and the sales of his products through a regular stall in the weekly market here, years earlier, had always done well – so at least he knew he would have a ready-made market for his products. He and his family rented a small terraced house at 13 Milk Street, and from there continued to sell their herbal pills, both through a small stall in the busy market, and door-to-door. Not content with this, Thomas set about forming an extensive (and expensive) advertising campaign; this was a huge risk, but he felt sure it was one worth taking. His first advert appeared in the *St Helens Intelligencer*, on 6 August 1859. He was proved correct; it was a huge success, and founded a very lucrative mail order business. It would be this new trade, bringing in such good revenue, that provided the capital required to open his first small factory in St Helens, located at 32 Westfield Street.

His son Joseph joined the business in 1866. Through a continued and vigorous advertising campaign, the company continued to expand, leading to the building of a new, much larger factory across the road, at the corner of Westfield Street and Water Street. Beechams will always be remembered in St Helens for this grand factory and offices, and in particular its impressive clock tower. This was built in 1885, at a cost approaching £30,000, with chimes said to closely resemble those of 'Big Ben'.

A Chemical Town

One of the town's most famous landmarks – Beechams' clocktower – was created in 1885. Its distinctive chimes were often said to closely resemble those of the famous 'Big Ben'. Despite the closure of the factory in the 1980s, the clock tower still survives today as part of the Technical College.
(*DW, AG, AG*)

For much of the next century the name Beechams, famous all over the world, was synonymous with the town of St Helens. However, in early years of the 1980s, Beechams, operating in a very competitive climate, chose to merge with one of its pharmaceutical rivals, Smith-Kline – changing the trading name to SmithKline Beecham. By the middle of the decade, the new company chose to terminate its predecessor's long association with St Helens, and move south to Harlow, Essex.

This came as a great shock and massive blow to the people of the town – and Beecham's mainly local workforce in particular. A long-term working relationship between the people of St Helens and Beechams had come to a sorry end. The company, and its effect on the town, would be missed.

Chapter Eight

THE CREATION
OF THE TOWN

L IKE MANY OTHER INDUSTRY-BASED TOWNS, St Helens was built quickly, with little forward planning: in simple terms, coal was discovered, which attracted the industry, which attracted the people, which created the town. In a very short space of time the town was established, though without the basic infrastructure it needed to sustain itself. Matters only began to change in this respect during the nineteenth century.

Local Government and Public Services

St Helens' first Town Hall had been built on Naylor Street, close to the Market Place, in 1839. It had been founded by a group of the town's more prominent businessmen, who had held a public meeting the year before, at which the sum of £3,000 had been raised by selling £10 shares. The driving force behind the creation of this, the new town's first official building, was Peter Greenall: he had been elected as treasurer of the group and had himself donated the sum of £300 towards the building's costs.

The Town Hall had been built with tall pillars, in an Italian style of architecture, by local architect George Harris. Apart from being the administrative centre of the growing town, it also held the new Magistrates Court, together with the town's first Police Station. Prior to this (and the passing of the 1829 Metropolitan Act) each of the four townships had its own constable, to maintain law and order; and the magistrates had previously held court in a rented room of the Raven Hotel on Church Street. With the building of the Town Hall, the town's police force was formed, with a total of thirty constables, and a senior officer, William Storey, who had gained promotion from his previous rank of constable for Hardshaw. By 1870, the police presence in the town had increased again: William Storey was now a Superintendent, and under him were an inspector, six sergeants and a further thirty-five constables.

Peter Greenall had stood for Parliament in the 1837 general election, for the seat of Wigan (as St Helens, at that time, was not a

St Helens' first town hall had been built on Naylor Street in 1839, in an Italianate style of architecture, by local architect George Harris. This building was initially shared by the Improvement Commissioners, local magistrates and police – it would be almost thirty years before the first St Helens Council was elected. At the time this picture was taken, around the 1860s, it was derelict, and to be honest, looking slightly worse for wear, having been replaced by a larger and more modern building on Corporation Street. (*DW*)

parliamentary constituency), but failed to be elected. That changed in the 1841 election, when the Conservatives were victorious, and so too was Greenall. Once at Westminster, Greenall promoted the town of St Helens, and with the passing of the Improvements Act (which Greenall himself was involved in preparing) he gained the approval of the Government in October 1844, to set up an Improvements Commission for St Helens. This was a body made up of fifteen local men, the majority of whom were businessmen, that could look anew at the infrastructure and the main problems affecting the town. The original fifteen Commissioners were as follows: John Ansdell, Samuel Bishop, David Bromilow, Robert Daglish, Fred Fincham, David Gamble, John Haddock, George Webster, Thomas Walmsley and, finally, Peter Greenall, who had been elected as chairman of the new body. However, his sudden death in the following year robbed the town of one of its greatest ever reformers. His work was continued, both in the capacity as chairman of the Improvement Commissioners, and other related matters, by David Gamble, by far his greatest supporter.

Until this time, the running of the services for each township –

water, housing, paving etc. – had been carried out by the overseers of each individual township, causing the quality and standard of the work to vary greatly. The creation of the Improvements Commission meant that this was united for the first time under a common body, offering a clearer overview of the work being done. The Commission set standards for housing, sewers, water, gas, roadways and other necessities.

Water

Peter Greenall had been the man responsible for the creation of the town's first water supply. His Hardshaw Brewery had, for a long time, had its own water supply which came from reservoirs at Eccleston, feeding into Eccleston Brook, and later into pipes increasing the water pressure to deliver it to the town centre. Greenall decided that there was sufficient water to supply both his brewery and the town, so in 1823 he had pipes laid along the town's main streets: Church Street, Market Street, Tontine Street and Bridge Street; Moor Flat (today known as Baldwin Street) was laid later.

Over the next twenty years, as the population of the town grew dramatically (between 1800 and 1851, the population increased from 8,000 to 25,000) and further streets and houses were built, further pipes were laid. With this increase in demand, the water coming from Eccleston simply failed to cope. Matters took a more serious turn during the drier summer months, when the reservoirs were easily depleted, and the quality of the water passing through the pipes was often of sub-standard quality, leading to complaints from both businesses and residents alike.

Following careful discussions amongst the overseers of the township of Eccleston, it was decided that larger reservoirs should be built there to ensure the town an all-year-round water supply, necessary to its continued development. This required an Act of Parliament; once this had been achieved, and the reservoirs constructed, the St Helens Waterworks Company was established to control the standards of drinking water and maintain its supply.

By the time of the setting up of the Improvement Commission, even with the new larger reservoirs in place, the water supply could no longer cope with the ever-increasing demands of the growing population, even though Eccleston supplied the town with around 150,000 gallons of water per day.

In 1850, the Commissioners applied to Parliament for another Improvement Act, concerning in particular the improvement to drinking water. The passing of this new Act would allow them to tap into what was then being referred to as the 'Rivington Scheme'. This was in

In 1850 St Helens Improvement Commissioners applied to Parliament for the right to connect to a proposed water pipe which was being built between Rivington Reservoir and Liverpool. Although this pipeline passed close to the outskirts of the town, the project suffered from delays and so St Helens had to find an alternative water source. The Rivington pipeline was finally completed in 1857. Evidence of this pipeline, which even today still supplies Liverpool, can be seen at Carr Mill Dam: the 'Nineteen Arches Bridge', is actually an aqueduct, carrying the pipe across the lake. From there it passes under Clinkham Wood and Moss Bank, before skirting around Cowley Hill (under Washway Lane) and through to Liverpool via Eccleston and Prescot. (AG) fact a significant undertaking, involving the construction of an underground water pipeline from the large reservoirs below Rivington Pike on the West Pennine Moors, all the way to Liverpool. This pipeline would pass close to St Helens, and it was possible (subject to the approval of the Government) for St Helens Waterworks Company to attach a separate pipeline to supply the town with all the water it required. Evidence of this pipeline, which today still supplies Liverpool, can be seen at Carr Mill Dam: the Nineteen Arches Bridge is actually an aqueduct, carrying the pipe across the lake. From there it passes under Clinkham Wood and Moss Bank, before skirting around Cowley Hill (under Washway Lane) and through to Liverpool via Eccleston and Prescot.

After receiving the necessary approval from Parliament in February 1851, the town's Commissioners discussed the matter with the surveyor, Thomas Hawksley, to locate the best point at which to connect to the forthcoming pipeline. Although the findings of his survey were positive, and connection to the pipe was feasible, eventual delays in its construction (it did not reach Liverpool until 1857) meant that St Helens could not wait, so an alternative source was needed.

With this setback, Hawksley was commissioned to investigate the

possibility of discovering natural underground reservoirs. As St Helens was built over a major coalfield, pockets of water trapped between the layers of coal were common, causing vast reservoirs to be created, fed by underground river systems. Exploration shafts were sunk in the most likely of places, in the hope of striking water. Test bores carried out around Eccleston proved to be the most successful; here water was discovered in abundance, trapped beneath the natural sandstone. Permanent shafts were created, and water pumping stations built above ground that could supply the town with around half a million gallons of water per day. This, combined with the existing supply, would enable the town to have water for all its needs, both residential and commercial.

Of the four townships, Sutton, despite reservations, had decided not to be part of the Improvements Commission. This decision doubtless annoyed the Commissioners, and others in the town, who wanted the important matters governed from the centre; nevertheless, Sutton pressed on alone, and for all the criticism it attracted in doing so, it managed its affairs rather well, investing in a building programme and improving the standard of roads too.

Matters only really came to a head in October 1866, when a severe case of cholera occurred at Peasley Cross: the cause was directly linked to the poor quality of Sutton's water supply, which drastically required improvements. The cost involved in sinking their own wells to find sufficient water for the needs of the large township would be high; what is more, they would be competing directly against the Commissioners' scheme. The residents of Sutton relented, and agreed to join the Improvement Commission.

Later, towards the end of the nineteenth century, the town would increase its water supply further still. Several of the collieries around the town such as Collins Green and Clockface would strike water during their search for coal. The latter found an underground water reservoir in 1890, capable of supplying in excess of 500,000 gallons per day, the majority of which they sold to the St Helens Corporation.

Incorporation

Regardless of the good work that the Commissioners did for the people of the town, they had their critics, and none greater than B. A. Dromgoole, proprietor of the *St Helens Newspaper & Advertiser*: he used his paper to publicise and condemn the failings of the Commission, and campaign vigorously for the right of incorporation for St Helens. These criticisms did not go unnoticed, for Dromgoole was accused of libel and legal proceedings were established against him: the matter was eventually settled out of court. Despite this, the campaign conti-

Victoria's statue has taken pride of place on Victoria Square, outside the town hall, since 1905. The people of the town had been grateful to her in 1868, when she granted St Helens its Act of Incorporation. In recent years, however, with the planned alterations to the square, the statue had to be relocated to the north end of the square. Residents of St Helens held their breath, hoping and praying that the statue would endure the move without damage. Thankfully it did. (*MF*)

nued, growing in strength, and several attempts were made to gain this right of incorporation, though without success.

In February 1865, the first public meeting was held to propose incorporation for St Helens; it attracted huge crowds. The chairman of the gathering was a local GP, Dr Robert McNicoll, who was himself one of the Improvement Commissioners (and later that year would become chairman of the Commission). After much discussion, the following resolution was passed:

> ... that the local governing bodies at present existing in the townships of Eccleston, Parr, Sutton and Windle, are various, inefficient and unsuited to the exigencies of the increasing population, trade and manufacture of these townships: and the economic, social and sanitary well-being of the districts therein comprising, imperatively call for an improved form of local government which only a Charter of Incorporation can alone supply.

This was sent to the Government of the day, and the following year, a Public Inquirer was sent up from London to look into the matter, although little came from this. Finally, after continually pressing the case at Westminster, the town's officials received word on 30 January 1868, that Her Majesty Queen Victoria was to grant the Lancashire town of St Helens the Charter of Incorporation.

Local elections followed in six designated wards to select the first eighteen councillors, three from each ward; in total, fifty-four candidates stood for election (many of the candidates and the successful councillors had previously served as Improvement Commissioners). There was a huge turnout for this, the town's first-ever election, and the people of St Helens were ready to use their democratic right to vote, something that had been denied them for so long. William Pilkington had been chosen as the Returning Officer, with Dr Robert McNicoll as his deputy (following the election, Pilkington made it known that he would be standing as a candidate at the next election).

The eighteen successful candidates to be elected as the first town councillors of St Helens were as follows: Eccleston Ward: James Bayley, J. Fidler, Robert McNicoll; Hardshaw Ward: Joseph Cook, Edward

St Helens' main thoroughfare was originally called Chapel Lane, though its name was later changed to Church Street. Today, it is still the town's main shopping street, and home to such stores at Marks & Spencer and Woolworths. *(AG)*

Johnson, L. W. Evans; Parr Ward: J. Greenough, R. Reeves, J. Wolfen-den; Sutton (East) Ward: Major Cross, W. J. Blinkhorn, Dr Taylor; Sutton (West) Ward: W. Roberts, James Radley, H. W. Todd; Windle Ward: David Gamble, H. Johnson, W. Webster.

The first official meeting of the newly-elected Council was held on 18 May in the former Improvement Commissioners Board Room at the Town Hall. During this first sitting, the aldermen of the town were elected, along with the Mayor. The position of Mayor was an unanimous choice: David Gamble. He had been proposed by Mr Wolfenden, and seconded by James Radley; his election was unopposed. The first five aldermen for the town were James Radley, L. W. Evans, Major Cross, Robert McNicoll and J. Greenough.

Later, the first committees were appointed, six in all, under the following headings: Paving; Highways and Sewers; Water; Sanitary; Lighting and General Purposes; Finances and Parliamentary. The year after the forming of the Council, Parliament passed the St Helens Improvement Act, which enabled the council to work on the waterworks, gas, roads etc. Although the new council initially rented the use of the Town Hall, they would purchase the building outright in 1870 for £2,150.

Gas

With the increasing demands of industry placed on the town, and the rapid growth in its population, the establishment of power services, such as gas and electricity, had been a necessity. The first gasworks in St Helens – built at Peasley Cross – was a private concern, which started life following the passing of an Act of Parliament on 24 March 1832. Included in the Board of Directors were such men as Peter Greenall, Richard and William Pilkington, James Bourne, William Bromilow, J. C. Gamble, Thomas Speakman and Lee Watson.

The company installed a series of gas lamps in the town's main streets, which replaced the earlier oil lamps. By 1845, the year of Greenall's death, there were more than fifty such gas lamps in operation within the town. In the years following his demise, the gas company was administrated by his brother, Gilbert Greenall. The company was re-structured seven years later, trading as the St Helens Gas Company Limited.

With the Act of Incorporation, moves were made by the new council to bring all of the town's services within their control. The gas company was purchased, by the St Helens Corporation, on 23 August 1877 for the sum of £130,000. The new company deemed it a priority to increase the number of gas lamps in service within the town, and within a few years expand this to incorporate the surrounding districts too. Through the years, the Peasley Cross site was both modernised and expanded, though within the confines of the industry that surrounded it. The need for expansion led to the construction of the Pocket Nook Depot in 1901. The Peasley Cross site was finally enlarged in 1929, when the former Kurtz Alkali works that surrounded it was bought for £7,000. In much later years, control of gas became a nationalised operation, and a new gasworks was built adjacent to Peasley Cross Lane.

Despite their Victorian origins, gas lamps remained in operation on the town's streets through to the 1960s, their familiar cross-shaped bar a common sight in the town until they were succeeded by electric light. The St Helens Gas Works at Peasley Cross was a major local employer, and the decision to down-size the works in the 1970s, with much of the trade relocating to Warrington, was deeply felt locally. Nevertheless, the site remained in operation, though with a smaller workforce, through to its complete closure in the mid-1980s.

Electricity

After gas, electricity soon took its place in the town. A small power station was built in Warrington Old Road, supplying a limited amount of power to businesses and some homes. Like the gasworks before it, this too was later taken into public ownership, by the St Helens Corporation in 1894, as it was deemed important to expand the supply of electricity throughout the town and districts, enabling more business in particular to benefit from the service.

With this increasing demand for greater power, a new, larger power station was constructed in Carlton Street, capable of producing sufficient output to cater for the whole town. Further demands on electricity came with the installation of electric-powered trams on the town's busy streets.

Like the gas industry, the electricity industry witnessed great change. Various independent power stations, located in towns throughout the country, were all later taken into national control with the passing of the Electricity Supply Act, 1926, and the subsequent forming of the national authority. This was divided into regional sections and St Helens was governed by the North West Electricity Scheme. The Carlton Street Power station remained in operation and would continue to supply the town's energy needs – and later still, the National Grid – until it too was eventually replaced in 1954. Its replacement was the new, much larger and up-to-date Bold Power Station, built alongside Bold Colliery, on the outskirts of Sutton. Bold Power Station would become a major employer and was a welcome boost to the local economy, and would remain in full operation through to the latter

The Creation
of the Town

Although in the early days of the town, the dead where buried in the many church graveyards – Jean Baptiste Francis Graux de la Bryure, the Frenchman who brought the art of glass-making to St Helens, is buried in the graveyard of St Thomas's Chantry – as the town continued to expand, a cemetery was needed. Land was found at Dentons Green, and this remains the borough cemetery to the present day. The Crematorium (BELOW) was added in the 1950s. (AG)

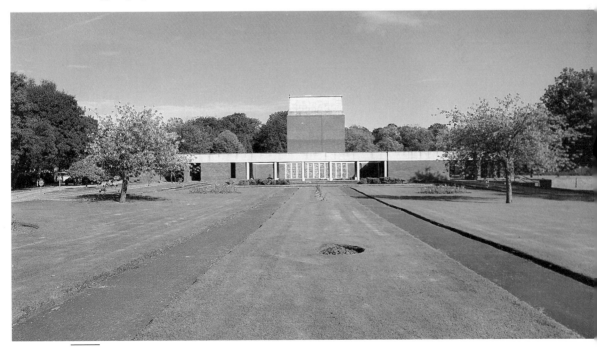

years of the 1980s. By the late 80s the rationalisation of the power industry meant that Bold Power Station was surplus to requirements, and was forced to close: its four huge cooling towers were later brought crashing down in spectacular fashion, watched by massive crowds of onlookers.

Education

Most of the early schools in the town came from the instigation of the churches: from the beginnings of the monastic houses, the church has played a large part in educating the population. Many churches held small literacy classes; in St Helens one of the first such classes was held at the Chapel of St Elyn, and Sunday schools were organised by Issac Sharp. Later, the nonconformist churches, such as the Presbyterians, Methodist and Congregational, combined to offer educational instruction to their congregations in 1806. The distinct shortage of space in all of these early classes meant that once a pupil had mastered the basic art of reading, and a little writing, he or she had to leave, giving up their place for someone else less fortunate.

The first recorded school in the town was built in 1670 by John Lyon, and referred to as the Old Grammar School. This was reserved for only the best of families and was not available to the common people. It survived through to the latter years of the eighteenth century, largely from funds donated by Sarah Cowley, before being demolished in 1797.

Its indirect replacement was an Anglican school, built at Moorflat in the same year the Old Grammar School closed its doors for the final time. This new school was called the Church of England School and opened in late 1797.

Other schools formed from the initial church Sunday schools, an example of which was the Nutgrove Methodist School, founded by the influential Nuttall family in the first quarter of the nineteenth century. However, generous donations were not reserved to church schools: Sarah Cowley, a local landowner, had died in 1716, and a charitable fund established in her name donated sufficient finances to form the Cowley School on land owned by Samuel Cross at College Lane in 1797; this was administered by the Reverend J. Gilliborn, and was in direct response to the opening of the Anglican school at Moorflat. Neither of these schools was particularly large, average attendances at each being fewer than fifteen. Attendances at both schools would rise and continue to rise through the following century: by the 1820s both schools had, on average, around thirty children, and by the following decade pupil numbers were in excess of eighty.

By the middle of the nineteenth century several privately-funded

The town's original Law Courts stood on East Street, until they were replaced by more modern buildings on Corporation Street. This town centre street disappeared with the construction of Tontine Precinct in the early 1970s. (*DW*)

schools had opened in the town, and for the first time in the town's fledgling history, its youth, regardless of their poor background, could gain a decent education. These little schools, such as the Congregational School and St Joseph's School, both at Peasley Cross, and the Holy Cross School in Parade Street, all of which originated in the middle of the century, still retained their religious links. By now areas of the town had several small schools to educate their children; in Windle alone there were fifteen schools retaining over four hundred pupils, and in Parr, Eccleston and Sutton, the schools collectively had attendances of more than two hundred. The original Cowley School, was looking worse for wear by the middle of the century, and was rebuilt in 1846, changing its name to the Cowley British School. Despite the change of name it was always referred to locally as 'Laceys', due to the larger-than-life presence of its new headmaster, Mr Newton Lacey.

By the middle of the nineteenth century, some specialist, private schools had opened in the town. These were fee-paying schools, only open to children whose parents were the more affluent members of society. Specialist girls' schools were established at Parr Hall and Eccleston Hall. Notre Dame School for girls opened at Eccleston in 1858, founded by a group of Sisters sent over from Notre Dame.

Originally they had created a one-room schoolhouse in rented terraced house in Hardshaw Street. Equally, West Park School, established strictly for Catholic boys, opened when three Brothers from De La Salle arrived in the town. They had been sent to assist the work of Father Patrick Hene, who had established a small school in a large detached house on Prescot Road.

The progress into a modern society caused a need to create a standard level of education. Industry required a level of literacy and numeracy that simply was not available. With this in mind, education took on a national role with the passing of the 1870 Education Act. This had been proposed by William Edward Forster, a minister in William Gladstone's first government. For the first time, it made it compulsory for all children – regardless of their background, or family circumstances – to attend school through to the age of ten. It also set up School Boards to monitor both schools and pupils. This led to the opening of more schools, some privately funded, others controlled by the state.

The Cowley Hill School opened in 1882, which contained places for one hundred and fifty boys and a hundred girls. It was considered at the time only right and proper that the sexes were kept apart, both for education and recreation, as even the playgrounds were divided. It would develop to become the town's most famous and wholly respected Grammar School. Other schools came about from the generosity of local wealthy families. The Pilkington family financed the foundation of the Windle Pilkington School, and David Gamble founded the Windle School, at Dentons Green, in 1898.

Public Health

The health of the town's inhabitants had been largely left to deteriorate through the second half of the eighteenth century and the first half of nineteenth. Although there were doctors within the town – such as Dr William Fildes – their prices, certainly in the eighteenth century, were prohibitive to the working class. The spread of disease during the nineteenth century had long been the concern of the more prominent members of the town, although it has to be stressed that the initial reasoning of Victorians had led them to believe that disease was something restricted to the working classes; in many middle-class homes it was thought that disease stopped at the front door! This reasoning fell down with the spread of such viruses as cholera and smallpox, which saw no class boundaries.

In 1873, Dr Robert McNicoll was appointed the town's first Medical Health Officer. He was an ideal choice, with a wealth of experience, not just medical but of local government too: he had been in general

THE FIRST MATRON, MRS. WALKER
AND HER STAFF.

St Helens Cottage Hospital was created from Sutton House, a detached property standing on Marshalls Cross Road, owned by the industrialist, Michael Hughes. This picture shows the first matron, Mrs Walker. (*Reproduced with the permission of the St Helens Local History and Archives Library*)

practice in Eccleston since 1848, and had been chairman of the Improvements Commission, before being elected as one of the town's first councillors and Aldermen following the Charter of Incorporation. His first report of that same year highlighted the need for a hospital to combat the infectious diseases that were endemic to the town's population. Contained in that report was an account of an outbreak of smallpox that had occurred in Pocket Nook, resulting in four deaths; the virus was suspected to have come from a family that had just located to the area from Liverpool. Later in the same year an outbreak of typhoid resulted in twenty deaths.

The need for a hospital had been evident for some years; with such a large workforce, employed in potentially dangerous employment, the requirement for good quality medical heath care was paramount. Peter Greenall, ever one to take a keen interest in the well-being of the people, first raised the issue of providing a cottage hospital for the town in 1840, though there was little in the way of a response to this request, and his death in 1845 closed the matter. The matter was raised again, in 1867, this time by Josiah Cook – though, once again, little came of it. It was only fully addressed when Andrew George Kurtz voiced the idea of funding a cottage hospital in 1872. Kurtz had made the solemn promise that, '… should a suitable site be found, to house such a hospital, [he] would provide sufficient funds to run it'. A local man, J. F. Allen, suggested the use of a detached house in Marshalls Cross known as Sutton House, which he was currently renting from the industrialist, Michael Hughes.

After the matter had been discussed at some length with Hughes, he agreed to its change of use and also offered to repair and decorate the premises prior to its occupation. Further donations to fund the medical equipment required came from the families of the Pilkingtons and Gambles respectively. Initially the founders were unsure as to the demands that might be placed upon the hospital, so only one of the rooms was used, with a total of nine beds; although within a short space of time, demand had risen so much that all of the rooms within the house were brought into use. The St Helens Cottage Hospital opened officially in 1873.

There was a total of 1,126 deaths occurring within the town that year, 598 males, 528 females. The death rate for St Helens stood at 24.74 per 1,000, which was higher than that of London at 22.2, though compared favourably with the town's north-west neighbours: Manchester was the highest at 30.0, while Liverpool stood at 25.8.

Although the St Helens Cottage Hospital had been the first to open, the Providence Hospital opened soon after. This had originally been founded by Mother Magdalen Taylor and her small group of nursing sisters, under the name 'The Poor Servants of the mother of God'. In 1881, the Reverend Father Cardwell had sought the assistance of Mother Magdalen, to help the poor and the sick. Initially this consisted of home visits, but soon they realised that they needed premises from which to tend the sick. They rented a couple of rooms in a terraced house in George Street in 1882. This house, situated in the passage off George Street leading through to the car park of the Raven Hotel, still survives today.

Mother Magdalen's real name was Mary Taylor, the tenth child of the Reverend Father Henry Taylor from Lincolnshire; she had worked as a nurse alongside Florence Nightingale, tending the injured soldiers during the harsh days of the Crimean War.

The demands being placed on these few tiny rooms of the house in George Street were to grow to a point were the Sisters could no longer cope. It was obvious that they would soon need to relocate to larger, more suitable premises. The problem facing them was that they needed to find large enough premises which they could actually afford. Their worries, however, proved unfounded, for ideal premises were to be offered to them free: the Walmsley-Cotham family, Lords of the manor of Hardshaw, who lived at Hardshaw Hall, were planning to relocate away from the noise and pollution of the industrial town to Springfield Hall at Eccleston, and were happy to donate their former residence for use as a hospital.

The Providence Free Hospital was opened by Cardinal Manningon on 15 September 1887. It would continue, operating independently of the St Helens Hospital, through to the mid-1980s, when it finally closed. The building was purchased by the Grosvenor Housing Association, soon after, and converted into flats, as well as its regional office.

The poor living standards in the town, together with the poor infrastructure, led to many health problems. With such a large population, and the demands of industry, the sewerage system was wholly inadequate. Although pipes had been laid under the main streets from 1800 and the surrounding streets in 1851 by the Improvements Commission, they all emptied their waste directly into the Hardshaw Brook, which, with the combined discharge, resembled a huge cesspool. Although there were mounting complaints from both businesses and residents from all over the town about the effect on the air quality and the noxious smell, little or nothing changed.

The atmosphere that hung over the town was putrid, and the surrounding alkali industry added to the misery. Dr Robert McNicoll complained to the Council on several occasions, pointing out that the town's many brooks (and Sankey Brook in particular) were contaminated with alkaline waste that ran off the town's mounting tips and into the brooks every time it rained. As the town's Medical Heath Officer, he pointed out that if nothing was done about this awful situation, a serious health problem could occur. Still nothing was done to resolve this. It would take serious outbreaks of disease to finally force the Council into action.

The town had witnessed two severe outbreaks of cholera, in 1849 and 1854, when many people had died. The first outbreak had been largely confined to the Sutton township, spreading as far as Peasley Cross and the outer edges of the township of Parr, though staying away from the centre of the town. Despite its localisation it accounted for almost one hundred deaths. The second outbreak spread throughout the surrounding area and therefore accounted for a greater number of fatalities. As severe as the outbreaks of cholera were, the Council were not prepared for the massive outbreak of typhoid in 1894. This affected much of the town's population, resulting in a great many deaths, which in turn placed excessive strain on the town's fledgling health care system. However, more importantly, the cause of this outbreak of disease was directly linked to the open sewer. As a direct result the town's sewerage system was completely overhauled, with Hardshaw Brook being largely enclosed soon after. Sections of this once-offensive brook still remain in the town today: open sections appear alongside the canal, near the railway; and a further section passes under Jackson Street its way to join the Sutton Brook (itself once so polluted that it was referred to as the 'stinky brook').

Public baths, today used exclusively for recreation, were originally opened to the public to boost cleanliness and health, as bathrooms, in the vast majority of houses in those days, were non-existent. The first public baths in St Helens, financed by Andrew Kurtz, opened in 1851 in Rimmer Street at the corner of Warrington Old Road and Warrington New Road. These had been built primarily for his workforce, though the public demand, due to a distinct lack of such facilities, led him to open them to all soon after. By 1890, they had been taken over by the St Helens Corporation and thus became the St Helens Public Baths. Public demand for their use was still so great that within a short while they were relocated to new, larger premises, on Boundary Road, where they remain to present day.

Expansion of Local Government

The original Town Hall in Naylor Street suffered a fire in 1871, which required substantial repairs. A second fire, in 1874, far more severe than the first, rendered the building beyond use, and it was abandoned except for the ground floor, which was used as a butcher's stables. The building was finally demolished in 1876, and once the site was cleared market stalls were erected there.

A new Town Hall was planned, this time in a location very different from that of the original. The Council had decided that it should occupy a site away from the busy shopping area. With this in mind, it was given pride of place, on a new site alongside Corporation Street. The building, designed by Liverpool architect H. Summers, was a much grander affair than its predecessor, with a clock tower and spire. A new police station was also built, attached to one wing of the Town Hall, though with its own separate entrance and courtyard. The new building was in use by 1887.

The Urban District of St Helens had been created in 1845, expanding the boundaries of the town slightly, although greater expansion occurred in 1865 when the town became a borough. Although the town was growing in stature, it still did not hold its own representation in Parliament; it fell within the greater parliamentary seat of Wigan (which had been gained by Peter Greenall in 1841, and later, following his

This photograph, taken in the 1890s, shows the current Town Hall. (*DW*)

queen's square & Town Hall. St. Helens.

death, by his brother, Gilbert). This lack of a voice in Westminster was only rectified in 1885, when finally the town gained its own parliamentary status, and its first Member of Parliament was elected. Four years later, its profile was raised further when it became a county borough.

Political Representation

St Helens, following many requests to Parliament, finally acquired the right of parliamentary representation in 1884. The people were able to put their newly-acquired right to vote to the test in the general election called in the following year, when the St Helens electorate stood at 8,291 people. Such was the excitement and anticipation within the town that the turnout for this first election was a massive 89.8%.

Politically, the town was divided between the two big parties – the Liberals and the Conservatives. Both parties began seeking out prospective candidates. The Liberals were the more popular of the two parties, and were soon judged to be the favourites, particularly with their choice of candidate. David Gamble was their clear choice, a political heavyweight, having served as chairman of the Improvement

Commission and as one of the town's first councillors, and unanimously chosen as the town's first-ever mayor. The Liberals were well supported, and Gamble was himself a popular figure in the town and noted for his generosity. He was backed by his friend Andrew George Kurtz who, like Gamble, was a generous man, having founded the St Helens Cottage Hospital. Both Gamble and Kurtz was local industrialists, their alkali factories employed many and so they felt that they had sufficient support to achieve victory in the election.

The Conservatives looked for a candidate of similar political weight and local standing. Their obvious choice was William (Roby) Pilkington, a man of standing equal to, if not greater than that of Gamble. However, to the party's amazement, he turned them down. Sir Harry Seaton-Karr, son-in-law of William Roby, became their second choice. He was backed by other significant figures within the town such as the Bromilow family, colliery proprietors, and Robert Daglish of the St Helens Foundry. The party's fear was that Seaton-Karr was a stranger to the area and lacked local knowledge. The highly influential Pilkington family were divided over politics: William Roby was a staunch Conservative, while his cousin, William Windle was Liberal.

The two candidates campaigned throughout the town, and as the election neared, the race seemed extremely close. Both candidates held their breath and waited for the electorate to decide. The result was much closer than had been predicted, though Gamble, who at the outset had been the clear favourite, lost by a mere 57 votes.

However, what swung the election victory to Seaton-Karr in the final outcome had little to do with local politics, and had everything to do with the fate of Ireland. Parnell's passionate speeches on Home Rule for Ireland swayed the large Irish vote within the town towards the Conservatives, whom Parnell had claimed would be more sympathetic to their cause than the Liberals.

In political terms, St Helens was to prove to be a strange town in its early days, for despite the success of the Liberals on the town council, they would find gaining a seat in Parliament beyond them. The town was to prove to be a Conservative stronghold. Seaton-Karr retained his seat through several elections. At the next general election, held in the following year, where his Liberal opponent was A. Sinclair, Sir Harry increased his majority to 217 votes. In the 1892 general election, the Liberals fielded W. R. Kennedy as their candidate, who put up a good challenge and although he failed to get elected, he reduced Seaton-Karr's majority to 59. In 1895, the final general election of the nineteenth century was called. This time Seaton-Karr's opponent was J. Foster. Despite a good campaign, the Liberals were on the wrong end of a political swing, and Seaton-Karr was returned with a much increased majority of 609.

Chapter Nine

LIFE IN VICTORIAN
ST HELENS

O F ALL THE TOWNS within the county of Lancashire, St Helens was the last to gain a charter to hold a regular market. This honour was only achieved in 1780, consisting of a handful of stalls clustered around the Chapel of Ease, in Chapel Lane. It was to remain there until a more permanent site was found years later. However, the creation of a regular market was far from the creation of a town; that accolade would be awarded during the Victorian years.

Religion

A great many communities formed around churches and St Helens can also trace its origins in this way, as it formed around the medieval chapel-of-ease, thought to have been built during the fourteenth century, and later took its name from it. The chapel would remain in its original humble state until the end of the eighteenth century, when it had to be enlarged slightly to cope with the increase of its congregation, as the local population had started to expand. Within a few years, the arrival of industry caused the population to overflow the capacity of the chapel, and a new, larger chapel was deemed necessary. From this time through to present day, the dedication of the chapel changed from St Elyn to St Mary. This chapel would form the basis of the church that followed later. In 1816, a tower was added to the structure, and bells installed that had originally hung in Liverpool's Church of St Peter (until its demolition). It reached the status of St Helens Parish Church in 1852, finally severing its traditional links with Prescot.

It was once fair to say that religion was at the core of any society, and that churches formed a vital part of developing that society, providing a direction and purpose to the standard of life and general well-being of the inhabitants. This was certainly true in the Victorian era, as the people then – as opposed to now – were regular churchgoers. The Victorian town was blessed with more than its fair share of churches and chapels, catering for a host of religions.

The oldest surviving religious site in the town is the ruined Catholic chantry, dedicated to St Thomas, today standing within the borough cemetery. This structure, often referred to (wrongly) as Windleshaw Abbey, was built in 1435 by Sir Thomas Gerard of Windle Hall. It remained in use and good order through to the sixteenth century, when it was visited by the King's Commissioners, during the period of Dissolution of the monastic houses. Though being of lowly stature compared to the priories and abbeys, it is not recorded as to what was found here. It is known that in the following century, Papists ransacked the place, and in 1627, the enclosed graveyard was used as a secret burial ground by local Catholics, buried here in the dark of night.

Another interesting old chapel in the town is that of the Quaker Meeting House at the end of Church Street. The Quakers (or to give them their correct title, Society of Friends), came to the town after a local farmer, George Shaw (who came from Bickerstaffe originally),

The oldest surviving religious site in the town is the ruined Catholic chantry, dedicated to St Thomas, today standing within the borough cemetery. This structure, often referred to (wrongly) as Windleshaw Abbey, was built in 1435 by Sir Thomas Gerard of Windle Hall. (*AG*)

An old and a modern picture of the Quaker Chapel, proving that through the years it hasn't changed. Compared to other religious houses, the Quaker Meeting House is perhaps less dramatic. However, its simple exterior befits its peaceful surroundings, standing within its own grounds at the end of Church Street, and in many ways is as impressive as any grand church building. Built in the sixteenth century, it is the town's oldest surviving place of worship. (AG, DW)

rented the use of a barn to Roger Taylor, who created the Quaker chapel. Their presence in the town was not always welcome, however: in 1678, fifteen local Quakers were accused of holding meetings in secret, which was contrary to the Protestant Act. Quakers were persecuted across the country and their founder, George Fox, was arrested and imprisoned in Lancaster Castle on several occasions. Only following the passing by Parliament of the Act of Toleration, in 1689, were they finally allowed to live in peace.

Following their freedom, the meeting house in St Helens became the centre of Quaker activities throughout South Lancashire. A small private burial ground was created at the rear of the chapel, and after sometime, a garden of remembrance was added alongside. This still exists today, in the centre is a rounded boulder, said to be of glacial origin (a similar boulder can be seen in Sutton Park).

Through the years the Quakers became a wealthy organisation, and this was certainly true of the St Helens groups, who proceeded to purchase large areas of land in the town. This land, in the centre of Hardshaw, included such streets as Church Street, Bridge Street, Tontine Street, Shaw Street and George Street (the latter two were named after the farmer who had donated the original barn which formed the basis of their chapel). As the town continued to develop, and the population grew rapidly, the Quakers sold sections of their land, at a profit, to developers who built both houses and shops. This action was openly condemned by other churches and some people in the town: in fact such was the level of anger towards the Quakers that they had to vacate their chapel for a period during the nineteenth century, for safer locations elsewhere. Later, after the uproar had faded, they returned.

Today, the meeting house is still there, set in a picturesque garden that makes it look all the more attractive. The sundial above the main entrance is dated 1753. During the later years of the nineteenth century, the Presbyterians were allowed to hold services here while their new church at the corner of Hardshaw Street and Tolver Street, was under construction.

The Presbyterian church was completed in 1868, and with its distinctive double spires it soon became a local landmark. It closed some years later, with the combining of the Congregational Church, forming the United Reform Church. Today, the famous double spires have gone, and the church is looking the worse for wear, now used as a discount furniture warehouse.

The arrival of the Pary's Copper Works in the town in 1776, attracted by the businessman John Mackay, brought with it many of the company's original workers from Anglesey. This influx of Welsh people into the town led to the creation of several small Welsh Chapels. One of these stood directly behind the Presbyterian Church, in Hardshaw Street: it survives today, although no longer used as a chapel, as home to a builder/decorators workshop. Another Welsh chapel still stands in Sutton Oak, at the junction of Sutton Road and Lancots Lane, built in 1840 using copper slag from the Pary's works.

Throughout the centuries following the Reformation, many nonconformist churches began to form, largely due to the intolerance of the Church of England. Followers of these churches suffered persecution like the Quakers, yet remained loyal to their beliefs: they became known as Dissenters or Independents. One such breakaway religious group was the Congregational Church, which formed in opposition to the Common Book of Prayer. As they could not afford churches or even chapels, they often held their services in the open air. In St Helens, they held their first meeting in a room they had hired in the Fleece Hotel. At that meeting donations were collected from the congregation, to add to larger donations they had received from influential local people, such as Sarah Cowley. It was these collections that funded the first Congregational Chapel which was built on Ormskirk Street, and would remain in use through to 1826.

With the congregation growing in number all the time, a new, larger church was built in 1826 on the same street, a little further along than the original. This building also had to be enlarged later, once in 1869 and again in 1883, to cope with the ever-increasing numbers. Such was the popularity of the Congregational Church that smaller chapels were built in the surrounding districts, such as Haresfinch and Peasley Cross.

Other nonconformists included the Methodists, who had also been persecuted for their beliefs. Denied places of worship, they too held open-air meetings, or met in the homes of friends and fellow believers (or in some cases, public houses). The local authorities viewed these meetings as potential trouble, and would often break up the gatherings on grounds of public order.

The Methodists had been attracted to St Helens by the invitation of Joseph Harris who, in 1780, was the manager of the Pary's Copper Works. He was a close friend of the Methodists' founder, John Wesley, and in 1782 invited him to stay at his home in the town next door to the Navigation Tavern, in Grove Street. Apart from holding their early meetings at Harris's house, they also used a joiner's workshop in Market Street.

In later years, as tolerance to varied religious beliefs grew, the Methodists were allowed to construct their own chapels. The first to be built in St Helens was in 1800 on Market Street, and was soon followed by another in nearby Tontine Street. These chapels were often referred to by locals as 'singing chapels' as the congregation

sang loudly. In 1899, a new, much larger chapel was built in Corporation Street, which became their main chapel.

The Salvation Army came to St Helens in the 1880s, feeling that such a new industrial town would have plenty of people worth saving. They were not made at all welcome, facing open aggression towards them on the streets, and violence. Nevertheless, in the true spirit of the 'Sally Army' they stayed here and persevered, putting up with the verbal abused and violence, to spread their word of hope and salvation. They established their Citadel in Milk Street in 1889, and stayed there for many years.

Catholicism was given a well-needed boost in 1849 with the arrival of Father Ignatius Spencer, sent by Father Domonic Barberi from Liverpool. St Helens lacked churches and chapels, and Catholics here had to travel far and wide to attend Mass. Father Spencer had been invited to the town by John Smith, who owned land in Sutton and was willing to donate sufficient space for a monastery to be built. The result was St Anne's Monastery, which opened later the following year, and survives to the present day. Such was the following of Catholics that another church was created at Peasley Cross, dedicated to St Joseph, in 1857 (this church survived through to the 1990s, before falling congregations caused its closure and demolition).

Other churches were built, both in the town and the surrounding districts. St Mark's church, on top of Cowley Hill (with its tall spire a local landmark) was built in 1883, designed by architect James Gandy and funded by David Gamble. Also in North Road is Lowe House

The Presbyterians and the Congregational Churches have been active within St Helens since the latter years of the nineteenth century. The United Reformed Church, located at the top of King Street, is a modern-looking, almost futuristic building, which was opened in 1972, following the amalgamation of the Congregational and Presbyterian churches. (AG)

Lowe House Church has, through the years, become one of the town's most famous landmarks, with its tall Gothic tower and green dome. It had been created on the wishes of Winifred Lowe, widow of John Eccleston, lord of the manor of Eccleston. Built on a piece of land she owned off Crab Street, it was completed in 1793. (AG)

Church, gaining its name from its founder, Winifred Lowe, widow of John Eccleston, Lord of the manor of Eccleston. She had vacated Eccleston Hall following her husband's death in 1742 to live in a large rented house at Cowley Hill, part of which she used to hold mass for the local Catholics. As her congregation continued to expand, she decided that a church of their own was needed. The location for such a church was a patch of land which she owned off Crab Street. Construction began in 1790, though sadly she would never witness its completion, as she died three years later (she is buried in the altar of Lowe House Church).

Housing

St Helens had expanded rapidly from a rural backwater into an industrial town. This was reflected in an editorial in the Chambers *Edinburgh Journal* of 1846, which stated that 'St Helens seems to have been built in a hurry, the attentions of the inhabitants being so absorbed in advancing manufacturers that they would care little about the kind of houses they should provide for themselves'. This picture, though set in the middle of the nineteenth century, could easily have described St Helens in the second half of the previous century. It had been the dramatic change from a quiet, rural backwater into an industrial town, almost overnight, which had caused the population to rise rapidly, and would continue to rise, as more and more people were attracted to the new town. Apart from the Irish coming to the area with the construction of the Sankey Canal, and the Welsh with the Parys Copper Works, more came from across the north west, in search of employment, as the change to industrialisation had deprived many of jobs in traditional trades.

Tontine Street was one of the town's earlier streets, built in 1794, by the Tontine Insurance Society, though like many later streets to be added to the town, it contained poor, inadequate housing. (*Reproduced with the permission of the St Helens Local History and Archives Library*)

The initial answer to this growing problem came from the very companies that were attracting the people to the town in the first place. In simple terms, the businesses had to offer accommodation to their new workforce if they hoped to retain their services here. Many firms built rows of terraced cottages or houses close to the factories; rather than generosity on the part of the employer, it was so the workers were always on hand. Early examples of these were the cottages John Mackey built for his workers at Ravenhead, a concept which was copied soon after by Michael Hughes to house his Welsh workforce. Further examples of workers' houses were the terraced rows built by the Pilkington Brothers, which stood at the rear of their Grove Street works for many years, until they were later demolished to make space for more warehouses.

By the middle of the nineteenth century the population of the town had increased to around 30,000, by 1875 to 48,664 – and by the end

of the century the population was rapidly approaching 90,000. All of these new arrivals had to be housed somewhere, and the lack of housing became a real problem.

The building of workers' houses continued. Pilkingtons, for instance, built a row of terraced houses – called 'Factory Row' – for workers at their Ravenhead site in 1854, which still exists to the present day (making them possibly the oldest surviving residential properties in the town). This process was continued for miners too; single storey stone cottages once stood on Coalpit Lane (modern-day Mertonbank Road) in the 1850s, used by local colliers and some of the alkali workforce too.

The largest proportion of basic terraced housing was constructed between the 1840s and 1860s throughout the town. During the second half of the century the number of houses continued to increase rapidly, passing the 10,000 figure in 1880.

Although St Helens, compared to its industrial neighbours Manchester and Liverpool, did not have its residents crowded into grim cellars, many of the very early workers' cottages were of sub-standard quality and little more than slums. Terraced rows of back-to-back houses, with

no yards, doors or even windows to the rear, were dark, damp and unhealthy, and common throughout the town. But in those times any housing, no matter how poor, was better than no housing at all.

The low standard of housing in the town was something that Peter Greenall was deeply concerned about, and had been clear in his mind when he helped to pass the 1843 Improvements Act through Parliament. For many years he had vigorously campaigned for better housing locally, and had founded the St Helens Building Society in 1824 to build decent housing for his large workforce. The success of this house-building venture meant that once his own workers had been helped, he continued to have houses built, on his own land, for other people of the town. He also purchased extra land, on which other like-minded developers could build decent housing.

The long-awaited improvements to the state of the local housing came with the forming of the Improvement Commission in 1845 (though Peter Greenall, its founder, would not live to see it); they insisted that all the dwellings within the boundaries of the Commission

Poor housing, was the bane of the St Helens population. Squalid rooms, with little or no ventilation or running water, and much of it rented, meant that many families lived in appalling conditions. The courtyard pictured here once stood off Marshalls Cross Road, and gives an insight into the living conditions within the town prior to the implementation of the 1930 Slum Clearance Act. (*Reproduced with the permission of the St Helens Local History and Archives Library*) had to meet certain standards of decency. To ensure that these standards were rigorously met, houses were inspected on a regular basis thereafter. However, despite the Commissioners' greatest efforts they were working against the tide. St Helens from the 1840s was witnessing a boom, and as industry expanded so too did the population, causing a shortage of housing once again. Despite the Commissioners' insistence on maintaining standards, poor-quality housing was erected in the town to cope with the ever-increasing demand; and as the majority of the houses were rented, unscrupulous landlords could get away with leasing inferior dwellings, regardless of the Commission's guidelines.

Westfield Street, close to the town centre, was a good example of this in practice; the early houses there were built in simple square patterns, to maximise the number of houses they could erect in the space available. The houses were small, damp and the overall quality of design and workmanship was low. Many were built in courtyards

Later more terraced houses were built, such as these shown at the rear of Westfield Street. As the town was modernised further in the 1970s, all of these houses were demolished. (Reproduced with the permission of the St Helens Local History and Archives Library)

where rooms were rented individually, and where entire families could be crowded into one room.

Later, other streets were added to this development, such as Lowe Street and North John Street, with other smaller streets in between. All of these houses were simple dwellings, though built to a higher standard than their predecessors: these were the basic two-up-two-down, with individual outside toilets, but they were a great leap forward from the early slums which had just one or two rooms, and communal privies. These improved terraced houses spread across the town, particularly in the coal mining areas and villages of Sutton, Parr, Peasley Cross, Thatto Heath and Sutton Manor.

The larger detached and semi-detached houses came to the town much later in the century, built for the more affluent: the managers, proprietors and directors of the factories and other businesses. These were built away from the noise, smoke and pollution of the industrial town, in areas such as Eccleston and Cowley Hill, which became areas of distinction, reserved for the leaders of industry. Many of these bigger and better houses still stand today. For a good many years, however, the mainstay of housing in St Helens was the humble terraced house, and this was something that could not be addressed until the second half of the next century.

Creating the Town Centre

Chapel Lane, the centre of the former Hardshaw township had just a few cottages during the eighteenth century, though later it would expand, changing its name to the now more familiar Church Street. Other streets were added: Bridge Street, and adjoining that, Tontine Street, built in 1794, following the arrival of the Tontine Insurance Society. The next terraced street to be built was Market Street, linking Tontine Street to Church Street. These four streets now enclosed a field owned by the Society of Friends; knowing that the developing town needed a permanent market, they donated this field to that purpose: the Market Place was built in 1833. This was an immediate success, as on such a large area more stalls could be brought in, and more people from surrounding towns were attracted to shop here. Within a decade much of the market area had been covered by a roof supported on iron pillars, though open on all sides, which protected both stall holders and customers from the majority of the elements.

Through the years, as the town continued to grow, new streets were added such as Hardshaw Street, Barrow Street, Baldwin Street (which was previously called Moor Flat), and Ormskirk Street. The first Market Hall was built in 1851, designed and built by architect George Harris, who lived in Tontine Street. It stood next to the original Town Hall in Market Place (later this was demolished and further stalls took its place). A covered market was erected in 1888 on the former site of the old municipal buildings; this, along with the Market Hall, were very busy places, with popular stalls such as the Penny Bazaar owned by Michael Marks (and later, Spencer). The old Market Hall was demolished in 1962.

Another famous store in the town is, of course, Tyrer's in Bridge Street. This was founded by William Tinsley Tyrer in 1887, with his first store in Liverpool Road. Young William had previously worked for Dromgoole's from the age of fourteen. His first job for them was working as an assistant in their printer's shop, but he had to vacate the position fairly quickly after it was discovered that the ink affected his skin, causing him to come out in a particularly nasty rash. Dromgoole's retained his services, however, transferring him to a position within their clothing store on Liverpool Road.

Bernard Augustus Dromgoole had been born in Warrington in 1819, though his family moved to St Helens later. His first business had been a pawnbrokers, which he opened in small premises on Liverpool Road in 1853, later expanding into the clothing store where William Tyrer worked. Apart from his business interests, Dromgoole was also a freelance journalist, contributing copy to some of the region's newspapers including the *Intelligencer*. This eventually led him to forming a newspaper of his own in 1860, the *St Helens Weekly News*. This paper continued to grow in popularity, and within two years had changed its name to the *St Helens Newspaper & Advertiser*, and was printed in Dromgoole's own print shop.

William Tyrer had learned his trade at Dromgoole's, and within a few years felt confident enough to branch out on his own. He opened his first store on Liverpool Road only a few doors down from that of his former employer, and was later joined in the business by his brother, Richard.

The first Post Office in St Helens opened in Church Street, operating from the front room of a terraced house close to the chapel of St Elyn. As the population of the town increased, so too did the amount of post it handled, forcing a move to larger premises. This move came in 1866, to new premises built on the former site of the King's Inn at the end of Church Street. The larger, purpose-built premises could now cope with the ever-increasing mail. It remained there through to the early 1970s, and only had to move following the planned construction of St Mary's Precinct. With its move, in 1972, to yet larger premises, at the bottom of Bridge Street, it gained the title of General Post Office; with a separate sorting office in Liverpool Road.

Public Houses

St Helens had its fair share of breweries, and with all the town's industries providing such a thirsty workforce, public houses were in abundance. The earliest recorded public house, the King's Inn, stood on Chapel Lane close to the Chapel of St Elyn. It opened in 1629 run by Thomas Martindale of Moss Bank and was finally demolished in 1879, to make way for the building of the town's first ever Post Office.

Due to the harsh, dusty working conditions in the coal mines, glass works, copper and iron foundries, liquid refreshments were in great demand, even if only to wash down the dust! In the very early days of the industrial town, it was common practice for public houses to send beer down the mines (and to other industries) to be consumed by the men as they worked; this led to drunkenness and fighting. Drunkenness was so common within the workplace in St Helens that mine owners and even trade unions complained that workers would often still be drunk, or at the very least hung-over when returning to work the following day. Eventually such behaviour led to the practice of drinking at work being prohibited, though that did not stop them drinking in their own time!

It is claimed that, by the middle of the nineteenth century, there

Shopping developed throughout the Victorian era. In St Helens, as the number of shops opening in the town increased, so too did the number of streets. Here is a classic picture of Bridge Street in the 1890s. To the right of the picture, the covered market, containing fruit and vegetable stalls, can clearly be seen – it would remain in operation through to the late 1960s. (*DW*)

were almost two hundred public houses open for business within the town. They were to be found on every street in the town and surrounding districts. Bridge Street, for example, had at one time no fewer than fourteen public houses, and many of these were right next door to one and other, yet they all did good trade. The fourteen in question were as follows: The Bee Hive, The White House, The Black Horse, The Shakespeare, The Red Lion, The Queens, The Cock & Trumpet, The Nelson (the only one of the original public houses that still survives today), the Adelphi, The Black Bull, The Crooked Billet, Old House at Home, The Volunteer, and finally, the A1 Vaults.

Bridge Street was one of the most popular streets in the town in the early days, particularly among the working classes, although it was frowned upon by the more respectable members of society. It was the type of street that attracted undesirable people: the likes of 'bookies' runners' busy taking bets, and fringe political groups, who would hold gatherings, either in the public houses (if they were allowed) or out in the street itself. Some of these gatherings – or open-air political meetings if you prefer – could become pretty rowdy and often violence would break out when opposing gangs met.

Many of the public houses, if not on the main busy streets, were located close to the pockets of industry and their customers (who could pop in for a 'swift 'arf'). Some of these still survive today, albeit modernised: the Phoenix Inn, standing on Canal Street, was once the Phoenix Tavern, and has been serving Pilkingtons' workers since the latter years of the nineteenth century though it was named after the Phoenix Colliery, which stood off Burtonhead Road, and its miners would have been its initial clientele. Similarly, the Hope & Anchor on City Road stands close to Pilkingtons' Cowley Hill works, and has been there since the factory opened although its neighbour, the Brown Cow Inn, has long since disappeared. The Navigation Tavern, which once stood at the end of Grove Street, was owned by William Bate (who also had canalside premises where he repaired barges), and was popular with glass-workers in its day; it was only demolished in the late 1980s. The Raven Hotel, at the end of Church Street, is another old establishment which still survives today, although its former neighbour, the Fleece Hotel (which was originally a coaching inn) was demolished in the late 1980s. The Sefton Arms, standing between Baldwin Street and Ormskirk Street, has been serving customers since the early years of the nineteenth century.

With so many public houses in the town selling so much ale, it is understandable that drunkenness was common. This was a hard, working-class town, where workers in the coal, glass and iron industries gathered in public houses. This would often led to fights, drunken behaviour and public disorder – offences of this nature were the most common to be seen by the magistrates courts. It is recorded that the average number of persons hauled before the magistrates for drunkenness in the second half of the nineteenth century was between 500 and 600 per annum.

Drunkenness led to street fighting, sometimes ending in open pitched battles in the streets. A common feature was an activity known as 'purring' where two men, who had fallen out while in a drunken state, would attempt to kick one and other in the shins until one or other collapsed. Living in nineteenth century St Helens was nothing if not colourful!

In spite of its sometimes rowdy behaviour, the town had its more peaceful aspects too. Throughout much of the nineteenth century, St Helens, like many other towns in the country, had its own town cryer. George Houghton was employed by Peter Greenall to walk the streets and pass on news to the people at the top of his voice. Greenall, always a man with the good of the people at heart, felt that everyone, regardless of their circumstances, should be entitled to hear the current news first-hand: in those times, although newspapers did exist, their prices were beyond the income of the average working man.

Leisure and Recreation

As the town began to develop, and gain a large overcrowded population, it became vital that places of leisure and recreation were made available. Leisure was many facets varying from the joy of walking in open spaces, visiting the theatre, watching or taking part in sport, or having the chance to read literature. If the town was to progress from simply being a working environment, it had to attempt to supply the population with all of these.

Public Libraries

Public libraries are not just a source of education, but also vital to the recreation and culture of a town. St Helens Libraries developed from the founding of the Mechanics Institute, in 1852, which was housed in the original Town Hall. This library was exclusive to the members of the Institute. A meeting was held in January 1854 to discuss the expansion of the library at the Institute, and the Earl of Derby was invited to address the gathering. Gilbert Greenall MP, (brother of Peter Greenall, who died in 1845) was the chairman, and other prominent members there included the Pilkingtons, Bromilows and Gerards. Also present was Robert Daglish of the St Helens Foundry, who made it clear from the outset that he opposed the expansion of the library if it remained exclusive to the Institute: he

TECHNICAL SCHOOL AND CORPORATION STREET ST HELENS.

Adult education received a massive boost in 1895 with the opening of the Gamble Institute, which also became the permanent home of the public library, which it remains to present day. The building cost £20,000 to build, all of the costs being covered by a generous donation by David Gamble. This picture also shows Victoria Square when it was still a busy thoroughfare, used by trams and carts alike. (DW)

wanted it made public, open to all, and would donate the sum of £100 if this became so. His actions were echoed by the others at the meeting, who agreed with his statement. In total, the sum of £600 was raised that day.

A new library was established in the Town Hall soon after, and the generous donations were used to purchase new books. Although the library was now public, it was not free: books were loaned to members of the Mechanics Institute for an annual subscription of two shillings, while it was four shilling to non-members. Although in real terms these subscriptions were low, they were still beyond the disposable income of the general public, who were understandably reluctant to join the library because of it. This fact, added to the overall low income the library was actually receiving, meant that it was unable to replace books or invest in additional material, and soon became run-down. The situation became so severe that, in 1869, the library was taken over by the newly-elected Council. New books were purchased, and within three years the library was declared free to all.

Following the fires at the original Town Hall in Naylor Street, a new library was designed for inclusion in the newly-completed Town Hall on Corporation Street. This was officially opened by Mayor Joseph Cook on 20 August 1877. In the early days of this new library, even though it had become free to use, the premises were not fully open to the public. Books were kept behind counters, closed off from the general public, who had to ask the librarian for the book they wanted. They were not allowed to browse and select their choice themselves.

As the new library was such a huge success, used by the large majority of the population, the next step was to open a branch library within one of the surrounding districts. A committee met to discuss this matter in November 1883: demand was greatest in Sutton Oak, and so it was agreed that, providing suitable premises could be located, the first branch library would open there. In February 1887, a former shop on Sutton Road was converted into the town's first branch library. It carried a stock of around 5,000 books, and was an immediate success, proving the committee right in their choice of location. Other similar branches were planned: the first of these was at Thatto Heath, following a sizeable donation from Andrew Carnegie, which opened on 3 November 1891. This was followed, in 1894, by a similar-sized branch in Parr.

Although the education of the young of the town had been set in motion, illiteracy amongst the adult population was rife. Following the Act of Incorporation, the Town Council turned its attention to the matter of education: a School Attendance Committee was established in 1877 to ensure that the youth of the town could and should gain a decent start in life coming from a sound education. The passing of the 1889 Technical Education Act (which ensured that one penny from all tax paid by residents went towards education), suggestions were made within the Council that a technical college should be created within the town. David Gamble, former Mayor, and one of the leading campaigners for the development of St Helens, was inspired to donate sufficient finances to cover the cost of construction of such a college: the Gamble Institute was the result, the cost of which reached £20,000. Gamble himself laid the foundation stone in a ceremony in October 1894; and the building was completed and opened, in a grand ceremony, by the Earl of Derby on 5 November 1896. It also housed an improved public library, where, for the first time, people could select their own books from the shelves. The Technical College was housed on the upper floors and held night classes aimed at adults who had not gained an education as children. This was a great success, attended by many in the town, and later led to the creation of the town's Technical College.

Parks and Open Spaces

Like many other towns, St Helens Council sought to create parks which would be open to all. The creation of wide-open spaces was also vital to residents' health, if only to escape the pollution and poor

Three aspects of Cowley House, within Victoria Park. John Ansdell, a local solicitor, commissioned local architect, George Harris, in 1851, to design and build a grand Victorian mansion in the centre of his estate, which he named Cowley House. However, following his death in 1885, his widow sold both the house and the wonderful parklands surrounding it to St Helens Council. Originally opening as Cowley Hill Park, it changed its name to Victoria Park in 1897 to mark the Queen's Jubilee. Throughout the years, Victoria Park – or Vicky Park as it is referred to locally – has been one of the town's most popular parks, with winding paths, beautiful gardens, bowling greens and ornamental ponds. At its centre the 'big white house', once the home of the town's museum, today has been taken over by Age Concern. As for the park itself, it is still popular, though not quite as pristine as it used to be. (MF, DW, MF)

atmosphere created by the town's many industries for a while: from a distance, St Helens' location could easily be determined by the black cloud of smog that hung over it.

The first of the town's parks to be opened was Thatto Heath Park. The creation of this had long been campaigned for by B. A. Dromgoole, who lived at Thatto Heath at the time. The Council purchased a section of the open heath land there, which they developed, planting trees and bushes, creating paths and adding seats etc. There had been many objections to this, some from the locals who, although they were getting a park, objected to losing the heathland where they had traditionally roamed and grazed their cattle. By far the strongest objections came from Samuel Taylor, Lord of the manor of Eccleston, as the chosen section of heath bordered his estate. Nevertheless, despite these objections, the planned park went ahead, and St Helens' first public park opened in 1884.

The second of the town's parks to be created was Victoria Park; although at the time of opening it was Cowley Hill Park, it changed its name in 1897 to celebrate Queen Victoria's Jubilee. The grand opening ceremony was headed by David Gamble, the Mayor, along with other distinguished guests and dignitaries.

This land had previously been a private estate owned by John Ansdell, a local solicitor. He commissioned the local architect, George Harris (who had designed the first Town Hall) in 1851, to design and build a grand Victorian mansion in the centre of his estate. Previously Ansdell and his family had lived at Greenbank, though the success of his legal practice and other business dealings had brought about this great change in status. However, following his death in 1885, his widow had chosen to vacate the mansion and move instead to Rainhill. She sold both Cowley House, and the wonderful parkland surrounding it to St Helens Council.

Following the creation of the park, Cowley House was used for many years as the town's museum. The park itself has all the hallmarks of a typical Victorian park, with rhododendrons, ornate paths and gardens, a Gothic duck pond and traditional bowling greens. Apart from the classical house in the centre, which in recent years has been restored, it still has huge greenhouses, and the famous ornate Italian fountain, donated by Sir Henry Doulton and erected in May 1897. Through the years, this was one of the town's most popular parks.

Although Samuel Taylor had objected to the creation of the first park at Thatto Heath, he would later propose the creation of another. Formed from a large section of his estate, it opened to the public in 1893, called Taylor Park, after its benefactor. It would become famous for its long, rhododendron-lined paths, its boating lake, and aviary, created in an old abandoned quarry. Two other parks were established

Entertainment for ordinary people increased in the later years of the Victorian era. Of all the theatres open in the town during this period, the Theatre Royal soon became the town's premier theatre. It had originally opened on Bridge Street in 1847, though this picture shows the later version, on Corporation Street, which opened in 1890. This more modern Theatre Royal was the victim of a fire nine years later, which caused it to close for a time before reopening. The building was purchased by the Pilkington family in 1960, and underwent massive refurbishment. The Theatre Royal remains popular through to the present day. (DW)

in the town established later in the century, Queens Recreation Park and Parr Recreation Ground, were both purchased by the Town Council in 1899. The park epitomised Victorian life, as the middle classes strolled around the ornate paths on Sundays during the summer, to the sound of the brass bands playing on the bandstand.

Apart from parks, the Victorians of St Helens had a variety of theatres to visit. The first recorded theatre opened in the town in 1847 at the bottom of Bridge Street. Another early theatre was in Milk Street, owned by a man named Haydock, which formed the basis of the first Theatre Royal, though it relocated to Corporation Street in 1890. This more modern Theatre Royal was the victim of a fire nine years later, which caused it to close for a time before reopening. It became the premier theatre in St Helens, attracting large audiences.

'When the "Saints" come Marching In'

The origins of popular spectator sport lie in the latter years of the nineteenth century. As the standard of health of the working classes improved, along with diet and, equally important, leisure time, the quest for sport gained more momentum. The football teams so popular today started around the 1870s; Liverpool and Manchester both formed teams in this era. For the industrial town of St Helens, however, the quest would not be for football, but for rugby.

Surprising as it may appear, the origins of the St Helens Rugby League Club trace back to a German, by the name of William Hermon – or Hermon the German, as he became affectionately known in the town. He had come to St Helens in the late 1860s to work for Pilkingtons, filling a gap left by the departure of George Pilkington, the company's chemist. Apart from being a trained industrial chemist, Hermon was also a keen rugby player. The problem was that at that time, there was no rugby played in the town. Hermon could often be seen on his days off, kicking a rugby ball around.

By the early 1870s some rugby was being to be played in the region, and some northern towns – such as Wigan – had already formed teams. This inspired Hermon to create a rugby team in the town. First he enquired amongst his workmates, but with little enthusiasm there, he resorted to placing adverts in the local press, and was overwhelmed at the response. It transpired that within the town there was a growing need for the creation of such a team. The like-minded individuals met and trained on waste ground off Boundary Road.

By 1874 a team had been formed. Not having a ground of their own at this stage, use of the Cricket Ground off Boundary Road was secured. Within a couple of years the 'Saints', as they were already being referred to, were playing fixtures with neighbouring towns. The

Northern Union League was formed in the 1890s, and St Helens played their first match in September 1895. By the following year, the Challenge Cup had been created, and would be played over the winter season of 1896/97. Saints fared well in this new competition, with Tommy Foulkes (who became a local celebrity) as their team captain and found themselves in the final, playing against Batley on 24 April 1897. In what turned out to be a pitched battle – referred to as the Battle of the Roses – Saints put up a valiant struggle, though they came out second best to Batley on the day.

By the turn of the century, the increasing demand for rugby in the north saw the creation of a new league to rival that of the Northern Union, though St Helens would not join this for another three years. This new 'league' would form the division between Rugby Union and Rugby League. Throughout the twentieth century, and through to present day, the Saints would prove to be one of the best sides in Rugby League, building up a rivalry with their neighbours Wigan equal to any rivalry that exists in football.

Chapter Ten

TWENTIETH-CENTURY COAL MINING

THE TWENTIETH CENTURY would witness great changes in the coal mining industry – some for the better, some for the worse. One thing is for certain: at the start of the century, when the coal industry was a major national resource vital to the industrial heartlands of Britain, no one could have predicted its extinction by the close of the century. To late Victorians that would have seemed an impossibility, yet to us, as citizens of the twenty-first century, we know it to be the case.

The century began well for coal mining, for as the production of coal increased to supply the ever-growing demand, so too did the workforce. St Helens collieries mirrored the nation trend: in 1890 the workforce employed in the mines was around 3,000, yet just a decade later that figure had more than doubled.

Attempts to improve working conditions in the mines had continued. The passing of the Eight Hours Act in 1909, restricting the hours miners could be expected to work, was broadly welcomed, and succeeded in attracting more people into the coal industry. However, it should be stressed that the change in legislation did not always bring changes in working conditions. Many colliery proprietors resented the restrictions to the hours worked by their employees, and many simply chose to ignore these laws. Sutton Manor Colliery was reported for this on 31 July 1914, for instance. However, since the introduction of limited working hours and improvements in conditions underground, the numbers of colliers were rising and by the 1920s there were in excess of 25,000 people working in the local coal mining industry.

St Helens collieries occupied a huge chunk of the South Lancashire Coalfield – which in total covered more than 217 square miles. From this coalfield came some of the finest coal. Some of the more famous seams on the South Lancashire Coalfield were in St Helens, such as Ravenhead Main and Rushy Park. By the 1920s the town was full of working collieries; at one count there was almost ninety in operation, though things were far from being rosy for the workers.

Clockface was the last of the town's collieries to be modernised. The new section of the colliery was opened on 4 August 1939 by W. Foster JP, Lady Balniel and the Earl of Balcarres. Part of the funds for the cost of this new addition to the mine came from the Central Miners' Welfare Committee. Further modernisation of the colliery occurred in the 1950s, to both above- and below-ground workings. Today, this part of the former colliery is used by an engineering business. (*British Coal Corporation copyright*)

A Workers' Revolution

Although there was employment aplenty within St Helens, like the rest of the country, times were hard. Wages were poor. Miners still worked long hours, and in an industry that still required modernisation. The daily work was a hard graft. Wages that had been set in an earlier agreement were about to be significantly reduced, as the mine owners conspired to reduce costs. Understandably, miners and their union – led by president Herbert Smith – condemned the announcement of reductions to their already meagre wage packets. Strike action was threatened, in an attempt to get their bosses to see sense; it had no effect. Stanley Baldwin's Conservative Government held talks with both parties, and offered to inject £23 million into the privately-owned coal industry, in an effort to maintain wages and avoid industrial action, but to no avail. A Royal Commission was established, chaired by Herbert Samuel, though its findings, published in the March of 1926, were inconclusive and therefore made little difference.

The miners' strike began on 1 May 1926. Support for the miners' plight came from the National Union of Railwaymen and the Transport and General Workers Union. Such was the feeling of outrage across the country at the poor handling of the miners that other trade unions soon offered support. Matters escalated, and within forty-eight hours the TUC had called a General Strike. Across the country workers

downed tools; factory after factory closed; the country was at a standstill. Now the bosses would listen – they would have to – or so thought the workers. The General Strike of 1926 ought to have held both the bosses and the Government to ransom. It ought to have brought about a change in the plight of the working class. It did neither. Within days, the solidarity of the strikers began to wane, and by 12 May the General Strike was abandoned.

The miners' strike, which had been the match that might well have lit the revolution, continued, and brought hardship to the country, including St Helens. As the people went without, some sought drastic measures to survive. The spoil heaps of the many collieries around the town, which covered a large area, always held an amount of usable coal that had become mixed in with the spoil, and through the years the locals would walk the tips, picking up pieces of coal for their fires.

St Helens' mining heritage came to an end on 28 May 1991, with the closure of Sutton Manor Colliery. In an effort to celebrate and to remember that St Helens was in fact built on coal, a statue was commissioned and erected on the road-island at the top of King Street. *(AG)*

During strikes, and the 1926 strike in particular, so large was the number of people taking coal that many of the tips became unstable. At Clockface, for instance, the tip was so undermined that it threatened the nearby railway track. The police were called on several occasions by the colliery proprietors, and those people caught on the tips were arrested, to appear before the magistrates the following day.

The strike came to a sorry close in December. The miners, their families facing near-starvation, were forced back to work. The reductions in pay – the catalyst that caused the industrial action in the first place – were implemented regardless. The coal proprietors had won: the miners had lost.

A Period of Modernisation

By the 1930s, the majority of the town's collieries still in operation had undergone some modernisation: for instance Ravenhead had its surface equipment replaced in 1922. Clockface Colliery, for some inexplicable reason, had not. This was, in fact, the last of the town's collieries to be fitted with a modern bath house. The new section of the colliery was opened on 4 August 1939 by W. Foster JP, Lady Balniel and the Earl of Balcarres. Part of the funds for the cost of this new addition to the mine came from the Central Miners' Welfare Committee. Further modernisation of the colliery occurred in the 1950s, to both above- and below-ground workings.

Although its neighbour, Bold Colliery, remained idle for a short period following its closure in the 1930s, it was later purchased by the Sutton Heath & Lea Green Collieries Ltd and reopened. Coal was extracted from the Yard seam initially, which was located nearer the surface, to bring in the much-needed revenue to fund the changes. Meanwhile, work was carried out to extend the original shaft to a depth in excess of 900 yards to reach the rich Rushy Park seam. Despite this investment, Bold was in decline: for although it employed almost 700 men, its output was running well below its expected output of 200,000 tons per annum. Regardless of this, it struggled on.

Nationalisation

Throughout the war years, the British Coal Industry had worked to full capacity. Men not called up to fight had instead signed up to work 'in the underground', keeping the nation's mines open. The Bevin Boys ensured a regular supply of coal to the nation's factories, thereby fuelling the war effort. It was a sterling effort, and one to be commended. Following the end of hostilities the nation returned a Labour government – the first to hold a parliamentary majority. This turned

out to be a reforming Government: creating the NHS, and nationalising industry and the railways.

By far the biggest change to the coal industry came in 1947, with the Labour Government's nationalisation programme. The forming of the National Coal Board meant that, for the first time in coal mining history, all miners were employed by the same boss: this meant the standardising of both conditions and, most importantly, wages. Locally, St Helens Collieries, and the other smaller mines around the town, formed the North West Division of the National Coal Board. During the period of change from private ownership to that of the National Coal Board (NCB), some of the smaller, less productive collieries were closed by their new masters, while others, such as Bold, Clockface, Sutton Manor and Ravenhead all received new investment. At the time of nationalisation there were just over 1,000 men employed at Ravenhead Colliery, and output was up to 260,000 tons per annum.

Of the town's four main collieries, Bold underwent the greatest redevelopment. Here, the new National Coal Board invested a massive £5 million into reorganising and modernising the colliery, making it one of the most modern and productive in the region. This revamping process was carried out between 1948 and 1956, and included the

Ravenhead Colliery, the last of St Helens' 'town centre collieries' closed on 18 October 1968 after more than two centuries of production. Although the colliery had ceased extracting coal, it continued to operate above ground, sorting coal for other collieries, for a further three years. (*British Coal Corporation copyright*)

winding gear and above ground workings being completely rebuilt,
making the colliery the most up-to-date, modern pit in the area. The
investment was worth it, however, for production reached almost
300,000 tons per annum by the latter years of the 1940s, and during
the 1950s in excess of 700,000 tons.

The massive investment programme of the NCB continued into the
1950s. The primary objective of this was to develop modern and
efficient mines that could yield economic coal supplies for at least the
next hundred years. The South Lancashire Coalfield, which had been
actively mined since the eighteenth century, still had vast resources
of workable coal. In the St Helens region, the modernisation of both
Bold and Sutton Manor led to the suggestion that another 'super
mine' could be created. Test bores were carried out from the late
forties in an effort to discover the best location for the new colliery.
The result was Parkside Colliery at Newton-le-Willows which would
later become one of St Helens collieries with the changes to the
counties in April 1974.

Newton Park Farm was purchased in early 1955, and on 13 July the
NCB gave the official announcement on radio and television that the
new colliery was to be built, at a cost approaching £10 million, that

would employ almost 2,500 men. Work began on sinking the shafts and constructing the above-ground buildings, including the two distinctive concrete towers, in early 1957. The colliery was officially completed and opened in April 1964.

While the 1960s saw massive investment in some collieries, restructuring of the industry led to a number of the town's older collieries closing. Clockface Colliery, although a profitable concern for much of its life, had entered a period of decline. Compared to its neighbours at Bold and Sutton Manor, which worked the same seams, Clockface was now uneconomical. After giving sixty-one years' service, the colliery was given notice by the NCB in October 1965 that they were planning to close it. It was thought that the closure of the mine would take four or five months to implement fully, and during this time the workforce would be significantly reduced, though the majority of the workers would be taken up at other local collieries. What coal reserves were still under Clockface would not be lost, for they were accessible from both the neighbouring collieries of Sutton Manor and Bold. There was great sorrow locally at the closing of the pits. Local councillor, John Quinn, himself a former miner, told the *St Helens Reporter* that it was 'like losing a member of the family'.

Clockface was not the only casualty. Ravenhead Colliery, the last of the 'town centre collieries', was also scheduled for closure. Ravenhead, which had once been one of the most productive collieries in the town had, in later years, had its problems: like many of the town's coal mines, it was prone to flooding. So severe was the problem that when the Alexandra Colliery stopped production in 1925, its pumps were used to extract water from its neighbour. In spite of its continued problems with flooding, production grew at Ravenhead through the years.

Ravenhead had a glorious history. It was while working at Ravenhead Colliery that James Anderton (later area manager for the NCB) designed and pioneered the Anderton Shearer Loader, a device that was later adopted throughout the coal industry. A monument to this great invention, along with a column dedicated to James Anderton, who died in 1999, now stands on the island of the Linkway Road, near the former location of Ravenhead Colliery (another statue, dedicated to the years of coal mining in the town, stands on the road island at the top of King Street, in the town centre).

However, throughout the 1960s, whereas Bold Colliery had seen its workforce rise to around 1,500, other collieries were witnessing a fall in their personnel. By the time of its closure in 1968, Ravenhead's workforce had dropped to below 500, yet its daily output reached 850 tons. When the colliery closed on 18 October 1968, it did so quite simply because there was no more coal left to be mined. Although

the mine was closed, the workings above ground were kept employed for a further three years, sorting coal that was brought in from outside. Later, following the removal of the winding gear, the former colliery buildings were used by alternative businesses (including a concrete works and a road haulage firm) though in more recent years the buildings were vacated and stood derelict, prior to their demolition to make space for the new retail park.

For St Helens, the closure of Ravenhead meant that all its coal mining activities were located to the south of the town, principally in two collieries: Bold and Sutton Manor, with Parkside included from 1974. It is perhaps fair to say that the town was no longer the significant coal mining area it had once been, though the remaining collieries continued to thrive.

The 1984/85 Coal Strike

Throughout the years since the National Union of Miners (NUM) had been founded, it had gained a great deal of power and influence, which manifested itself most since the industry had been nationalised, and more significantly during 1960s and 1970s, when it wielded a powerful hold over successive Governments. Strikes – or just the threat of them – had brought several Prime Ministers to their knees.

The miners had brought down Edward Heath's Conservative government by demanding a wage increase of thirty-five per cent. The Government – while in the middle of an energy crisis – had attempted to keep the miners on side by appeasement; though their offer of half the increase that had been called for was deemed an insult and led to the calling a strike in February 1974. This strike resulted in the calling of a general election later that month, in which the Government asked the question 'Who governs Britain?' The answer, one might say, was the miners, for the result of the election was a Labour victory, and Harold Wilson giving the miners their full wage increase.

The power of the NUM changed with the election of the Margaret Thatcher in 1979. As a minister in Edward Heath's Government, she had witnessed at first hand the power of the miners' unions, though unlike her predecessors – of either political persuasion – she was not prepared to be dictated to. The leaders of the NUM – and Arthur Scargill in particular – angered at the reorganisation of the mining industry, and the threatened pit closures (Bold had been threatened with closure as early as 1983, though it had later been withdrawn) under the leadership of Ian McGregor, set about to test her resolve.

The 1984/85 miners strike (although perhaps called for the best of reasons), did not go the way the union had planned, and had a devastating effect on the coal industry – something it had never set out to do. Certainly, with the benefit of hindsight, the greatest flaw was the refusal to hold a national ballot, which meant that the strike was seen as unlawful, and the Labour Party – traditionally the miners' greatest ally – was unable to back the strike wholeheartedly. It would be the refusal to hold a ballot that would cause many of the NUM's own members to later question the validity of the industrial action.

The action leading up to the strike had started in the February and early day of March 1984, though the strike itself did not begin until Tuesday 15 March, when all work ceased at St Helens' three remaining collieries: Bold, Sutton Manor and Parkside. Picketing of the colliery gates started that evening, bringing the collieries to a complete standstill. As the strike gathered pace throughout the mining communities of the country, 'flying pickets' came into the town from Yorkshire pits. Of the three collieries, Parkside seemed to be the least committed. Some miners there resented the fact that there had been no ballot on strike action, and some were willing to work. As a result, certainly in the early days of the industrial action, the majority of the flying pickets were outside Parkside Colliery.

Initially the strike was not seen as a long-term affair by either side in the dispute, and it was confidently thought by the NCB that the industrial action would be over within a fortnight. How wrong they were. The strike was to be a battle of wits, with defiance on both sides, neither side wanting to show weakness to the other. This thought process made any form of negotiation, no matter how minor, almost impossible.

A good example of this attitude was the matter of maintenance. Initially some safety work was carried out at the pits, simply to ensure the long-term viability of the coal faces. However, later this also stopped. This action – or rather inaction – would have serious consequences. Two months into the strike, and with repair work having ceased at Bold and Sutton Manor, the NCB stated that the condition of one of the Bold faces, known as T26, was of grave concern; in fact this would continue to deteriorate to a point were it was no longer workable. Bold's three other faces were also cause for alarm. The NCB claimed that £2 million of machinery was at risk if maintenance work was not forthcoming. Despite this warning, the NUM dismissed the safety claims as scaremongering, stating it was simply nothing more than 'NCB propaganda'.

As the strike entered its second month there were signs that not all of the striking miners were of the same mind. Within St Helens, the miners of the Bold and Sutton Manor collieries were the most defiant (some might say the most militant), refusing to return to work. However, some miners at Parkside returned to work in April. This led to miners from the other two pits, along with flying pickets, increasing the picketing at Parkside and who described the workers as 'blacklegs'. Violence followed.

By the end of April the striking miners' families were suffering. The strike was now six or seven weeks old, and the families had gone without any income in this time. Being on strike also meant that they were denied any form of state benefits. As a result, St Helens Council organised free school meals for the children of striking miners.

As the summer months arrived, the picketing at Parkside Colliery began to turn ugly, with the pickets taking out their frustration on the 'blacklegs' and the police. Missiles were thrown, fighting occurred and a great many miners were arrested.

To boost support for the strike, and to keep morale high, a march through the town was organised and held on Saturday 5 May. Beginning at the car park adjacent to Birchley Street, the march passed in front of the Town Hall and through the town centre, leading to a massive gathering at Sherdley Park. The march was led by NUM General Secretary Peter Heathfield, and hundreds of miners and their families took part in the show of solidarity. In Sherdley Park, speeches were made by miners' leaders and prominent members of the Labour council, vowing that the strike would continue.

By June, the matter of coalface maintenance had been put back on the agenda. By now the situation at Bold was so severe that some miners agreed to work – with the approval of the NUM – if only to repair and maintain the two other coal faces, T22 and T29. Unfortunately, the T26 coal face, which had been the cause for concern soon after the strike had begun, was now beyond repair. A conservative estimate is that around 30,000 tons of coal were lost as a result.

During the year-long strike, the whole town came out in support of the miners and their families. Marches and demonstrations were held, speeches were made, and generous donations were kindly given to the miners' families who were struggling financially. The greatest worry for the striking miners was how to feed their families; a concern shared by members of the town's Labour Party. By July St Helens Council decided that food should be delivered to the families of striking miners, paid for by the rates. The cost of this act of generosity was estimated at £70,000. This was something that did not go down too well with all ratepayers, resulting in strong letters to the newspapers. Nevertheless, further help came in August, when it was announced that St Helens Council were to offer 100% rate rebates to striking miners: this was also met with anger by many residents in the town, who pointed out that the council was taking other non-payers to court! And opposition parties pointed out that the council was in a deficit by £1.7 million. In spite of this condemnation, the Council went further still, setting up a fund to support the striking miners, and asking council workers whether they would like to contribute a percentage of their wages, which, they pointed out, could be deducted more efficiently by direct debit.

The strikers were given a much-needed boost on Saturday 18 August when NUM President, Arthur Scargill, arrived in the town to address a meeting held at the rear of the Bold Miners Club. By now the strike was twenty-three weeks old. Over 1,500 people turned up to hear the speeches, which were reported in the *St Helens Star* on 23 August. Also addressing the crowd was Councillor Marie Rimmer, who urged the miners to 'keep on going, we'll not fail you'.

By October the strike was showing signs of weakening when a growing number of miners, annoyed that there had not been a national ballot, were returning to work at Parkside. These miners were taking a big risk – some might say taking their lives in their hands – for the atmosphere was not pleasant; miners were attacked, many of their homes were vandalised, and their families persecuted. So severe was this persecution, by once-fellow miners, that many chose to leave the town and never return.

November saw the split in the strike widen, with the first few miners reporting for work at both Bold and Sutton Manor Collieries. Although this was contested by the NUM, the first coal came out of the two St Helens collieries since the strike began. By the following month, with more miners returning to work, there was a growing feeling that many more wanted to return, but were understandably fearful of the consequences. By the new year, after what would have been a poor Christmas for the families of striking miners, there were moves on the part of the NUM to negotiate, though there were also claims that Margaret Thatcher was interfering in these negotiations. The NUM claimed that she had her own objective – to crush the trade union movement.

Throughout January, February and March, the NCB ran a poster campaign calling striking miners back to work, saying that they should think to the future. This appears to have been successful in St Helens, for attendances at the town's three pits continued to increase. In an effort to counter this, the NUM organised another rally and visit from Arthur Scargill to the town, scheduled for early March. This, however, never took place.

On 1 March, with more than half the miners back at work, the NUM finally admitted that they had lost the year-long battle. It was therefore decided that the remainder of the striking miners should march back to work. At 8 a.m. on Tuesday 7 March, the miners returned. A crowd of over one thousand strong marched alongside their wives and children to both Bold and Sutton Manor collieries, singing what had become their battle hymn: 'Here we go, here we go'. Defeated, but still defiant.

And so what had the strike achieved? For despite its length, despite the powerful and emotive speeches that were made, and despite the pickets and the fighting that occurred between miners and police, (which divided communities, then and after), the management of the NCB, the Conservative Government, and Margaret Thatcher in particular, did not given in to the NUM. In the end, after a period of twelve months out of work, a period of twelve months without any wages, the miners were forced to return to the collieries, defeated. Though they returned defiant, it was a humiliating climb-down. Worse still, the neglect of the mines during the year-long strike meant that by the time it was over, many – including Bold Colliery – were no longer safe to operate and had to close. What might have been the NUM's finest hour had ended as its worst. Nationally, as well as locally, the coal industry would never recover: between the start of the strike in 1984 and the closure of the majority of the country's mines in 1992, the number of people employed within the British coal industry would be reduced from more than 270,000 to fewer than 20,000.

Sutton Manor Colliery, which had opened in 1906, would prove to be the last working colliery in St Helens. Although it too was affected by the 1984/85 coal strike, its coalfaces and underground workings were still safe to operate when the strike ended, unlike its neighbour Bold Colliery which had been so badly damaged by the strike that it had to close soon after.

The colliery had had a chequered past. It had been threatened with closure in 1968, along with Ravenhead, though had been reprieved the following year. It witnessed £200,000 of investment four years later. Without this investment it was claimed that the colliery would have closed within seven years. Indeed by 1980 the mine was showing an increase in production almost reaching 400,000 tons per year.

An announcement, three years later, of further investment – totalling £14 million – made its future look secure. However, the colliery had made a loss of over £9 million by the end of 1986 – making it the most uneconomic pit in the region – resulting in 250 jobs being lost, reducing its workforce by one-third. The following year brought with it more gloom: the NCB informed Sutton Manor that if output did not reach 12,500 tons per week by the end of November 1987, then the colliery would close. This threat inspired the reduced workforce to increase productivity to a point were it smashed all previous records, in an attempt to ensure the colliery's life. Although they had failed to reach the target – its highest production figure was 10,000 tons per week – the NCB were so impressed that the colliery was given a reprieve.

By the late 1980s, however, British Coal itself was in grave difficulties – the annual report of 1988 shows a loss £37 million. The 1990 report was little better and led to calls for the closure of a quarter of its 41 pits: Sutton Manor Colliery was on this list, with a closure date of 28 June 1991.

This announcement came as a massive shock to the people of St Helens. A campaign was started, backed by St Helens Council – including Dave Watts, Deputy Leader – to keep this, the last mine in the town, open. Ultimately, the campaign failed to alter opinion, and the colliery closed on Friday 30 May, one month early due to continual machinery breakdowns and problems underground. Today, apart from the colliery gates and some of the former spoil heaps, nothing remains above ground: the buildings, winding gear and workings have all been demolished and cleared away.

Throughout the relatively short years of its existence, Parkside Colliery became one of the most efficient and productive collieries in the country. Being such a modern pit, it weathered the effects of the coal strike more easily than others, and soon returned to full production once the strike had ended. Production increased steadily from the mid-1980s into the 1990s, and Parkside held a significant position in the now-reduced coal industry. In 1990, for instance, it produced almost one million tons of coal.

Ravenhead's above ground workings. Winding gear like this once dominated St Helens' skyline, but not any more. St Helens was once a proud coal mining town, employing thousands of miners, and providing quality coal for the nation. Today, that mining heritage has been largely overlooked. One might expect that for a town built on coal it would celebrate its heritage; it has not. As each of the collieries closed the winding gear and the buildings were demolished, effectively wiping away any evidence that they were ever there. For a town that once boasted over one hundred collieries, modern St Helens offers little in the way of its mining heritage – and that, in my opinion, is a crying shame. (*British Coal Corporation copyright*)

Rumours of further pit closures still echoed throughout the industry, and every miner feared that his colliery would be the next to be axed. In the time that followed, Parkside experienced trouble on the coalface with flooding – something that had not occurred for more than a decade. It was a bad omen, for it offered the excuse needed to suggest closure. The decision that had been feared the most came on 31 March 1993: Parkside was no longer a viable concern and was scheduled for closure. It was not alone, for the Government announced that the remaining 31 pits were to close, signalling the end of 31,000 jobs in an already decimated industry.

Protest at the closure of the remaining collieries formed around the Women Against Pit Closures group. Some of their members camped on the perimeter of Parkside Colliery in the January of 1993. They were still there six months later when Parkside closed; the last workers

left on 4 June 1993. In October, some of the protesters – led by Arthur Scargill's wife – broke into the colliery and staged a sit-in on top of the towers. They were forcibly removed. Later that same month, as a result of their actions, the NCB turned off all power to the colliery. Demolition of the site began in the following March. Nothing whatsoever of the former colliery survives today.

In St Helens town centre, the NCB offices, which stood at the corner of Corporation Street and College Street, also closed. The closure of the mines had a huge effect on the local economy and swelled the dole queue accordingly. Thousands of ex-miners were faced with life on the dole, and ahead of them would be countless failed job applications, and endless retraining courses: although eventually many of the ex-miners would find work again, it would not be in their chosen profession.

In more recent years, opencast mining has proved successful, removing much of the quality coal lost through 'pillar and stall' workings. Locations such as Ravenhead, which has been opencast twice (first in the 1980s, and again a decade later) by United Gravel Company of Wrexham, have actually yielded vast amounts of coal. Other sites in the area have proved equally productive; currently a substantial opencast mine is operating near Garswood, extracting coal from the former Gerard family estates.

Despite the loss of the local coal mining industry, reminders of its early days often come back to haunt the people of the town. When shafts were originally sunk throughout the area in search of the elusive coal, many of these went unrecorded. Old shafts, that have since been built over and long since forgotten about, unexpectedly reappear from time to time. One example of this was a former completely unknown shaft that was suddenly discovered when a row of old terraced houses in Bryn Street behind the Town Hall was demolished in the early 1990s. Obviously a builder had erected these houses at the turn of the century, right over the shaft, and people had lived there ever since, not knowing what was right under their feet! Thankfully, no tragedy ever occurred, and the shaft has since been capped.

Our Coal Mining Heritage

For a town that once boasted over one hundred collieries, modern St Helens offers little in the way of its mining heritage. Where the colliery spoil heaps once encircled the town, today they are no longer to be seen. In the summer of 1996, St Helens Council purchased the former colliery sites of Bold, Sutton Manor and Clockface, for the bargain price of £1 each. It was a deal that would see them earmarked for a period of redevelopment, creating a 'wasteland to woodland' experience.

Today, those former industrial sites are 'country parks' covered in topsoil and trees, where the town's former miners can take solace while walking their dogs.

Although I welcome the transformation of these derelict sites into areas for recreation, in many ways I would have liked to have seen the process taken a stage further. It would have been a more fitting tribute to the town's coal mining heritage if, when the axe had fallen, one of the former collieries – say, Sutton Manor as the last colliery in the town – had been preserved as a heritage centre. Using the above ground working as a visitor centre – in the same way as the World of Glass utilises the former Pilkington glass house – it would have been a constant reminder to the people of the town, its visitors, and most importantly to the generations that follow, that St Helens was quite literally built on coal. However, the workings at Sutton Manor and all other collieries were demolished, and today, all the town has to show from its long and distinguished coal mining heritage are a couple of tasteful monuments and its memories, both of which will undoubtedly fade with time.

Chapter Eleven

LIFE IN TWENTIETH-CENTURY ST HELENS

*T*HE CITIZENS OF ST HELENS celebrated New Year's Eve, 1899, with great hope, looking forward to the excitement of entering a new century. However, at the dawn of the following morning, with the euphoria of the night left behind, the new century would look little different than the one they had left. They were, after all, still Victorians – and would remain so for another twelve months or so. The new century would bring massive changes, though in the early years life was little different. If change in the living standards of the people was to come, then surely the creation of the Labour Party would prove to be a step in the right direction.

A Safe Labour Seat

The new century was to bring radical changes to the political arena, nationally as well as locally. The number of eligible voters in St Helens had reached 10,763: the first general election to be held in the new century came in 1900. Political opinion locally had not changed from the previous century, and so Sir Henry Seaton-Karr, the town's Conservative MP, witnessed victory for the fifth time, beating his Liberal challenger, C.A.V. Conybeare with a majority of 1,898. However, although this was to be his best-ever victory (producing his greatest majority), it was also to be his last. For times were changing, and at the next general election in 1906, the Labour Party fielded their first candidate, Thomas Glover.

The arrival of the Labour Party within the town had come with the founding of the St Helens Trades and Labour Council in 1890. In 1900 the Labour Representation Committee had been formed in London, just prior to the founding of the Independent Labour Party. The appeal of a socialist party, a party ready to fight for the working man, found an immediate and most welcome home in St Helens; and so the result of the 1906 election was that Sir Seaton-Karr lost, and in spectacular fashion. Labour's majority was 1,411.

There were two general elections in 1910. The first, in January, saw Glover beat the new Conservative challenger, R. P. W. Swift, though

These two pictures show the town hall at the turn of the twentieth century. Here the clock tower still retains it impressive spire. However, a fire, started accidentally by a workman's blow lamp, devastated the Town Hall in 1913. As a result of the damage, whose cost exceeded £20,000, the decorative spire above the town hall clock was demolished. (*DW*)

TOWN HALL, VICTORIA SQ ST HELENS

177

with a majority that had been almost halved. The Conservatives were regaining the ground that had been lost. This comeback reached full steam by the time of the second election of that year, held in December, and Rigby Swift beat Glover, albeit with a majority of just 264. By the time of the next scheduled election, the country was at war with Germany, and so all elections were suspended for the duration.

In the election of 1918, against the backdrop of the war, when the Liberal Prime Minister David Lloyd George promised 'a land fit for heroes', the people not only wanted, but expected change. In St Helens, Swift lost his seat to a new Labour challenger, Sir James Sexton. By now the number of eligible voters in the town had increased significantly to almost 45,000. Sexton won with a majority of 4,000. He would prove to be a formidable MP: holding the popular vote, he would win the next four elections and match the record of success that had been set by Seaton-Karr.

Within the twentieth century, the modern town of St Helens has become a safe Labour seat along with its neighbours Wigan and Warrington. It is often remarked that a prize bull could get elected here, as long as it wore a Labour rosette! However, Labour MPs from St Helens are often returned to Westminster with some of the highest majorities in the House.

Incidents

St Helens' original Town Hall had been the victim of a disastrous fire in 1874, which led to the rebuilding and relocation of its more modern replacement two years later; uncannily, this too was the victim of a serious fire in 1913. A blow-lamp, used by workmen carrying out routine general maintenance to the clock tower on 9 June of that year, started a small fire which soon got out of control. Even though the local fire service were called, bringing their single fire-pump, and were assisted by the Pilkingtons' fire service, the blaze had taken hold and would take sometime to bring under control. The result was the destruction of the top of the clock tower in particular its spire, and the main hall. It was later estimated that the total cost of the damage caused by the fire and smoke was in the region of £20,000. The clock tower's ornate spire was beyond repair, and had to be demolished; it was never rebuilt. The clock tower itself, which had sustained some damage, was repaired, and left with a flat top and a flag pole. Repairs were carried out to the Town Hall itself, and it was returned to its former high standards in time for the Royal Visit by King George V and Queen Mary on 8 July.

The Church of St Mary, the centrepiece of the town since its founding, was a victim of fire just three years later. The blaze was

St Helens Parish Church had been created from the town's original chapel-of-ease, which had been extended in the latter years of the eighteenth century, changing its dedication from St Elyn to St Mary. Its tower was added in 1816. This picture was taken around the beginning of the twentieth century. Sadly, however, this church was completely destroyed by fire in 1916 and had to be demolished. Its successor, the current parish church, was completed within the next decade. (DW)

started by a suspected electrical fault on 2 December and the damage was so severe that it had to be completely demolished, as it was feared that the structure was unsafe and beyond repair. Construction of the new, even larger church began in earnest, once the demolition and clearing of the site had been completed. The new church of St Mary was built to a design proposed by architect W. D. Caroe, and would cost in excess of £70,000 to complete. It opened to its congregation in 1926, and it is this church, with its tall tower, that today occupies the central position on the town's main shopping street.

A Town Full of Churches

St Mary's was not the only church to have witnessed rebuilding during this century. A familiar landmark in the modern town is Lowe House Church on North Road, with its Gothic tower and large green copper dome. Although the Catholic church had been founded in the nineteenth century this structure dates from 1929, when it was completely rebuilt at the request of Father Riley.

The Methodists, who had been active in St Helens since the 1780s, saw their main chapel on Corporation Street, built in 1899, demolished

Parish Church, St. Helens.

in 1973 to make way for the construction of new local government offices called Wesley House. As part of the arrangement a new, ultra-modern chapel was added to Wesley House, which remains to this day the centre of the Methodists.

The Congregational Church, which had stood on Ormskirk Street since 1826, was eventually demolished in the mid-1970s to make way for the construction of the new National Westminster Bank. However, following the amalgamation of their church with the Presbyterians, a new, United Reform Church was built at the far end of Ormskirk Street in 1972, although the completion date was considerably delayed after mining subsidence was discovered on the construction site: in the early days of mining there had been a colliery here too!

Public Health

The change from the end of nineteenth century to the twentieth was not remarkable for a town such as St Helens. After all, the town was still full of heavy industry, life was hard, work was long and arduous, and the living conditions of the working class were still very much the same – poor. However, the new century was to see great improvements to the state of the public health of the town's residents. St Helens Cottage Hospital, founded in 1873, had increasing numbers of patients, which had placed a burden on the authorities to enlarge the facilities there. North-west architects Briggs & Wolstenholme were commissioned to extend the hospital, which they completed in 1902–4, building three new wards and a separate nurses' home to the rear. The new extended hospital handled almost five hundred cases in 1903 – though this figure would rise to over one thousand within the decade.

The greatest change to the perception of public health came with the foundation of the National Health Service in 1948: the concept a simple one, medical care for all, free at the point of need. The creation of the NHS has changed the standards of health in the second half of the twentieth century, though the burden on the service throughout the years has been a heavy one, and a problem that successive Governments have tried to solve. In St Helens, the closure of the hospital's Accident and Emergency facilities in the late 1980s was met with strong local opposition. Despite the petitions and objections, the plans were enacted upon and the facility closed, leaving the town's residents dependent on the A & E of Whiston Hospital (located at least four miles away). Further complaints led to the concession of a Minor Accident Unit opening at St Helens Hospital in the early 1990s. St Helens Hospital itself has seen further expansion under the control of the St Helens and Knowsley Health Authority Trust in the 1990s.

As the town's population continued to expand into the twentieth century, the St Helens Cottage Hospital underwent a process of expansion and modernisation. This picture, taken in 1928, shows the work carried out by local architects Briggs & Wolstenholme. By this time the traditional 'cottage hospital' had virtually disappeared. (DW)

Housing

Despite the improvement to the town's hospital, the state of its housing did not help to improve the standard of health. The problems created by the sudden creation of the town in the eighteenth century had manifested itself in even greater difficulties throughout the nineteenth century. The massive growth in the town's population placed great stress on the available housing, resulting in slums being built just to accommodate the residents attracted here.

Poor housing in industrial towns such as St Helens continued into the twentieth century. The passing of the 1930 Slum Clearance Act gave the local authorities the power they required to demolish the worst of the nineteenth-century housing: masses of the worst type of housing, cramped, damp and dingy rooms and basements were seized from unscrupulous landlords and knocked down. Their replacements were council house estates in areas of the town such as Portico, Parr, Thatto Heath and Sutton.

However, under the strict terms of the Act, only the worst homes could be demolished. Many which were only slightly better than the slums escaped demolition. It was these homes, traditional terraced housing, that would form the basic living quarters of the town's residents long into the twentieth century and beyond.

These homes, many of which still stand today (though modernised) largely consisted of two rooms downstairs – a parlour and a kitchen/ sitting room – and two bedrooms above: the typical two-up, two-down. The kitchen area had a white pottery sink, with a single cold water tap, and a pantry attached. There was no bathroom in the house, the toilet was down the yard, and bathing was done in the tin bath, normally placed in front of the fire. Although there was no hot running water, it could be supplied either by putting a large pan on the fire, or – for the more fortunate – by a separate boiler within their range. Although electric lighting had been available around the turn of the century, few homes actually had it installed, and still relied upon gas lighting. The houses were heated by coal fires – with one in every room – and the coal itself was stored outside in the yard in the coal bunker. The coal man made regular weekly deliveries of coal, his arrival heralded by the barking of all the local dogs! The front room, or parlour, was the pride of place of the vast majority of housewives, kept spotlessly clean and used for only the grandest of occasions; for normal, everyday living the family remained in the sitting room/kitchen area. This type of household remained in towns like St Helens through to after the Second World War. Although some improvements had begun to take effect in the early years of this century, the First World War intervened and work was halted. This work recommenced following the Great War; new houses were built in the town throughout the 1920s and 30s, though as before, work was interrupted by the arrival of yet another World War.

Improvements in Public Transport

The replacement of trolley buses with motor buses gave a real boost to public transport, as longer routes could be established. These became more frequent by 1929, and initially met with some confrontation from the local bus operators whose areas these long distance services were passing through. Matters came to a head, and the regional authorities held a meeting to discuss the situation in the hope that a plan could be formulated to allow these long-distance services to operate more freely. The authorities were reluctant to impose a strict plan of action upon the individual bus operators, suggesting that it would be better for all concerned if a system of co-operation could be reached. Following further discussions in 1933, a system emerged where long-distance buses were allowed to pass through rival districts.

All the early motor buses had been single-deckers, but as the routes expanded, and greater numbers of passengers were using the services, double-deck buses were installed on most of the routes by 1933. Nevertheless, despite the usefulness of such buses, some routes had

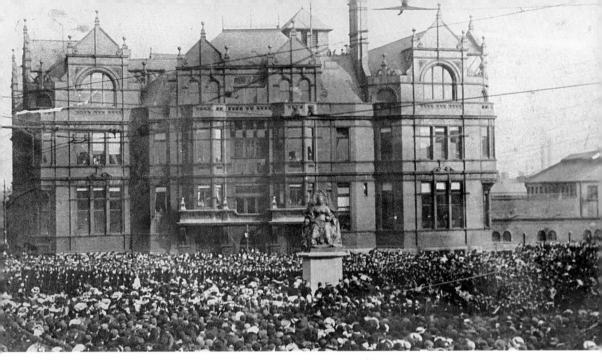

A massive crowd gathers outside the Gamble Institute for the unveiling of Victoria's statue in 1905. Queen Victoria, who had died four years earlier, was held in great respect and affection within St Helens, best remembered locally, perhaps, for having granted the town its Act of Incorporation in 1868. (*DW*)

to remain the sole preserve of single-deck buses, mainly due to the low height of some of the bridges. It is only in recent years that some of these offending bridges have been given greater clearance. Yet, even today, there are still one or two bridges within the town that for one reason or another cannot be altered, and although double–deck buses do not use these routes they are still a problem for tall lorries. Also, when open-top double-deck buses were first introduced, many of the town's bridges had signs fitted warning passengers not to stand! A good example of this was the railway bridge on Peasley Cross Lane.

Although St Helens had its own bus operator, and a depot, it did not possess (until recently) its own bus station: one of the unusual features of the town was that the bus stops for the various routes were scattered along almost all of the town centre streets. Some of these were on Baldwin Street, outside Helena House; Water Street, opposite Beecham's factory; and of course, several more stops around Victoria's Square. Only during the 1990s has St Helens acquired a bus station, built on land off Bickerstaffe Street eliminating the need for stops scattered around the neighbouring streets and making the task of finding the correct bus much easier.

Road Improvements

As well as public transport, the motor car brought increased mobility for people. The early car enthusiast had the freedom of the open road – or rather, lane, for by the turn of the century the roads were still narrow and often winding. Progress through towns was often slow and the flow of traffic restricted. Long distance travel was a slow and laborious process, and as a result the movement of goods was often kept to the railways.

The residents of St Helens benefited greatly from the construction of the East Lancashire Road. This was the first of the new 'super' roads, built, in this case, to connect the cities of Liverpool and Manchester with a single direct route, avoiding the previously slow and winding journey along the A57. Although plans had been drawn up as early as 1913, the Great War intervened before construction could commence. The respective councils of Manchester, Liverpool, St Helens and Warrington had reconvened meetings to discuss the possible route of the new road in the 1920s, and the plan gained Government approval in 1926, with an estimated cost of construction set at £2–3 million.

The road would pass St Helens to the north of the town and required a cutting through Windle Hill. John Brodie, Liverpool's chief engineer, was given the daunting task of overseeing its construction. The workforce for the project were hired from local sources along the proposed route, and in the case of St Helens came as a welcome boost to the local workforce still experiencing difficulties from the Depression. Work commenced on 29 April 1929 when the first sod was cut by Sir John Aspell, chairman of Lancashire County Council's Highways Committee. The road was built in sections, with each local area responsible for the construction of its own section, and was unique at that time as it was made of concrete, with a tarmac surface. The highway was completed by the end of June 1934, and officially opened on 19 July by King George V.

The demand for better roads continued throughout the 1930s. Traffic from St Helens through to the coast at Formby and Southport had seen an upsurge but once again, the poor country roads were not a match for the level of traffic they were receiving. A new road was planned that would take traffic in a more direct route, and away from the tiny villages. Construction of the new road, the Rainford bypass, began in February 1939 and although progress had been made by the September of that year, the declaration of war with Germany affected its continuation. Although construction was officially suspended in March 1941, within a couple of years the road was being used for military purposes, and would remain in military hands through to 1946. In the following years work recommenced, led by James Drake. The road took on higher status soon after with the decision to create the A570 route (linking Warrington, St Helens and Southport) and the speedy completion of the Rainford bypass was given priority. The completed highway opened for traffic in 1950.

The centre of Victorian shopping in St Helens was the Market Hall and Covered Market, built in 1851 and 1888 respectively, and they continued to dominate the town centre for much of the twentieth century. This photograph, taken in the 1960s, shows that they were still in use and still popular among the town's shoppers at that date. Sadly, within a few short years the bulldozers would move in and demolish this classic building, making way for the construction of the Tontine Precinct. (*DW*)

Life through Two World Wars

Following the declaration of war on Germany on 4 August 1914, volunteers were hastily recruited in the town centre. The recruiting, which took just three days, was not difficult as the young men of St Helens – like elsewhere in the country – answered the call to arms, and were prepared to fight for 'King and Country'. By 4 September their numbers were sufficient to create the Eleventh Battalion of the South Lancashire Regiment. Made up of local lads, the battalion was referred to locally as the 'St Helens Pals', and were temporarily housed at the barracks created at the old London & Manchester Plate Glass Works on Robins Lane, Sutton Oak.

The First World War was a particularly hard time for the soldiers stationed abroad; the South Lancashire Regiment saw action on the Western Front, and many lost their lives at the Battle of the Somme. For the locals, little really changed, as the war was, after all, far away.

However, on 12 April 1918, an incident occurred that was to change that situation. It had been known for some time that the Germans were using Zeppelins to bomb allied territories, though no one suspected that they would come in this direction; however, on that fateful day a lone Zeppelin (it had been part of a force of five, which had become detached from the flight and had lost its way) dropped two bombs on St Helens. Thankfully, due more to good luck than planning, no one was killed, however, the same Zeppelin and the others dropped more bombs on the Kirkless Ironworks at Wigan, killing five people in the process.

During the years of the Great War, many of the town's traditional industries turned to war work. The former site of the Manchester and Liverpool Plate Glass Company in Sutton was purchased by the Ministry of Defence, which used it for munitions work, together with a small barracks on site for security. The glass companies, including Pilkingtons, Fosters and UGB, were also heavily involved in munitions production.

The Armistice of 11 November 1918 came as a great relief to many in the town and the victory was celebrated on the Town Hall steps; further celebrations were held with summer parades of the following year.

The years between the First and Second World Wars were a blessed peace. However, with the increasing difficulties with Germany, the declaration of war in September 1939 came as little surprise. The initial call-up for the armed forces had come in the summer of 1939, though the Territorials had already received their papers and were mobilised accordingly. Not all the men in St Helens were called up for active service: being a major coal mining town, many were required to stay behind and ensure the continuation of coal production for industry and the vital war effort. This was as part of the reserved occupation scheme, though in the case of the coal miners, they were better known as the Bevin Boys.

To aid the war effort the ladies knitted sweaters for 'our brave boys at the Front', and the much-depleted resources were boosted with paper drives, rubber drives, and other fundraising efforts. The shortages caused by rationing were something that the people simply had to come to terms with; they meant long queues for almost everything and, more often than not, simply going without. The slogan 'dig for victory', promoted by the Government, saw people given allotments where they could grow their own produce and perhaps keep a few chickens etc. The iron railings and park gates of both Sutton and Victoria Park were taken for the war effort, leaving their pillars standing alone – as they still do today.

The town's inland location and its low military status meant that

This picture shows the rear of the Market Hall and the Covered Market (in the top left-hand corner, the light coloured brickwork is the Savoy Cinema). This street would be filled with stalls, and packed with shoppers, particularly on Saturdays. All this section was demolished in the 1960s. (*DW*)

compared to its neighbour Liverpool it was not a prime target for the Luftwaffe. Nevertheless, public air raid shelters were erected throughout the town, and council houses were equipped with Anderson Shelters in the gardens (in fact, many of the town's older houses still possess them to this day – though more often used as garden sheds now): despite this effort by the local authorities, the majority of residents in the town much preferred to remain in their homes during the raids, taking to hiding under the stairs. During the long Blitz of 1940–1, St Helens suffered little real damage, but the constant threat of air raids meant that the night skies had to be watched with vigilance by the local ARP. Blackouts were strictly enforced, accompanied by the familiar call of 'Put that light out!' The long summer evenings were often highlighted by the dogfights occurring hundreds of feet up in the sky over St Helens.

To guard the shores while our forces were abroad, the Local Defence Volunteers (LDV) were formed, consisting of men too old or too young

SEFTON PLACE, ST HELENS.

to fight in the regular army: despite their official name (the Home Guard as they were later called) they were often referred to as Dad's Army, as depicted in the popular BBC series. Although the town held no strategic military position, there were soldiers stationed here, though the majority of them were Territorials: 'C' company were stationed at Sherdley Hall, for instance, and trained in the grounds of the Hughes estate. Defences were prepared to counter the threat of invasion; obstacles were placed alongside the major highways, and natural defences such as the Sankey Canal were reinforced with 'pillboxes' erected along its length.

The town's relatively close proximity to the USAAF Burtonwood air base meant that the locals saw their fair share of Yanks. They filled the pubs and dance halls, charmed the local young ladies and infuriated the local lads; but all's fair in love and war!

When VE day came in May 1945 the people of St Helens celebrated both the victory and the end of the long war years, and waited for their loved ones to return safely home, although those involved with the war in the Pacific would have to wait until August. However, with the war finally at an end, people settled down to normal life once

Life in St Helens moved at a more gentle pace in the Victorian era, as this picture of Sefton Place clearly shows. Today, that same location is a busy crossroads in the centre of the town! The Sefton Arms is still there, though, as busy as ever. On the left-hand corner now stands Wilkinsons' Home and Garden Centre. (*DW*)

more, and the authorities returned to more mundane matters, such as housing, education and public health.

Education

The turn of the century saw a further commitment to education of the young. The passing of Arthur Balfour's 1902 Education Act had started the process by abolishing the school boards and replacing them with education authorities, which oversaw the building of new secondary schools and brought in, for the first time, medical inspections in schools. Later in the same year, the St Helens Council formed an Education Committee. Its principal purpose was the expansion of education throughout the borough, which would lead to the formation of state schools in and around the town, covering the areas of greatest population, such as Sutton, Parr, Thatto Heath and Eccleston.

A further boost to education was the passing of H. A. L. Fisher's 1918 Education Act. This extended the boundaries of education by increasing the school leaving age from ten to fourteen, and offered part-time secondary education to those between the ages of fourteen and sixteen.

The three Education Acts passed between 1870 and 1918 had paved the way for a modern education system; however, the most significant change came with the passing of Rab Butler's 1944 Education Act. This replaced the largely ineffective Board of Education with the new role of Minister of Education, and significantly it called for the school leaving age to be raised from fourteen to fifteen within three years (with the proviso that by 1970, it would increase to sixteen) and made schooling free for all.

Leisure and Recreation

The Victorians' move into 'leisure and recreation for all' was pursued with some conviction into the twentieth century. In particular, their indulgence in the written word was continued with the further expansion of the town's free library system begun in the previous century. This was as much for leisure as education: despite the creation of schools in the previous century illiteracy was still widespread, particular among the poorer working classes, and the increased access to books was thought essential.

In 1904 another branch library was built on Horace Street, overlooking the Queens Recreation Park, for the residents of Newtown; this is still in use today. In the following year, Eccleston's Carnegie Library opened, funded by David Gamble, and built on land owned by the Greenalls who had sold it to the Council for the nominal price of just ten shillings. Later, a further branch opened in Sutton Manor, serving the miners and their families working at Sutton Manor Colliery. Although Thatto Heath library had been extended in 1902, demand was so great that a new building, built on a corner of Thatto Heath Park, was opened in 1915, where it remains to this day.

The town's theatres remained popular through the first half of the twentieth century. By far the most popular was the Theatre Royal on Corporation Street. During its heyday, it attracted top performers, including the great Rob Wilton who always began his amusing tales with the line 'The day war broke out . . .' In spite of its general popularity, the theatre was forced to closed in 1957 due to a lack of funding. However, after a short while the premises were bought by the Pilkington family, who had the theatre rebuilt and redesigned. The result was a thoroughly modern theatre with increased seating, which opened its doors again in 1960. This is the Theatre Royal that survives today.

The growth of industry within the town led to greater demand for electricity. This aerial picture shows the first of the town's power stations, at Carlton Street, which remained in operation through to it being superseded by the larger, more modern Bold Power Station. (*Reproduced with the permission of the St Helens Local History and Archives Library*)

By the turn of the century, theatres had a rival which was a major threat to their very survival – moving pictures. Cinemas took off in a big way, attracting huge audiences that clamoured to see the latest Hollywood releases, and were thrilled by the performances of the American stars. Silent movies were eventually replaced by the first 'talkies'.

One of the first cinemas to open in St Helens was the Scala in Ormskirk Street, in 1911. Others followed: the Palladium on Boundary Road in 1923; the Capitol, on the corner of North Road and Duke Street, in 1929; and the Rivoli, on Corporation Street, in the same year. The Savoy, which was the last to open, in 1933, was the town's largest cinema. Other smaller cinemas opened throughout the surrounding districts such as Parr and Sutton. In fact, there were so many cinemas in and around the town, that people could visit a different one every night of the week! Of all the cinemas in St Helens the Savoy and the Capitol were by far the most successful. They were the largest, seating around 1,500 people, and would prove to have the greatest longevity; when the other cinemas had closed, these two were still showing the big movies of the day. As the decline in the cinema audiences continued, many became bingo halls, including the Hippodrome and the Rivoli; or worse, some became warehouses, cash and carry outlets, supermarkets, or even car showrooms. By the late 1970s and early 80s, cinemas were in major decline; even the Capitol fell victim to this downturn. Soon after the premises were sold, and emerged later as a sports centre which remains to this day, now owned by the YMCA. The Savoy fared better than its old rival: it lingered on, surviving the downturn, and screened major releases until the mid-1990s, before it too was forced into closure. It stood derelict for a while, looking the worse for wear, and soon became a real eyesore on Bridge Street. Several moves were made to acquire it as a private cinema, but these apparently failed to deliver. Despite its sorry appearance, when demolition began in late 2000 many residents in the town felt a pang of regret. As I write, a new building is rising from the ashes of the old cinema … yet another night club and wine bar, no doubt.

However, the story of the town's cinemas continues, with the construction of the new Cineworld multiplex centre at the corner of Bridge Street and Water Street (the former location of the Windle Pilkington School). The new cinema opened its doors to an eager audience in the spring of 2001.

Apart from the wealth of theatres and cinemas in the town, the creation of public spaces started in the later years of the nineteenth century was continued into the early years of the twentieth. A popular park, though smaller than most, is Sutton Park, which was created from land purchased from the Hughes family in 1903. A similar park, though smaller again, is Hardshaw Park. Standing alongside the railway, at the top of Shaw Street, this land was purchased from the executors of the Greenall estate in 1906.

The largest park in the town, and the most famous, is Sherdley Park. This was the former private estate owned by Michael Hughes, who bequeathed the land to the people of the town in his will. The Score (an old roadway) had been a right of way through the estate for years, but the removal of the tall perimeter wall by the early 1950s meant that the entire park land was open to public access for the very first time. The park became the most famous of the town's recreational areas following the creation of the St Helens Show in 1966, and it has been held there ever since, attracting huge crowds from throughout the north-west.

The last of the town's parks to be opened to the public was Haresfinch Park. This, like most of the other parks, was created from the purchase of a former private estate – in this case Haresfinch House. Through the years, several of the more prominent families in the area have lived here, including David Bromilow, one of the large colliery owners; L. W. Evans, one-time Mayor of St Helens; and later still the Gamble family, who need no introduction. Haresfinch House and its surrounding parklands were purchased by the Council in 1960; soon after the perimeter wall was taken down, and the house demolished; nothing whatsoever remains of it today.

The East Lancashire Road was constructed between 1929 and 1934. It passed close by St Helens, and not only improved transport links with both Liverpool and Manchester, but brought employment. This photograph shows the section passing the borough cemetery. This required a cutting through Windle Hill, and the construction of the bridge. The highway was officially opened on 19 July 1934 by King George V. (AG)

Chapter Twelve

ST HELENS:
A BRIGHTER FUTURE

*T*HE SECOND HALF OF THE TWENTIETH CENTURY could easily be described as the 'soft half of a hard century'. Since the Second World War this country and its people have witnessed significant change in the standard of living: better houses, better schools, improved public health, better roads: the list is endless. The town of St Helens had witnessed change too, though not all of it has been good. The second half of the century has seen the town enter its post-industrial phase, with the loss of much of its former industrial base, and the change to service industries instead of manufacturing. It has been, at times, an unsteady change, though one I feel sure will lead to a brighter future.

Post-War Housing Improvements

Following the landslide Labour victory in the 1945 General Election, the Labour-controlled council in St Helens embarked upon a huge house-building programme: massive council estates were created – in an attempt to cope with the growing demand for affordable housing within the town – in areas such as Parr, Sutton, Thatto Heath, Portico, Peasley Cross and Haresfinch.

Further building followed. Many of the older houses surrounding the town centre were demolished and rebuilt to a much higher standard. Those built off Westfield Street were demolished during the 1970s to make way for the construction of the new dual carriageway and large stores. To replace this loss of housing, the Council built blocks of flats nearby, though these too have recently been demolished. Unlike its neighbours – such as Liverpool and Wigan – St Helens refrained from the 'enlightened sixties' bandwagon of building high-rise flats. The flats in question, and others scattered around the town such as those at Peasley Cross, were 'maisonettes', standing no taller than two storeys high.

Much of the earlier private housing throughout the town, mainly in terraced rows, had been built with outside toilets and no bathrooms. Many of these were modernised, with bathrooms added through a scheme pioneered by the Wilson Government, though administered by the local councils via grants (examples of these houses can still be seen today, right across the borough). The town was awarded Development Status in 1966, creating more new houses.

St Helens was once filled with traditional cobbled terraced streets (epitomised in Granada's *Coronation Street*), but redevelopment through the years has seen their numbers diminish. The few that did remain began to be resurfaced during the 1970s. Manville Street and Cleveland Street, at Peasley Cross, were just two of the streets that were resurfaced early on; other parts of the town kept their cobbles until more recent years – Central Street and Gleave Street, for example, located behind the Town Hall, were only resurfaced in the mid-1990s. In Sutton Oak, Oxley Street, located off Robins Lane, still retains its cobbles and even its stone paving slabs and kerbs, proving that there is still work to be done.

In more recent years, improvements by the Council to existing housing estates, with grants from both central Government and Europe, have greatly benefited the lives of many of the town's residents. Once-declining estates have been turned around and given a new lease of life. The role of housing associations has also made a great difference to the number of affordable houses and flats available to rent. Apart

from constructing housing on their own sites, partnerships with the council have seen former Council houses and flats taken over and thoroughly re-modernised.

Post-War Education

In the later years of the twentieth century, state-funded schools spread throughout the town and districts. By the 1960s, the comprehensive system was adopted through all state schools. Nevertheless, despite this pressure to create the equality of the comprehensive system, some of the established grammar schools, such as Cowley, persevered with their high standards and the segregation of boys and girls.

The Cowley British School on College Street, first founded at the end of the eighteenth century, remained in operation through to 1910 by which time it had become run down and in poor stare of repair. Its demolition made way for the building of a new, more modern, school; this was called, quite logically, Central Modern, though, in more recent years, this too has been demolished.

Throughout the century there have been a great many new schools built within the borough. One of the last schools to be built in the town was Sutton High School; built on green fields adjacent to Sherdley Park, it opened to the first pupils in 1980. Apart from being the most modern of the town's schools, it could also boast the best of sporting facilities, as it was built alongside the Sutton Sports Centre.

This new school was an overflow from the original Sutton High School, which had been built off Robins Lane near Sutton Park at the turn of the century. Originally known as Robins Lane School, it initially housed infants, juniors and seniors in the same building. As new housing as built in Sutton, and the catchment area of the school expanded accordingly, a new, larger infants and juniors building was added during the years immediately following the Second World War.

The post-war years have witnessed a further expansion of the town's population, and in particular the number of young children, which has placed further burdens on the local education system. Schools such as Sutton High, working within restricted budgets, were forced to use mobile classrooms (which, in spite of their name, sadly became a permanent fixture in many of the playgrounds of our schools). This was a state of affairs which, in the case of Sutton High, finally led to the building of the new school.

However, in the latter years of the century the numbers of children within the borough has fallen, which has had the seemingly disastrous effect of schools being closed, boarded up, and in many cases demolished.

Undoubtedly one of the town's best loved buildings, the Gamble Institute takes pride of place on the south corner of Victoria Square. Today it is home to the town's public library, as well as its local history archive. (*AG*)

Road Improvements

Within St Helens town centre, the old roads and narrow streets created in the Victorian era desperately required improvement. By the mid-1950s, the Council had plans in place to widen some streets and demolish others in order to create an inner ring road, in an effort to reduce the traffic on town-centre streets such as Church Street and Ormskirk Street, and aid the flow of traffic on the outer edge of the town. The construction of the new road was commenced in 1959 and completed by the turn of the decade, developing the dual-carriageway, called Chalon Way, with the demolition of Tontine Street. The completion of the road allowed the building of the town's first multi-storey car park, on waste ground between Chalon Way and the canal, previously occupied by St Helens Foundry.

The days of motoring reached their heights in the 1950s. The build-up of traffic on the East Lancashire Road led to it being widened during the 1960s, creating a dual carriageway. Long before the construction of new 'super' roads such as this, there had been plans as early as 1937 to create a network of new superhighways, designed to connect the main cities of the country. However, the arrival of the Second World War, and the debts the country faced after it, caused the idea to be mothballed.

The concept was only resurrected in the late 1950s. However, this time around, the planners intended to base these new superhighways on the German autobahns – where traffic could travel in relative safety, at unrestricted speeds, over long distances. The motorway age was dawning. One of the first routes to be proposed was the north–south highway, designed to connect the full length of the country by a single road. On a local level, this would connect the industrial towns of Warrington, Wigan, Preston and Lancaster. The first taste of the future came with the construction of the Preston by-pass in 1959, which was later to form part of the M6 motorway. The construction of the M6 was divided into sections: the section between Newton-le-Willows and Ashton-in-Makerfield brought between 300 and 400 new jobs to St Helens, albeit temporarily.

Unfortunately, as successful as the M6 undoubtedly was, and despite its connection to the East Lancashire Road at junction 23, it passed too far east of St Helens to be of any real benefit to the town's transport developments. The closest of the motorways was the trans-Pennine M62 which started life in 1969, at Eccles, built in separate sections. The Burtonwood to Bold section – the nearest point to St Helens – was built in 1973, though benefited Warrington more than anywhere else. The completed motorway opened in 1976. However, the town of St Helens still lacked a modern infrastructure, and surprising as it

The town received a royal visit in the summer of 1977, when Her Majesty the Queen and Prince Philip attended a ceremony held in their honour outside the Town Hall as part of the Silver Jubilee celebrations. (*DW*)

may seem, it would have to wait almost thirty years for a motorway connection.

Building a Modern St Helens

Although St Helens had seen its boundaries expanded in 1889 when it became a county borough, by far the biggest change to the status of the town came in April 1974, when the Metropolitan County of Merseyside was created (along with Greater Manchester and Cumbria, it broke up the historical and traditional boundaries of the county of Lancashire). St Helens became one of the five metropolitan boroughs; Liverpool, Sefton, Wirral and Knowsley were the other four that made up the new county of Merseyside. It meant that St Helens was no longer a Lancashire town, and the traditional county border was moved just north of Rainford. Many people who had been born and bred in Lancashire wanted to remain Lancastrians; they resented the creation of Merseyside, and these objections rankle to this day. Nevertheless, this change in status expanded the town's authority and its boundaries, taking in districts such as Billinge, Rainford, Garswood, Rainhill, Newton-le-Willows and Earlestown.

The 1970s also saw significant changes to St Helens' local government buildings. The town's original County Courts, built on East Street in 1845, remained in use there through to 1972, when they were demolished to make way for the modern shopping precincts. Smaller courts were housed in Rexmore House on Cottam Street, where they remain to present day. The Magistrates Courts, which had formed part of the Town Hall complex, stood at the corner of Corporation Street and Birchley Street, attached to the police station. As the town expanded during the 1970s, the need for better facilities grew. Larger and more modern replacements were built on Corporation Street, on the site of the former Central Station, in 1972. In the same year, the police vacated their small station within the Town Hall for new, modern premises on College Street, where they remain.

St Helens' new, modern Law Courts opened on Corporation Street in the early 1970s, on the former site of the Central Station, to replace the original which had been demolished to make way for the construction of Tontine Market. (*AG*)

The Town Centre Shops

As the streets increased in number, so too did the stores, such as the Co-operative Society, who had expanded right across the North West from their humble beginnings in Toad Lane, Rochdale. In St Helens, they opened several small stores scattered throughout districts such as Peasley Cross, where their shop occupied the corner of Marshalls Cross and Sutton Road; their town centre site on Baldwin Street was their biggest venture.

Through the years, the Co-op became a major player in the retail trade within the town. However, by the 1950s, with other shops opening in St Helens and existing outlets looking to expand, the Co-op had to undergo a facelift. Work began in 1956, with some of the surrounding buildings being purchased by the company (particularly on Cottam Street) to provide the extra space needed for expansion. By the end of the following year the work was completed and the result was a grand affair known as Helena House, which occupied a much larger site surrounded by streets such as Baldwin Street, Cotham Street, Claughton Street and College Street.

This new store now held a prime position at the northern end of the town centre. This was a particularly busy area, with bus stops situated on Baldwin Street and Cotham Street. The store benefited from its position, developing through the years from a mere green-grocers (famous for its customer dividend), into a department store, selling clothing, household goods and furniture. In its day, the Co-op (pronounced locally as the 'Kworp') was one of the most popular firms in the town. As for the building itself, it was one of graceful architecture and had a large ballroom on the second floor, which was popular for dances and other occasions, particularly during the 1940s, 1950s and 1960s.

The old shopping area of the town, largely created in the nineteenth century, was a sprawling mass of narrow streets, each containing small, individual shops. It was Napoleon who referred to Britain as a 'nation of shop keepers', and that description was certainly true of old St Helens. However, changes to the shopping area had begun in the 1960s. The area of Westfield Street and Liverpool Road remained a busy and regular shopping route for a great many years, right through to the closing and the demolition of the shops there in 1963. Tyrer's, who had established their position in the previous century, continued to trade from their Liverpool Road premises (which had been extended through the years) until they had to vacate prior to demolition. Their choice of relocation – the corner of Bridge Street and Milk Street – could not have been a better prime site in the new town centre. Here they constructed much larger and more modern premises, which opened their doors in 1960 – St Helens' only true department store – and remain there to the present day.

As the modern town expanded the Post Office, located on Church Street, also needed to expand. It remained there through to the early 1970s, until the construction of St Mary's Precinct. With its move in 1972 to larger premises at the bottom of Bridge Street, it gained the title of General Post Office, with a separate sorting office located on Liverpool Road.

The 1960s and 1970s saw many changes occur in the town centre.

The Technical College, built on Water Street, had been started in 1958 but only reached completion at the turn of the decade. By far the greatest upheaval came when the old Market Hall was demolished in 1962, together with the shops and some of the streets that stood around it, to make way for the construction of the modern shopping precincts. St Mary's Precinct and market was the first of these to be built, opening in 1972, with its neighbour, Tontine Market, opening just two years later. The arrival of the modern markets, though a necessary progression, changed the appearance of the town – particularly in the area of Church Street and Bridge Street – forever. This change was welcomed by some and condemned by others in particular the older residents of the town who much preferred the friendliness and personal customer service received in the older markets, as opposed to the modern stores.

However, despite changes to local government and the redevelopment of the town centre, the town saw many changes for the worse through the 1970s and 80s. It was a hard time for the residents, as much of the industry that St Helens had once been famous for was closing. Greenall's brewery, a major employer in the town which had retained its Hall Street location since the eighteenth century (producing the strong pungent smells in the town centre that many people remember) closed in 1979. The Gas Works at Peasley Cross was reduced in size in the 1970s, and with much of its work moving to Warrington, by the 1980s the site had closed. Bold Power Station, an employer since the 1950s was no longer required, and closed in the late 1980s.

In more recent years, the town centre has witnessed some dramatic changes. These two pictures show modern St Helens: the first shows the Technical College, originally opened in the 1950s and extended over the years; the second highlights Safeway, opened on 4 July 1989, and part of the often confusing new road system. The town's new cinema has since been built in the foreground. (*DW*)

Beechams closed its St Helens factory and relocated south with the merger with Smithkline. And Sidac, a significant employer in the south of the town, also closed, not to mention the reduction in the town's principal industry, glass.

All of these closures, occurring in a relatively short space of time, were a major financial blow to the local economy, with many of the workers losing their jobs. Despite the shock that these closures caused locally, this was only the beginning of a process of change that would see St Helens lose many of its traditional industries. However, it was these very closures that enabled the town to begin to change. St Helens entered a long, slow and often painful period of regeneration.

The next great change to the appearance of the town's shopping areas came in 1984. Greenall's former Hardshaw Brewery site had been left derelict following demolition in 1979, and became a serious eyesore in the very heart of the town centre. However, within a few years, work had commenced on the construction of the Hardshaw Shopping Centre, which was to transform the town centre for the better. With the completion of the Hardshaw Shopping Centre in 1984, both Woolworths and Marks & Spencer – who had held prime sites for many years on Church Street – extended their stores backwards to join with the new shopping complex.

The former site of Rockware Glass was earmarked for the creation of the town's new Technology Campus, an overflow from the Technical College. Today this is now in full operation, training school leavers in a variety of useful trades. The former Beechams factory site was donated to the town by the company, and soon after work began demolishing large parts of the structure, with the important exception of the famous clock tower. In the 1990s the site was substantially remodelled, and now forms an important extension of the town's Technical College.

By the end of the 1980s, work began on demolishing and transforming the former industrial site of the old Peasley Cross gas works into a retail centre. Although the demolition of one of the town's two gasometers, seen as famous local landmarks, was a sad event for some of the town's older residents, the result was the creation of the St Helens Retail Park, containing such well-known stores as B&Q and Halfords.

However, in spite of the improvements in the town centre, other unforeseeable changes such as the shopping habits of the people, and increased competition from the ever-expanding supermarkets, put pressure on some of the long-established town centre stores. Many of these fell victim to the trend and closed. One of the more prominent victims was the Co-op. Unable to compete, it closed in the late 1980s, and the building itself was left empty. After it had been abandoned for a short while (and there was still some hope that some other company might well take the premises over) the vandals moved in, causing untold damage and turning it into a real eyesore. Sadly, demolition followed soon after, leaving the site empty, surrounded by wooden boarding for years and no less an eyesore. Although many varying rumours circulated regarding its future, some claiming that a new shopping precinct was going to be built on the site, others saying that a new supermarket had been earmarked, it remained derelict. Finally, in 1995, work commenced on constructing a new, modern store for the Wilkinson Home and Garden Group – who had previously occupied a large store within the St Mary's Shopping Centre, originally built for Fine Fare Supermarkets, at the opposite end of the town. The new store was completed and opened for business in January 1996. Perhaps not as architecturally pleasing as its predecessor, but a welcome arrival all the same.

Through the years the town's main streets – Church Street, Bridge Street, Westfield Street – remained busy, while others such as Hardshaw Street and Barrow Street began to change in style and the businesses attracted there. Hardshaw Street established itself as the financial centre of the town, with almost all of the main banks and building societies locating there. Barrow Street seemingly proved to be a des. res. to their corporate cousins, the estate agents, who in more recent years have almost dominated this street with their presence.

The town centre was extended with the opening of the Safeway superstore on 4 July 1989. Built on part of the former Pilkington

There have been many obvious benefits to the town following the opening of the Link Road in 1994 – surely the most obvious is the transformation of the former Ravenhead Colliery site (derelict since 1973), into the Ravenhead Retail Park seen in this picture. *(MF)*

Grove Street site, following the demolition of the former warehouses and Research and Development offices some years earlier, the store benefits from its canalside location. Nearby, the town's first *bona fide* hotel (previous hotels had been based on public houses) was built in 1991, the Chalon Court Hotel, though within a matter of a few years it had been bought by the Stakis group, and more recently it has become the Hilton Hotel. Safeway gained a competitor in the spring of 1991 in the shape of Asda, who built their new store off King Street. All of these new additions to the town benefited from the vastly improved road network.

During the 1990s further changes occurred to the town centre. The original shopping precincts built in the 1970s – St Mary's and Tontine – were looking a little long in the tooth. Redevelopment of the centres was started in the middle of the last decade of the century, completely transforming the shopping areas, and attracting new stores – such as British Home Stores – into the changing town. Many of the town's streets were pedestrianised to create safe areas for shoppers. Finally, the opening of the St Helens Retail Park at the end of the 1980s, on the site of the old gas works, became the town's first foray into the 'out-of-town' shopping experience; this has since been followed up by the construction of the new Ravenhead Retail Park on the former Ravenhead Colliery site in 2001.

Two Safe Labour Seats

Due to parliamentary changes at the 1983 general election, St Helens would have two seats to contest: the constituencies of St Helens North and South. In the St Helens North seat, John Evans stood for Labour, and Tony Rhodes for the Conservatives. For the first time in years, the Conservatives were in upbeat mood; they felt that the division of the constituencies, and their increasing popularity in the north of the town, meant that for the first time in over seventy years they had a real chance at gaining a St Helens seat. For St Helens South, Gerry Bermingham was the new candidate to stand for Labour, Richard Bull for the Conservatives and Philip Briers for the SDP/Liberal Alliance. In the end, despite the Conservatives' confidence of victory, St Helens North was won by Labour: John Evans gained a majority of 9,259 (the Conservatives polled just over 16,000 votes, compared to Labour's 25,000). In comparison, St Helens South was never in any real doubt: Labour won, with Bermingham polling more than 22,000 votes, and gaining a majority of 9,662.

John Evans contested the St Helens North seat at the consecutive elections of 1987 and 1992, both times retaining the seat for Labour. Prior to the 1997 general election, Evans announced his retirement.

For many years the bus stops for a variety of destinations were scattered around the town: some on Baldwin Street, outside the Co-op, some on Water Street, outside Beechams, others on Victoria Square; at times, finding the right stop for the right bus was a nightmare. The town was crying out for a bus station! In more recent years our prayers were answered with the opening of a bus station between Corporation Street and Bickerstaffe Street. At last, all the stops are in one place, and handy for the shops too! (*AG*)

OPPOSITE
The unexpected closure of Beechams factory in the early 1990s was a massive blow to the town, not only because of the loss of jobs, but also because the town centre could become blighted by a derelict factory, just when redevelopment was being to rejuvenate the town. Thankfully, Beechams' former offices have now transformed as part of the Technical College. (*AG*)

A new Labour candidate was sought and found in the shape of Dave Watts, Leader of St Helens Council (his replacement was Councillor Marie Rimmer, whom Watts had replaced a few years earlier). The election was a foregone conclusion, with Watts being returned with a healthy majority.

Gerry Bermingham was to prove a popular and hard-working MP. He contested and won the St Helens South seat at three more elections, before announcing his retirement prior to the 2001 election. It is of interest to note that had Bermingham stood in that election, and judging his popularity and safe majority, it is reasonable to assume that he would have won, he would have equalled the record of five election victories held by Sir Harry Seaton-Karr and Sir James Sexton.

It should be mentioned that for the 2001 election 'New Labour' chose to 'parachute in' Shaun Woodward, the Tory defector, as its preferred candidate for St Helens South – excluding popular locals such as Council Leader Marie Rimmer in the process, which did not please many of the town's ardent Labour activists. The 2001 election for the St Helens South seat was one of local contention, with an outcry against this ex-Tory. The protest vote was taken by up 'by varying degrees of Labour', with candidates standing against Woodward from the Socialist Labour Party and the Socialist Alliance. The result, however, was never really in doubt, for Woodward was safely returned as the Labour MP, albeit with a substantially reduced majority than that held by his predecessor. However, in fairness to Mr Woodward, in the short period that he has been an MP for the town, he has carried out some really good work, and so, despite his origins and his previous political leaning, he is rapidly gaining recognition within St Helens. If he continues the good work he has begun, I think the people of St Helens may eventually accept his as one of their own.

The Road to Riches

Throughout the decades of the twentieth century, the economic success of any modern town lay in its connection to the increasing road network and the region's motorways: this became all the more evident with the switch of freight from rail to road by the late 1970s. While many north-west towns (several of them neighbours, such as Warrington and Wigan) took the plunge and invested heavily in their road infrastructure, modernising their towns and as a result attracting new industry, St Helens did not. Instead it lagged behind: as traffic increased, it was forced to cope with the old, narrow roads – roads that had never been designed to cope with such a level of heavy traffic. This led to long and costly repairs to the ageing highways, which caused further delays, all of which created a picture of St Helens that was increasingly unattractive to modern industry.

Despite rumours circulating since the late 1970s that a new road was going to be built to link the town to the motorway network, this growing problem was only finally addressed in the early 1990s. The driving force behind this transformation was the new council leader Marie Rimmer, who was insistent that St Helens desperately needed this road modernisation.

After securing much-needed European funding, plans were unveiled for the construction of a new road connecting the town to the M62 motorway. The proposed route, leaving the motorway at Junction 7, would travel through Lea Green (stealing a section of Sherdley Park's Golf Course en route), and finally reach the town centre by crossing a section of waste ground once occupied by the spoil heaps of Ravenhead Colliery.

Work commenced in 1991, and continued through to completion in 1994 despite having exceeded its original budget. Further spin-offs

St Helens Town Hall square – Victoria Square – has received a makeover in more recent years, with the vast majority of it pedestrianised, it even makes the old town hall look a little more modern. (AG)

from the new road came to the town centre: the creation of a new dual carriageway system to handle the expected increase in traffic; and the closure of other roads (including Chalon Way created in the early 1960s) to develop one-way systems and larger pedestrian areas, which improved the town centre shopping areas.

The new road, finally named the Linkway, was heralded as the 'road to riches' in the local press. Its completion has increased expectation of new prosperity for the town. So has the new road brought the trade and prosperity that was so boldly predicted? On the whole, the answer is yes. In more recent years there has been much redevelopment of the land alongside the road, with the construction of the Sherdley Business Park on the former site of Sherdley Colliery, and the new Ravenhead Park, the planned new retail park earmarked for the site of the former Ravenhead Colliery, of which construction is already under way. In the May of 2001, the town received a huge boost with the granting of a further £11 million of European aid for further regeneration of former industrial sites. This new finance will enable the construction of the new stadium for the town's famous Saints Rugby League, from its traditional home on Knowsley Road to a 'super stadium' at a new location alongside the Linkway, on land once used by UGB.

With all of this new investment in the town, and its new found prosperity, it is clear that, for the first time in centuries, the future of St Helens looks bright once more.

Bibliography

T. C. Barker, *The Glassmakers, Pilkingtons 1826–1976*, Weidenfield & Nicholson (1977)

T. C. Barker, *Pilkington, An Age of Glass: An Illustrated History*, Boxtree (1994)

T. C. Barker, *Pilkington Brothers and the Glass Industry*, Allen & Unwin (1960)

T. C. Barker & J. R. Harris, *A Merseyside Town in the Industrial Revolution, St Helens 1750–1900*, Frank Cass (1954)

Geoffrey Bolt, *A Regional History of the Railways of Great Britain: vol. 10, The North West*, David & Charles (1978)

Charles Foreman, *Industrial Town: Self Portrait of St Helens in the 1920s*, David & Charles (1978)

F. W. Free, *Our Heritage in Eccleston & District*, Author (1971)

F. W. Free, *Our Heritage in Parr*, Author (1971)

F. W. Free, *Our Heritage in Sutton and Bold*, Author (1971)

F. W. Free, *Our Heritage in Windle*, Author (1971)

Tom Grundy, *The Miracle of Float Glass*, Author (1990)

Charles Hadfield & Gordon Biddle, *The Canals of North West England, vol. 1*, David & Charles (1970)

Roger Hart, *Vintage St Helens and District*, Hendon Publishing (1976)

T. B. Maund & M. J. Ashton, *Local Transport in St Helens, 1879–1974*, Venture (1995)

David Paul, *Voices of St Helens*, Tempus Publishing (2000)

Mary Presland, *St Helens: A Pictorial History*, Phillimore (1995)

Sister Dominic Savio, *St Anne's, Sutton 1850–2000*, Altrincham Publications (2000)

Geoffrey Senior & Gertrude Hennin, *St Helens As It Was*, Hendon Publishing (1973)

Frank Sheen, *St Helens: In the Making, Parts 1–6*, Jones-Sands Publications (1990–96)

G. Simm & I. Winstanley, *Mining Memories*, St Helens MBC Community Leisure (1990)

J. Norman Slater, *A Brewer's Tale*, City Press (1980)

'The Thursday Group', *A History of St Helens Libraries*, St Helens MBC Community Education Services (1977)

J. M. Tolson, *St Helens Railways*, Oakwood Press (1983)

C. H. A. Towneley & J. A. Peden, *Industrial Railways of St Helens, Widnes and Warrington*, Industrial Railway Society (1999)

Other sources

(documents contained in St Helens Local History Library & Archive)

COAL MINING:

Coal Miners Strike 1984–5, Newscuttings A 36.2

Bold & Sutton Manor Collieries, Newscuttings, C1900–1985 A 36.2

Sutton Manor Colliery, Newscuttings 1986–91 A 36.2 (DESK)

Ravenhead Colliery, Newscuttings, A 36.2

Richard Evans Ltd, *The Romance of Coal 1928* A 36.2

Bold Colliery Centenary Open Day 1976 information booklet A 36.2 (p)

Coal Mines St Helens & Wigan, annual tonnage, owners etc., pre-1860 B 36.2 (P)

Clockface Colliery, Newscuttings A 36.2 (P) (*St Helens Reporter,* 4 August 1939 and 23 October, 1965)

Coal Mining in St Helens 1540–1970, Patrick Gill, 1970A 36.2 (P)

Mining Disasters, reports from 1849 D 36.2 (P) ***

Abandoned mines in St Helens 1841–1971 A 36.2 (P) ***

THE SANKEY CANAL:

The Sankey Brook Navigation, report, J. R. Harris

RAILWAYS:

St Helens Railway Acts 1830 & 1838 A 35.7 (41.2)

INDUSTRIAL:

The McKechnie Story (published by the Company 1965).

VICTORIAN LIFE:

Medical Health Reports, 1873–1899

THE TWENTIETH CENTURY:

Medical Health Reports 1909–